The Revelation of Jesus Christ

Ingrid Florencia-Kirindongo, RN, MHA, MBA

"He that hath an ear,
let him hear what the spirit
saith unto the churches."

TEACH Services, Inc.
PUBLISHING
www.TEACHServices.com

World rights reserved. This book or any portion thereof may not be copied or reproduced in any form or manner whatever, except as provided by law, without the written permission of the publisher, except by a reviewer who may quote brief passages in a review.

This book was written to provide truthful information in regard to the subject matter covered. The author assumes full responsibility for the accuracy of all facts and quotations as cited in this book. The opinions expressed in this book are the author's personal views and interpretation of the Bible, Spirit of Prophecy, and/or contemporary authors and do not necessarily reflect those of TEACH Services, Inc.

This book is sold with the understanding that the publisher is not engaged in giving spiritual, legal, medical, or other professional advice. If authoritative advice is needed, the reader should seek the counsel of a competent professional.

Copyright © 2011 TEACH Services, Inc.
ISBN-13: 978-1-57258-675-8 (Paperback)
ISBN-13: 978-1-57258-676-5 (Hardback)
ISBN-13: 978-1-57258-677-2 (E-book)
Library of Congress Control Number: 2011941078

Published by

TEACH Services, Inc.
P U B L I S H I N G
www.TEACHServices.com

All scripture quotations, unless otherwise indicated, are taken from the King James Version Bible.

Scripture quotations marked "NKJV™" are taken from the New King James Version®.
Copyright © 1982 by Thomas Nelson, Inc.
Used by permission. All rights reserved.

Complete Jewish Bible Scripture quotations are taken from the *Complete Jewish Bible*, copyright © 1998 by David H. Stern. Published by Jewish New Testament Publications, Inc.
www.messianicjewish.net/jntp.
Distributed by Messianic Jewish Resources.
www.messianicjewish.net.
All rights reserved. Used by permission.

Foreword

"The book of Revelation opens to the world what has been, what is, and what is to come; it is for our instruction upon whom the ends of the world are come. It should be studied with reverential awe. We are privileged in knowing what is for our learning....

"The Lord himself revealed to his servant John the mysteries of the book of Revelation, and he designs that they shall be open to study of all. In this book are depicted scenes that are now in the past, and some of eternal interest that are taking place around us; other of its prophecies will not receive their complete fulfillment until the close of time, when the last great conflict between the powers of darkness and the Prince of heaven will take place" (*The Review and Herald,* August 31, 1897).

Table of Contents

Introduction 9

Chapter 1　The Revelation of Jesus Christ 22

Chapter 2　Jesus's Messages to You and His Church—Part 1 33

Chapter 3　Jesus's Messages to You and His Church—Part 2 48

Chapter 4　God's Throne 61

Chapter 5　Jesus the Lamb of God 67

Chapter 6　Jesus Opening the Seals 72

Chapter 7　Sealing of God's people 81

Chapter 8　The Trumpets' Warning of Catastrophes—Part 1 91

Chapter 9　The Trumpets' Warning of Catastrophes—Part 2 96

Chapter 10　Jesus and the Little Open Book 102

Chapter 11　Jesus' Two Witnesses—The Old and New Testament 110

Chapter 12　Woman Pregnant With Jesus 118

Chapter 13　The Dragon and Mark of the Beast 128

Chapter 14　Jesus's Last Three Messages of Warning 163

Chapter 15　The Bowls of God's Wrath 170

Chapter 16　God's Seven Last Plagues 173

Chapter 17 The Harlot Woman...182

Chapter 18 The Fall of Babylon..190

Chapter 19 Jesus the Word of God..195

Chapter 20 Vacation With Jesus for 1,000 Years......................................200

Chapter 21 Starting Over in the New Earth With Jesus 205

Chapter 22 Jesus the Water of Life...210

Bibliography 216

Introduction

Over the years in talking to my friends, colleages, neighbors, and Bible students, I've discovered that many of them are afraid of the book of Revelation. Some of them said that it was all symbolic, a sealed book, and very hard to read. Because it is hard to understand, it is scary. I have to confess, I was also afraid of the book of Revelation. I love reading stories in the Bible, but when it came to the book of Revelation, suddenly I was not interested because I couldn't understand it and the symbols. The beast with seven heads, fire, brimstone, and the plagues made me even more afraid.

I remember as a child growing up paying close attention while my mother gave Bible studies to her friends and neighbors. Some of her words that stuck with me to this day were from Revelation 6:15. She would quote this verse from memory and then plead with her students to get on Jesus' side so that they won't partake of the last plagues or have to ask the rocks and mountains to fall on them and hide them from Jesus' face (Rev. 6:15; Hosea 10:8). This made me wonder about the book of Revelation, and it caused me great anxiety.

But after God opened my eyes and understanding about the book of Revelation and its meanings, I came to love it. You see, the book of Revelation puts it all together from the beginning of this world to the end. The main point of the story is that God the Father, God the Son, and God the Holy Spirit loves us so much that God sent His only Son, Jesus Christ, to die for us sinners so that one day we can live with Him forever, provided we choose to follow God's commandments and keep the testimonies of Jesus Christ. I then realized that it's a great book and not scary at all.

The book of Revelation, in my humble opinion, is the most beautiful book in the Bible. Why? Because this book reveals God's love and His Son, Jesus Christ, to me. It gives me the full picture of who Jesus is, was, and is to come. As a matter of fact, the entire Bible is about Jesus. The Bible is God's Word and Jesus is the Word of God. Therefore, the book of Revelation reveals Jesus Christ to us. It reveals Jesus as the Son of God. He is Creator of this world, Redeemer, the Lamb of God, Son of man, Master, Teacher, the Great Physician,

The Revelation of Jesus Christ

the Prophet of Galilee, Lord, Savior, God, Emmanuel, Messiah, Comforter, Prince of Peace, Counselor, High Priest, Judge, Sheppard, the Light, Protector, the Truth, the way to God, the Living water, and King of kings.

I got so excited about what I discovered that I wanted to share everything I've learned with everyone out there who's still afraid to read the book of Revelation. You see, Revelation is all about Jesus the Messiah, and if you love Jesus, you will learn that He loved you first. He created you, died for you, and washed all your sins away in His blood so that you can be saved and live with Him forever. This is true longevity, and it is all free! What more can you ask for?

I've also learned that in order to understand the New Testament we must first have an understanding of the Old Testament. These two testaments go hand in hand and testify about Jesus from the beginning to the end.

A good example of this is when Jesus Himself told His perplexed disciples as they were on their way to Emmaus that the Old Testament scriptures—beginning with Moses, the Psalms, and all the prophets—told about Him (Luke 24:13-27). On another occasion while He sat and ate with His disciples, again he told them that all these things must be fulfilled which were written in the laws of Moses, and in the prophets, and in the Psalms concerning Him (Luke 24:44-48; John 1:45). And, in the New Testament Jesus spoke about Himself and His Father (Heb. 1:1-14).

According to Ellen White, the history of the life, death, and resurrection of Jesus cannot be fully demonstrated without evidence contained in the Old Testament. Jesus Christ is revealed in the Old Testament as clearly as in the New Testament. The Old Testament testifies of a Savior to come while the New Testament testifies of a Savior that has come in the manner predicted by the prophets. In order to appreciate the plan of redemption, the Old Testament must be thoroughly understood. It is the glorified light from the prophetic past that brings out the life of Jesus Christ and the teachings of the New Testament with clearness and beauty. The miracles of Jesus are a proof of His divinity, but the strongest proof that He is the world's Redeemer is found in the prophecies of the Old Testament compared with the history of the New Testament. Jesus said to the Jews: "Search the Scriptures; for in them you think you have eternal life: and these are they which testify of Me" (John 5:39, NKJV).

I like to read this same text from the Complete Jewish Bible. It says, "You keep examining the Tanahk because you think that in it you have eternal life. Those very Scriptures bear witness to me. But you won't come to me in order to have life!"

Introduction

Ellen White, goes on saying that, "a beautiful harmony runs through the Old and New Testaments; passages which may seem dark at a first reading, present clear interpretations when diligently studied, and compared with other scripture referring to the same subject. A careful search of the prophecies would have so enlightened the understanding of the Jews that they would have recognized Jesus as the predicted Messiah. But they had interpreted those predictions to meet their own perverted ideas and ambitious aspirations.

"The disciples had been confused by the interpretations and traditions of the priests, and hence their darkness and unbelief in regard to the trial, death, and resurrection of their Master. These misinterpreted prophecies were now made plain to the understanding of the two disciples [on the way to Emmaus], by Him who, through his Holy Spirit, inspired men to write them. Jesus showed his disciples that every specification of prophecy regarding Messiah had found an exact fulfillment in the life and death of their Master" (*Spirit of Prophecy,* vol. 3, pp. 209, 210).

Here is a message to everyone who uses the Bible to teach others, especially if they are teaching those who are new in the faith. If you teach or give them the wrong or false interpretation of the Bible, or cause those who believe in Jesus to sin, Jesus says that it would be better for you if "a millstone were hung around [your] neck, and [you] were drowned in the depth of the sea" (Matt. 18:6, NKJV). So beware of false teachers and false prophets. If you want to know the truth, go to God and His Son, Jesus Christ, for the truth. Don't go to the dead or psychic to learn about the truth. They don't know anything because they are dead. Here is a rule of thumb that Jesus gave us to abide by. Jesus said, "To the law and to the testimony! If they do not speak according to this word, it is because there is no light in them" (Isa. 8:19, 20, NKJV; see also 9:15, 16).

To begin, let us review the prophecies in the Old Testament so that we can get a better and clearer understanding of who Jesus is, was, and is to come. But before we do that, I want you to bow your head right now and ask Jesus to send His Holy Spirit to open your understanding of God's Holy Word.

Jesus told His disciples that Moses, the Psalms, and all the prophets witnessed about Him. They all wrote about Him. So let's go back to the Old Testament to review what they wrote about Him.

We know that Moses wrote the first five books of the Old Testament—Genesis, Exodus, Leviticus, Numbers, and Deuteronomy. David wrote Psalms, and the other prophets have their own name written on their books—Isaiah, Jeremiah, Zechariah, Ezekiel, Daniel, Micah, etc. The following chart covers the prophecies in the Old Testament writings about the Messiah and their

The Revelation of Jesus Christ

fulfillment in the New Testament. As Jesus said, "Do not think that I came to destroy the Law or the Prophets. I did not come to destroy but to fulfill" (Matt. 5:17, NKJV). Jesus came to fulfill everything that was prophesied or written about Him. In Psalm 22 David gave us a full picture or preview of the Messiah's life here on earth. How He would be despised by His own people, how He would be killed and suffer for our sins. Then in Acts 3:18 the apostles who walked and talked to Jesus and witnessed all that was prophesied about Him gave us the confirmation that all that was prophesied about the Messiah was fulfilled (see also Acts 26:22, 23; 1 Pet. 1:10-15).

Prophecies about Jesus Christ, The Messiah

The Messiah Must:	Old Testament Prophecies	New Testament Fulfillment
Be the Son of God	Ps. 2:7; Prov. 30:4	Matt. 3:17; Mark 1:1, 11; 5:7; Luke 1:32
Have eternal existence	Mic. 5:2	John 1:1, 14; 8:58; Eph. 1:3, 4; Col. 1:15-19; Rev. 1:18.
Be the seed of the woman who would bruise the serpent's head (Jesus bruised Satan's head when He defeated the devil on the cross.)	Gen. 3:15	Luke 2:25-32; John 1:14; Gal. 4:4; Heb. 2:14; 1 John 3:8
Be born of a virgin	Isa. 7:14	Matt. 1:18-2:1; Luke 1:26-35
Be the seed of Abraham and David	Gen. 12:3	Matt 1:1; John 7:42; Acts 3:25; Gal. 3:16; Heb. 2:16
Be of the tribe of Judah	Gen. 49:10; Mic. 5:2	Matt. 1:2, 3; Luke 3:33; Rev. 5:5
Be born a king of the line of David; be the King of kings	2 Sam. 7:12, 13; Ps. 2:6; Isa. 9:6, 7; 11:1-5; Jer. 23:5	Matt. 1:1, 6; John 18:33-37; Acts 13:22, 23; Rom. 1:3; Rev. 1:5
Come after the rebuilding of the wall of Jerusalem	Dan. 9:24-26	Matt. 2:1; Luke 3:1, 23
Be born in Bethlehem of Judea and be called out of Egypt	Mic. 5:1-5; Hosea 11:1	Matt. 2:1, 14-19; Luke 2:4-11

Introduction

The Messiah Must:	Old Testament Prophecies	New Testament Fulfillment
Be adored by kings and great persons	Ps. 72:10-11	Matt. 2:1-11
Have a messenger sent to prepare the way before him	Isa. 40:3-5; Mal. 3:1	Matt. 3:1-3; 11:10; Mark 1:2-4; Luke 1:17; 3:2-6; 7:27-28
Be anointed by God and be the Lamb of God	Isa. 11:2; 53:5; 61:1; Ps. 45:6-8	Matt. 3:16; John 1:29; 3:34; Acts 10:38; Heb. 1:8-9; 9:28; 1 Pet. 2:24
Speak in parables	Ps. 78:2-4	Matt. 13:34, 35; Mark 4:33, 34; Eph. 3:9
Engage in a ministry of healing, binding up the brokenhearted and proclaiming liberty to the captives	Isa. 42:18; 61:1-2	Matt. 11:5; Luke 4:16-21; Acts 10:38
Be a servant—tender, compassionate, meek, sinless—and bear the reproaches of others	Ps. 69:10; Isa. 40:11; 42:1-4; 53:9-12	Matt. 12:15-20; Rom. 15:3; 1 Pet. 2:22
Enter publicly into Jerusalem riding on a donkey	Zech. 9:9	Matt. 21:1-11; Mark 11:1-11; Luke 19:28-38
Have great zeal for God's house	Ps. 69:9; Isa. 56:7; Mal. 3:1	Matt. 21:12-24; Mark 11:15 Luke 2:27-38, 45-50; John 2:13-22
Be hated without reason	Isa. 49:7; Ps. 35:19; 69:4-9	John 15:24-25
Be rejected by men	Isa. 53:2, 3; 63:3, 5; Ps. 69:9	Mark 6:3; Luke 9:58; John 1:11; 7:3-5
Be rejected by the Jewish leadership	Ps. 118:22	Matt. 21:42; John 7:48
Be plotted against	Ps. 2:1-2	Acts 4:27
Be betrayed by a friend	Ps. 41:10; 55:13-15	Matt. 26:21-25, 47-50; John 13:18-21; Acts 1:16-18
Be sold for thirty pieces of silver	Zech. 11:12	Matt. 26:15

The Revelation of Jesus Christ

The Messiah Must:	**Old Testament Prophecies**	**New Testament Fulfillment**
Have His price thrown into the Temple treasury	Zech. 11:13	Matt. 27:6-7
Be forsaken by His disciples	Zech. 13:7	Matt. 26:31, 56
Be struck on the cheek	Mic. 5:1	Matt. 27:30
Be spat on	Isa. 50:6	Matt. 26:67; 27:30
Be mocked and insulted by men	Ps. 22:7-9	Matt. 26:67, 68; 27:31, 39-44; Mark 15:27-32; Luke 23:35-39
Be beaten	Isa. 50:6	Matt. 26:67; 27:26-30
Have soldiers cast lots for His garment	Ps. 22:18	Matt. 27:35
Be executed by crucifixion, His hands and feet pierced	Ps. 22:16; Zech. 12:10	Matt. 27:35; Luke 24:39, John 19:18, 34-37; 20:20-28; Rev. 1:7
Be thirsty during his execution	Ps. 22:15	John 19:28
Be given vinegar to drink	Ps. 69:21	Matt. 27:34
Be executed without having a bone broken	Exod. 12:46; Ps. 34:20	John 19:33-36
Be considered a transgressor	Isa. 53:12	Matt. 27:3; Luke 23:32
Be cut off	Dan. 9:24-26	Rom. 5:6; 1 Pet. 3:18
Be seen by Israel as pierced	Zech. 12:10	Luke 24:39; John 19:34-37; Rev. 1:7
Be a Savior, the one whose death would atone for humanity's sins	Isa. 53:5-7, 12	Mark 10:45; John 1:29; 3:16; Acts 8:30-35; Heb. 2:9
Be buried with the rich when dead	Isa. 53:9	Matt. 27:57-60
Be raised from the dead; conquer death through His resurrection	Isa. 53:9-10; Ps. 2:7-8; 16:8-11; 49:15; 86:13	Matt. 28:1-20; Luke 24:6-8; Acts 1:3; 2:23-39; 13:28-39; 1 Cor. 15:3-8; 2 Tim. 2:8

Introduction

The Messiah Must:	Old Testament Prophecies	New Testament Fulfillment
Ascend to the right hand of God as Judge	Ps. 16:11; 68:19; 110:1	Luke 24:51; Acts 1:9-11; 7:55; Rev. 3:21; (Messianic Jews 1:3)
Exercise his priestly duties in heaven	Zech. 6:13	Rom. 8:34; (Messianic Jews 7:25-8:2)
Be the cornerstone	Isa. 28:16; Ps. 118:22-23	Matt. 21:42; Eph. 2:20; 1 Pet. 2:5-7
Be sought after by Jews and Gentiles	Isa. 11:10; 42:1-4; 49:1-6	Matt. 12:18-21; Acts 10:45, 46; 13:46-48; Rom. 9:30; 10:20; 11:11; 15:10
Be the Passover lamb without blemish that takes away the sins of the world	Exod. 12:1-11; Isa. 53:7	John 1:29-36; 1 Cor. 5:8; 1 Pet. 1:18-19; Rev 5:6-14; 7:14; 21:22-27; 22:1-4
Be the Passover sacrifice with no bone broken	Exod. 12:46; Num. 9:12; Ps. 22:17; 34:20	John 19:31-36
Be lifted up as Moses lifted up a serpent	Num. 21:8, 9	John 3:14, 15; 8:28
Be hung upon a tree as a curse for our sins	Deut. 21:23	Gal. 3:13
Feel forsaken by His Father	Ps. 22:1	Matt. 27:46; Mark 15:34
Be the Ruler of this world	Ps. 2:7-8; Dan. 7; 8	Rev. 12

To summarize the above table, we've compared the Old and New Testament and seen the connection between them. They all point to Jesus, His love for you and me, and the gospel. We've seen how they go in sequence of what has been prophesied about the Messiah and how it was fulfilled. The last and final chapter is still in the end time, which I believe we are in now. At the end after Satan and sin is destroyed; Jesus, the King of kings, will rule the universe for eternity.

Jesus is the only one who fits all the above descriptions, and He's the one who did it all as predicted; therefore, there's no doubt in my mind that Jesus is the Son of God—the Messiah. It was Jesus who spoke to Moses in

The Revelation of Jesus Christ

the burning bush (Exod. 3:4). It was Jesus who performed all those miracles in Egypt (Exod. 7). It was Jesus who provided manna for the Israelites in the wilderness (Exod. 16:2-35; Deut. 8:2-3). It was Jesus who gave Moses the Ten Commandments (Deut. 6:13, 16; 10:20). It was Jesus quoting His words back to Satan in the wilderness (Matt. 4:4; Luke 4:4-21). And it was Jesus who said to the Jewish leaders that "before Abraham was, I AM" (John 8:58). I've learned that it was the voice of Jesus who spoke through the prophets starting from Adam in Genesis to John in Revelation. So my brothers and sisters, *Jesus is the Messiah.*

For further study, please read the following scriptures: Deuteronomy 6:13, 16; 8:3; 10:20; Nehemiah 11:1, 18; Psalms 22; 91:11, 12; 95-100; 104-106; 121; Isaiah 9:1-7; 21; 24; 40:3; 53; 55; 56; 58; 59; 60; 61; Micah 5:2; Jer. 31:15; Malachi 3:3.

Based on the fulfilled prophecies that we've examined thus far, we now have proven that God's Word is true and that He does what He says. Jesus' first mission was completed as predicted—all of the prophecies happened according to God's word—so now God the Father is going to tell us how His Son's final mission will be completed at the end of this world. This analysis has increased my confidence in God's Word even more. No other book in this world can compare to the Bible. The Bible is God's Word; and Jesus is the Word of God.

In addition to the comparison between the Old and New Testaments, it is important to understand the parables, symbols, and pictures that Jesus used to get His message across to His servants as was predicted in the Old Testament (Ps. 78:2-4) and fulfilled in the New Testament (Matt. 13:34, 35). The Bible teaches us that He will speak in parables so that only His servants will know and understand what He is saying while on the other hand His enemies will be in total darkness, unable to understand (Isa. 6:9, 10; Matt. 13:3, 9-15; Mark 4:34; Luke 8:10). So we find it to be the same in the book of Revelation. It was written and presented in symbols so that God's servants who have a sincere heart and are guided by the Holy Spirit can understand it. Another reason was because He did not want His enemies to construe and destroy His words. Today, the army uses this same tactic. When they go to war, they send messages to their headquarters in codes so that their enemies won't know what's being communicated. Their people, however, can decode the message and get the information.

My mother did the same to us children. Whenever my parents were talking grown-up talk, they would use different language or symbols that we as

Introduction

children could not understand what they were saying. Mother did it on purpose because she did not want us to understand and follow their conversation.

Therefore, in order for us to understand the book of Revelation, we need to pray and ask the Holy Spirit to guide us and open our understanding to decode the symbols of Revelation to be able to understand it. Take a few minutes to pray before you continue reading. Now let's begin decoding the symbols. Most of the answers to decode the symbols of Revelation are in the Bible.

Symbols of Revelation and Their Literal Meaning

Angel	Messenger	Dan. 8:16; 9:21, Luke 1:19, 26; Heb. 1:14
Babylon	Religious apostasy/confusion	Gen. 10:8-10; 11:6-9; Rev. 17:1-5; 18:2, 3
Balaam, doctrine of	Compromise	Num. 22:5-25
Bear	Destructive power	Prov. 28:15; Dan. 7:5
Beast	Kingdom, government, political power	Dan. 7:23
Bread	Word of God	John 6:35, 51, 52, 63
Binding of Satan	Chain of circumstances	Isa. 14:12-20
Black, darkness	Moral darkness, sin, apostasy	Exod. 10:21-23; Jer. 4:20-28; Joel 2:1-10; John 12:35; Acts 26:18
Bottomless pit	Earth in chaos, torn up, dark, and empty	Gen. 1:1, 2; Isa. 24:1-4,19; Jer. 4:23-28; Rev. 20:1-3
Bow	Success in battle against evil	Ps. 7:11,12; Ps. 45:4,5
Candlesticks	Seven candlesticks in the holy place of the sanctuary of the Seven Churches	Exod. 25:31-40
Crown	Kingship, victory	2 Kings 11:12; 1 Chron. 20:2; Ezek. 21:26, 27; 1 Cor. 9:25; 2 Tim. 4:7, 8; James 1:12
Cup	Meted out suffering; judgment	Ps. 11:6, 75:8; Isa. 51:17, 22-23; Jer. 25:15-17; 49:12
Day	Literal year	Num. 14:34; Ezek. 4:6

The Revelation of Jesus Christ

Door	Opportunity and probation	Luke 13:24,25; 2 Cor. 2:12; Rev. 3:20
Dragon	Satan, the old serpent, devil, the adversary	Ps. 74:13,14; Isa. 27:1; 30:6; Ezek. 29:3; Rev. 12:7-9
Eagle	Speed, power, vision, vengeance, protection	Deut. 28: 49; Hab. 1:6-8; Rev. 12:14
Eating the book	Assimilating the message	Ezek. 3:1-3; Jer. 15:16
Egypt	Symbol of atheism	Exod. 5:2
Eye salve	Holy Spirit to help us see truth; discernment to understand the Word; antidote for spiritual blindness	Ps. 119:18; John 16:7-13; Eph. 1:17-19; 1 John 2:20, 27
Faithful witness	Christ	John 3:11; 18:37; Rev. 1:5; 3:14; 19:11
False prophet	Apostate Protestantism	Rev. 13;13, 14; 16:13, 14; 19:20
Fire	Holy Spirit	Luke 3:16
Four corners of earth	Four directions of compass	Jer. 49:36
Forehead	Mind	Deut. 6:6-8 Rom. 7:25; Ezek. 3:8,9
Fornication	Illicit connection between church & world	Ezek. 16:15,26; Isa. 23:17; James 4:4; Revelation 14:4
Four Beasts or Living Creatures	Heavenly beings with special responsibilities	Revelation 5:8-10; 4:6-9; 6:1-7; 14:3; 15:7; 19:4
Garments	Covering of righteousness	Gen. 35:2; Isa. 61;10; Isa. 52:1; Zech. 3:3-5; Rom. 13:14
Gold	True riches of heaven, faith, scripture	Ps. 19:7-10; Gal. 5:6; James 2:5; Job 23:10
Hand	Symbol of word	Ecclesiastes 9:10
Harlot	Apostate church/religion	Isa. 1:21-27; Jer. 3:1-3, 6-9
Harvest	End of World	Matt. 13:39
Heads	Major powers, rulers, government	Dan. 7:6; Dan. 8:8,22; Revelation 17:3,10
Hidden Manna	Christ	John 6:49, 50, 53; Matt. 13:44

Introduction

Horn	King or Kingdom	Dan. 7:24; Revelation 17:12 Zech. 1:18,19 Ps. 89:17,24; Dan. 8:5, 21, 22
Horse	Symbol of battle; special representatives/angels	Exod. 15:21; Isa. 43;17; Jer. 8:6; Ezek. 38:15; Zech. 10:3
Image	A likeness	Gen. 1:26; 5:3; Exod. 20:4; Deut. 4:25; Rom. 8:29
Incense	Prayers of God's people	Ps. 141:2; Rev. 5:8; 8:3, 4
Israel	True followers of Christ	Rom. 2:28, 29; 9:6-8; Gal. 3:29
Jezebel	Immorality, idolatry, apostasy	1 Kings 21:25; 2 Kings 9:22
Lamb	Jesus/sacrifice	Gen. 22:7, 8; John 1:29; 1 Cor. 5:7
Lion	Strength; Jesus Christ	Gen. 49:9; Ps. 7:2; Rev. 5:4-9
Lamb's wife	New Jerusalem	Rev. 19:7-9; 21:2, 9, 10
Lamp; light	Jesus, Word of God	John 9:5; John 1:9; Ps. 119:105; Rev. 4:5
Locusts	Destruction; destructive agencies	Deut. 28:38; Joel 1:4
Lord's Day	The Sabbath	Exod. 20:10; Isa. 58:13; Matt. 12:8
Man child	Jesus	Ps. 2:7-9; Rev. 12:5
Mark	Sign/seal/mark of approval or disapproval	Ezek. 9:4; Rom. 4:11; Rev. 7:2, 3
Measuring rod	God's law God's word	Eccles. 12:13, 14 Isa. 8:19, 20; 2 Tim. 3:16, 17; James 2:10-12
Merchants	Advocates of Babylon's teachings	Isa. 47:11-15; Nah. 3:16; Rev. 18:3, 11, 15, 23
Moon	Permanence; Moses' system of types and sacrifices	Ps. 89:35-37
Michael	Christ	Exod. 3:2; 14:19; Josh. 5:14, 15; Isa. 63:9; John 1:1-3, 10, 14; 5:27-29; 6:38; 17:5, 24; 1 Thess. 4:16; Titus 1:3, 4; Jude 9;
Mystery of God	The gospel	Eph. 1:9, 10; 3:9; 6:19; Col. 1:26, 27
Morning Star	Jesus	Rev. 22:16

The Revelation of Jesus Christ

Mountains	Political or religio/political powers	Isa. 2:2, 3; Jer. 17:3; 31:23; 51:24, 25; Ezek. 17:22, 23; Dan. 2:35, 44, 45
New Jerusalem	The holy city of heaven	Rev. 3:12; 21:2
Oil	Holy Spirit	Zech. 4:2-6; Rev. 4:5
Open Door	Unlimited opportunity	Hosea 2:15; John 10:7-9; Acts 14:27; 1 Cor. 16:9; Col. 4:3
Rainbow	Token of covenant keeping	Gen. 9:11-17
Reapers	Angels	Matt. 13:39
Red (color)	Sin, corruption, persecution, destruction	Ps. 75:8; Isa. 1:18; 26:21; Jer. 46:10 Ezek. 32:6,11; Nah. 2:3
Reign	Seat of will, affections	Ps. 7:9; 16:7; 26:2; 73:21; Prov. 23:16; Jer. 17:10
Second death	Lake of fire	Rev. 20:14; 21:8
Serpent	Satan	Rev. 12:7-9; 20:2
Sickle	Symbol of harvest; end of the world	Matt. 13:39; Rev. 14:14
Sodom	Moral degradation	Gen. 19:4-14; Jer. 23:14; Ezek. 16:46-55
Stars	Angels	Job 38:7; Rev. 1:16, 20; 12:4, 7-9
Seal	Sign, mark, and seal mean same thing	Ezek. 9:4; Rom. 4:11; Rev. 7:2, 3
Sword	Bloodshed, destruction	Isa. 3:25; 13:15; Jer. 48:2; Acts 12:1, 2
Testimony of Jesus	Spirit/gift of prophecy	1 Cor. 13:2; Rev. 19:10; 22:9
Thief	Suddenness of Jesus' coming	1 Thess. 5:2; 2 Peter 3:10
Time	Literal year	Dan. 4:16, 23, 25, 32; 7:25; 11:13; Rev. 12:6, 14
Tongue	Language/speech	Exod. 4:10
Twenty-four elders	A group redeemed from earth	Rev. 4:4; 5:9, 10; 7:9-14
Two-edged sword	God's Word; sword of Spirit	Eph. 6:17; Heb. 4:12; Matt. 10:34; Isa. 49:2

Introduction

Waters	Inhabited area; people and nations	Rev. 17:15
White robes	Victory and righteousness	Isa. 61;10; Zech. 3:1-5; Gal. 3:27; Rev. 3:5; 7:14; 19:8
Winds	Strife, commotion, "winds of war"	Jer. 25:31-33; 49:36, 37; 4:11-13; Zech. 7:14
Wine	False doctrine/teachings; Jesus blood of atonement	Jer. 25:15-18; 51:7; Matt. 26:21-29
Woman, pure	God's true church	Isa. 51:16; Jer. 6:2; 2 Cor. 11:2; Eph. 5:22, 23
Woman, impure	Apostate church	Ezek. 16:15-58; 23:2-21; Hosea 2:5; 3:1; Rev. 14:4
Wrath of God	Seven last plagues	Rev. 15:1

Now that we've learned the meanings of the symbols of Revelation, please feel free to refer back to them as needed. While reading passages in Revelation if you can't picture what it is saying or understand it, pray and ask the Holy Spirit to illuminate your mind, then replace the symbol with the meanings above and you'll be able to understand it.

Now that we have covered that information we are ready to start reading the book of Revelation, which is the Revelation of Jesus Christ. In other words, it is an explanation of Jesus Christ, who He is, what He did, and what He will do.

You are about to discover Jesus in the book of Revelation. But before you start, please bow your head right now, pray again, and ask God for a blessing of the Holy Spirit to open your understanding of His words; and talk to you personally through His Word.

In each chapter I will share with you what I've learned and researched along with giving you quotes from other authors on the same topic. I will also give you some applications as to how you can apply everything you read and learn to your personal life. This will help you to experience the joy and love of getting to know Jesus in the book of Revelation. At the end the choice is yours to decide who you want to give your heart to or who you want to serve and worship. I hope and pray that you will make the right choice.

Chapter 1

The Revelation of Jesus Christ

Revelation 1:1-3

"The Revelation of Jesus Christ, which God gave unto him, to shew unto his servants things which must shortly come to pass; and he sent and signified it by his angel unto his servant John: Who bare record of the word of God, and of the testimony of Jesus Christ, and of all things that he saw. Blessed is he that readeth, and they that hear the words of this prophecy, and keep those things which are written therein: for the time is at hand."

The first five words of Revelation tell us who this book is going to reveal or unveil: "the Revelation of Jesus Christ." Here in a nutshell John tells us that in this book God reveals His Son, Jesus Christ, and it behooves us to believe Him because this is the duty of all men. This is the purpose of our being or existence. (1 John 5:1, 10-13).

Now let's examine the steps of how Jesus' revelation was passed down to His servants. First, God the Father gave His Son, Jesus Christ, His revelation. Here God is revealing His Son, so that His servants will understand the things that are about to take place. Second, Jesus signified it by His angel; He put in signs and symbols and commissioned His angel to give it to John. Third, His angel gave it to John and explained to him the things that he did not understand so that he could write it in a book for all of us to read.

Angels are ministering spirits who do God's bidding (Heb. 1:14). The angel's mission was to tell and explain the revelation to John so that he could testify about it and share it with those who have an ear and want to read, listen, and obey God's commandments. Fourth, John was instructed to write it down to instruct humanity so that you and I can read it and hear what God

The Revelation of Jesus Christ

is telling us. Fifth, John sent it to the seven churches. Wow, have you noticed that this world consist of seven continents (North America, South America, Africa, Australia, Asia, Europe, and Antarctica). I truly believe that these seven churches are representative of Christians in the seven continents of this world.

You may ask, why did God give Jesus His revelation and who are His servants? God in His wisdom trusted His Son with His words. God loves us just as much as Jesus loves us, and through His Word He is sharing with us secrets about the future of this world and the things that are going to happen very soon so that we will not perish for lack of knowledge (John 3:16). His servants are those who serve Him and do what He asks them to do. They serve Him and listen to His words and believe Him. If you have ears to listen what God is telling you and are willing to obey and serve Him, then you are His servant.

You do not have to be of Hebrew descent or a Jew to be God's servant. Jews and Gentiles who are willing to follow Jesus Christ are His servants because God does not show favoritism or partiality of person (Rom. 2:11; 1 Pet. 1:17). We are all God's children.

In the beginning, God spoke to our forefathers Adam and Eve and Moses face to face (Gen. 2:15-24; 3:8-10; Num. 12:6-8), but after sin entered the world, it created a barrier between humanity and God. So God then started to speak to His people through His prophets (Num. 12:6). In order to restore that relationship between man and God, Jesus offered to die for us. Every human being, every descendant of Adam and Eve has sinned and must die, "for the wages of sin is death" (Rom. 6:23). But Jesus Christ became the sacrificial Lamb and died in our place so that we can be saved and restored back to the Father provided we ask for forgiveness of our sins, obey His commandments, and keep the testimonies of Jesus Christ. God's love for humanity is evident in the following scriptures:

Isaiah 40:11; Ezekiel 34:23; Luke 11:28; 20:9-18; 24:44-49; John 3:16; 10:11; 11; 14:6; 20:31, Acts 4:12; Romans 5:8; Hebrews 13:20; 1 John 1:9.

In the parable of the husbandman in Luke 20:9-18, God is giving us another parable to teach us how His own Son was despised and killed by His enemies. In the example, the husbandman is God the Father, His servants are His prophets, many of whom the Jewish leaders killed, and the son is Jesus Christ.

So now that Jesus died for our sins, He became the gap between humanity and His Father. Jesus restored the broken human relationship with His Father. God the Father now is speaking to His servants/people through His Son Jesus Christ (Heb. 1:1-3; 1 John 5:10-12).

The Revelation of Jesus Christ

Jesus became the gap between heaven and earth to bring us back to the Father. So, my friends, it does not matter where you're from, what language you speak, how rich or poor you are, how fat or skinny you are, how ugly or pretty you are, how tall or short you are, how healthy or sick you are, what culture, tribe, or nation you belong to, what area you lived in, where you moved to, or what church you go to. As long as you have an ear, this message is for you. God the Father wants everyone to know the prophecies and message about His Son, Jesus Christ, so that they can be saved.

By the way, there's no secret about the book of Revelation. A book that reveals secrets and information can't be a sealed book. God the Father shared the information with us and entrusted it in the right hand of His Son to pass it on. God also promised to bless those who read and hear the words of this prophecy provided they keep those things that are written in it (Luke 8:21; 11:28). Wow, how hard can it be? In Revelation God reveals the beginning, the future, and the end of this world to us. He shows us the good, the bad, and the ugly. He has made it plain so that we can make an informed consent. If we choose His side, which is the good side, and do what He says, He will bless us with true riches and eternal life. The choice is yours to receive this free gift. Praise God what a love.

God is a wonderful God who loves us and would not do anything without telling us about it first. In Amos 3:7 we read, "Surely the Lord God does nothing, Unless He reveals His secret to His servants the prophets" (NKJV). And in Deuteronomy 29:29 Moses tells us that "the secret things belong to the LORD our God; but those things which are revealed belong to us and to our children forever" (NKJV). So here God is revealing His Son to us and the future of this world as it is coming to an end.

Therefore, it is true that the book of Revelation is all about Jesus Christ fulfilling what was written about Him (Luke 24:44). The Bible shows His love for humanity as shown through Creation (Gen. 1:1-28), His love of the world and sacrifice to redeem sinners (John 3:16), and His Second Coming (John 14:1-3), which is His crowning act to save man and restore their relationship with God the Father.

In the book of Revelation I've learned that Jesus Christ is the beginning and the end, the Word of God, the Good Shepherd, the Lamb of God, the lover of our souls, and the Son of God and Son of man. I've learned that He will fight His enemies, take charge of this world, and reign forever as King of kings.

In John's old age God gave him this revelation to tell everyone who has an ear what will come to pass in the closing chapters of this earth history. So please note that with God there is no retirement age. Even in our old age God is still able to use us and work with us if we allow Him.

As we've learned, there is a true harmony between the Old and New Testaments. We can't read the book of Revelation without having some knowledge of the Old Testament, especially the books of Moses, the prophets, Psalms and Daniel. They all speak about Jesus Christ. The testimonies of Jesus is the spirit of prophecy (Rev. 19:10). The Old and New Testaments go hand in hand. The books of Revelation and Daniel mirror and follow each other. Both Daniel and John saw Jesus and fell as death at His feet. They both lost all their strength in the presence of Jesus (Rev. 1:17; Dan. 10:5, 6). In Daniel 7 through 12, God gave us a glimpse of what was coming at the end of time, and He told Daniel to seal the book until the time of the end. But in Revelation 10:10, 11 and 22:10, God told John to take the open book and prophesy again about many peoples, nations, tongues, and kings and to unseal the book because the end is at hand for the fulfillment of what was written. The whole Bible talks about Jesus. Genesis starts with the beginning of the world's history, Creation. and His mission as the Lamb of God, and Revelation shows us how the world will finally come to its end and what we can do to be saved.

This book utilizes the whole Bible, the Old and New Testaments, to help us understand God's Word, His prophecies and parables, and the mysteries that He's revealing to us. The Old and the New Testaments testify about Jesus Christ. So to learn about Jesus, we must read both of them to get the picture.

Revelation 1:4-8

"John to the seven churches which are in Asia: Grace be unto you, and peace, from him which is, and which was, and which is to come; and from the seven Spirits which are before his throne; And from Jesus Christ, who is the faithful witness, and the first begotten of the dead, and the prince of the kings of the earth. Unto him that loved us, and washed us from our sins in his own blood, And hath made us kings and priests unto God and his Father; to him be glory and dominion for ever and ever. Amen.

"Behold, he cometh with clouds; and every eye shall see him, and they also which pierced him: and all kindreds of the earth shall wail because of him. Even so, Amen. I am Alpha and Omega, the beginning and the ending, saith the Lord, which is, and which was, and which is to come, the Almighty."

As human beings we all are searching for peace in this world. Peace of heart and mind—peace and tranquility instead of wars and rumors of wars; peace and quietness instead of constant arguments, fighting, and bickering one toward another. But this peace can only come from Jesus. He's ready to give us this peace if we only ask Him. "Peace I leave with you, My peace I give to you; not as the world gives do I give to you. Let not hour heart be troubled, neither let it be afraid" (John 14:27, NKJV; see also John 16:33; 1 Cor. 1:3; and 2 Cor. 1:2-5).

Jesus Christ is the faithful witness, the firstborn from the dead. This means that He was with God from the beginning of creation and He was raised from the dead and went to heaven to become our ruler and King. And He will come back again riding on clouds of angels, and every eye shall see Him. When Jesus comes back the second time it will not be a secret event. There's no such thing as a secret rapture, because He said every eye will see Him. "For as the lightening comes from the east and flashes to the west, so also will the coming of the Son of Man be" (Matt. 24:27, NKJV; see also Ps. 50:3; 97; Luke 17:24; Acts 1:9-11; 2 Pet. 3:10-12).

Moreover, Jesus went on saying that even those who condemned Him will also see Him (Zech. 12:10; Matt. 26:64). Those tribes of the world who during their life chose not to listen, read, do God's will, or keep His commandments will wail when they realize their mistake of not following Jesus or accepting His free gift of salvation. Don't let this happen to you. Now is the time to make your decision and accept Jesus's free gift of eternal life.

God loved us so much that He sent His Son to die in our place, washing away our sins in His blood. After we are washed in His blood, He makes us heirs to His Father's kingdom. Hebrew 9:22 tells us that "without shedding of blood there's no remission of sin" (NKJV).

Revelation 1:9-16

"I John, who also am your brother, and companion in tribulation, and in the kingdom and patience of Jesus Christ, was in the isle that is called Patmos, for the word of God, and for the testimony of Jesus Christ. I was in the Spirit on the Lord's day, and heard behind me a great voice, as of a trumpet, Saying, I am Alpha and Omega, the first and the last: and, What thou seest, write in a book, and send it unto the seven churches which are in Asia; unto Ephesus, and unto Smyrna, and unto Pergamos, and unto Thyatira, and unto Sardis, and unto Philadelphia, and unto Laodicea.

"And I turned to see the voice that spake with me. And being turned, I saw seven golden candlesticks; And in the midst of the seven candlesticks one like unto the Son of man, clothed with a garment down to the foot, and girt about the paps with a golden girdle. His head and his hairs were white like wool, as white as snow; and his eyes were as a flame of fire; And his feet like unto fine brass, as if they burned in a furnace; and his voice as the sound of many waters. And he had in his right hand seven stars: and out of his mouth went a sharp twoedged sword: and his countenance was as the sun shineth in his strength."

Everyone who chooses to be on Jesus' side will have tribulation, be hated by the world, and have a cross to bear. Jesus said "if anyone desires to come after Me, let him deny himself, and take up his cross, and follow Me" (Matt. 16:24, 25, NKJV; see also Mark 8:34, 35; 10:21; John 15:18).

That means exactly what He said, deny yourself, put others before yourself, pick up your cross, and follow Him. Denying yourself means to put others first and yourself last. Love others just as you love yourself. And picking up your cross means that your whole life will and must be changed forever; you will go through some pain, trials, tribulation, persecution, and difficult and hard time. You will experience discouragement at times, and people will hate you for no reason, try to kill you, give you up to the authorities, talk about you, lie about you, fire you from your job, and remove themselves from you, but you still have to bear this cross and love and forgive them. But guess what Jesus promises us for going through these terrible times—He promises that anyone who loses their life, family, and/or possessions for His name sake will find it again (Matt. 10:16-39).

I've learned that the book of Revelation unveils the battle between good and evil. Jesus Christ is the good, and Satan the evil. The whole point is for us, as created human beings, to learn about this battle and choose which side we want to be on. There are only two sides: Jesus or Satan. The choice is yours. You cannot be neutral because there's no neutrality in this battle—you're either on Jesus' side or Satan's.

At the end of the day what's your choice going to be? Jesus or Satan? The choices are as follows:

Jesus – He *is* "the way, the truth, and the life" (John 14:6, NKJV).

Satan – He is *not* the way. He is a liar, does not stand for truth, is a murderer, and is full of lies, deceit, darkness, and death (John 8:44).

Everyone must choose one or the other. But today Jesus is advising you that there's only one way to God, His Father, and that is through Himself, His Son. If you hear his voice, do not harden your heart. Let Him come in to your heart and save you. If you want to live forever then choose Jesus because He said He's the only way that leads to life eternal. The Bible is clear that every knee shall bow at the name of Jesus (Phil. 2:10; see also Phil. 4:6).

Think about it this way. Whenever you buy a car, a machine, or a piece of equipment, you follow the instructions written in its manual to the letter because you want your car and/or equipment to last a long time. Well, God created us and gave us the Bible and the Ten Commandments as our manual to teach us how to live and be saved through Jesus Christ. Let's read the Bible and practice what it says so that we can live forever with Jesus.

John picked Jesus Christ as his Savior, and therefore, was banned to the island of Patmos. In the opening chapter of Revelation, he is giving us a quick history to let us know how he ended up on the island of Patmos and how he received the revelation of Jesus Christ.

John was picked up from among his friends and companions in the faith and brought to the priests and rulers. His crime? Preaching about Jesus Christ. His sentence was to be exiled on the Isle of Patmos. This was just a ploy that Satan used to silence him from preaching about Jesus Christ.

But little did his enemies know that that's where God was able to work with him. Sometimes we get very upset when our world is turned upside down, but later on we'll discover that it was the best thing that could have happened to us. So, my brothers and sisters, don't fret and fuss when things go wrong or don't go your way. Instead, say like Paul, "In everything give thanks; for this is the will of God in Christ Jesus for you" (1 Thess. 5:18, NKJV). We need to learn to be content in all kinds of situation we're in. Although it is hard, painful, and disappointing, with Jesus we can still go on and be content because we know that "all things work together for good to those who love God, to those who are the called according to *His* purpose" (Rom. 8:28, NKJV).

According to Ellen White, "God has spoken unto us by His Son, whose we are by creation and by redemption. Christ came to John, exiled on the isle of Patmos, to give him the truth for these last days, to show him that which must shortly come to pass. Jesus Christ is the great trustee of divine revelation. It is through Him that we have knowledge of what we are to look for in the closing scenes of this earth's history. God gave this revelation to Christ, and Christ communicated the same to John.... He was the last survivor of the first chosen disciples.... The instruction to be communicated to John was so important that Christ came from heaven to give it to His servant, telling him to send it to the churches....

He bade John write in a book that which should take place in the closing scenes of this earth's history" (Manuscript Releases, vol. 20, p 150).

According to Uriah Smith, "Every fulfillment of prophecy brings its duties. There are things in the Revelation to be observed, or performed. Practical duties are to be fulfilled as the result of an understanding and accomplishment

The Revelation of Jesus Christ

of the prophecy. A notable instance of this kind may be seen in Revelation 14:12, where it is said, 'Here are they that keep the commandments of God, and the faith of Jesus'" (*Daniel and the Revelation*, vol. 2, p. 8).

So, here God is revealing His Son to us and our children. It's not a mystery or secret; He's opening and revealing to us the things that will shortly come to pass as this earth's history is winding down and coming to its end.

John said that on the Lord's day he was in the "Spirit" and heard God's voice. My brothers and sisters, in order for us to be connected with God and hear His voice, we have to believe in His Son, Jesus Christ, and be spiritually minded. We can't come to Him in our human intelligence or speak to Him without His Son and the Holy Spirit. We have to be connected to God the Father through His Son so that we can understand Him (1 John 5:1).

We need to stay connected to Jesus in order to make it as is demonstrated in the parable of the vine and the branches (John 15:5-21).

If we want to know Jesus and hear His voice, we need to be connected with Him spiritually. Spiritual things are spiritual (Dan. 12:10; John 3:8; 18:37; Rom 8:6; 1 Cor. 2:8-16; 1 John 4:1, 2).

John heard a voice on the "Lord's day." Now the question is, what day is the Lord's day? According to the Bible, the Lord's day is the seventh-day Sabbath (Gen. 2:1-3; Exod. 20:8-11). God created the Sabbath on the seventh day of Creation—the Sabbath is the only day that God blessed and sanctified; He made it special.

Furthermore, the fourth commandment is the only commandment that God placed an emphasis on to "remember." God knew that people would forget or try to switch things around; therefore, He made the emphasis to "remember the Sabbath day, to keep it holy" (Exod. 20:8, NKJV). He knew that people would one day say that it does not matter which day you worship God on as long as you worship Him. That's why He said, "Remember the Sabbath day." He knew that people would one day say that the Sabbath is only for the Jews. That's why He said "remember" to everyone who has an ear. He knew that one day people would think to change the Sabbath day of worship to Sunday worship. That's why He said, "Remember the Sabbath day." So my brothers and sisters, let us not forget to keep God's Sabbath day holy.

According to the Bible, who is Lord of the Sabbath? Let's turn to Mark 2:28 and Luke 6:5 for the answer. In both texts it says that the "Son of Man is also Lord of the Sabbath" (NKJV). Therefore, if Jesus is Lord of the Sabbath, then the Sabbath is His holy day. In Isaiah Jesus Himself called the Sabbath His holy day. "If you turn away your foot from the Sabbath, from doing your pleasure on My holy day, and call the Sabbath a delight, the holy day of the Lord honorable, and shall honor Him, not doing your own ways, not finding your own pleasure, nor speaking your own words, then you shall delight yourself in the LORD; and I will cause you to ride on the high hills of the earth, and feed you with the heritage of Jacob your father. The mouth of the Lord has spoken" (Isa. 58:13, 14, NKJV).

Now, how do we know that the seventh-day Sabbath falls on Saturday? Let's go back to the Bible. According to Genesis 1, the days of creation week started in the evening after sunset (Gen. 1:5, 8). The sequence is that the evening and the morning were the first day, the evening and the morning were the second day, etc.

Whenever the Sabbath or Saturday is mentioned, it is referred to the seventh day of the week; and when Sunday is mentioned, it is referred to as the first day of the week. Read the following texts for further study:

End of Sabbath starting the first day of the week, which is Sunday (Matt. 28:1).

Jesus risen on the first day of the week, which is Sunday (Mark 16:1, 2, 9).

Friday is the preparation day for the seventh-day Sabbath (Luke 23:54; 24:1).

Early on the first day of the week, which is Sunday (John 20:1, 19; Acts 20:7).

So, here we have learned that Sunday is the first day of the week. Therefore, Monday is the second, Tuesday is the third, Wednesday is the fourth, Thursday is the fifth, Friday is the sixth, and Saturday is the seventh, which is the Lord's day (Gen. 2:2; Exod. 16:29; Deut. 8:12-14; Heb. 4:4, 10). Thus the Sabbath is to be kept holy from evening, sunset, on Friday to evening, sunset, on Saturday.

The next question is for whom was the Sabbath made? The Sabbath was made for us—for you and me. It does not matter if you are a Jew or Gentile; black or white; brown, red, or yellow; tall or short; fat or skinny; beautiful or ugly; or healthy or sick, the Sabbath was made for you.

Just as the Sabbath in the fourth commandment was made for us to remember and to keep Holy, the rest of the ten commandments were made for us to keep and abide by. We cannot pick and choose which commandments we will abide by. We must abide by all of the ten commandments.

The last question is when does God want us to stop worshipping on the Sabbath? The answer is never. "'And it shall come to pass that from one New Moon to another, and from one Sabbath to another, all flesh shall come to worship before Me' says the LORD" Isa. 66:23, NKJV). Read the following texts for further study: Isaiah 65:17; 2 Peter 3:13; and Revelation 21:1. We will always worship God on His Sabbath day as He proposed it to be.

Are you willing to obey God and worship Him on His holy day? If you are then you should do the following:

Search the scriptures for yourself to find out about God's holy Sabbath day, which is His holy day that *He* instituted.

Read it; listen to God's voice; and obey Him.

Are you willing to do God's will as you're getting to know Jesus Christ in the book of Revelation?

If Satan, the enemy, has you bound by alcohol, drugs, sexual immorality, lying, cursing, worshiping God on a day that He did not institute, hatred toward others, stealing, coveting, worshiping your possessions, taking God's name in vain, or breaking the commandments, God is ready to break you loose from his grasp. Just ask God to help you; He's the only one who can take you out of the devil's grip. You're not a match for him. Only Jesus can help you.

According to Ellen White, "The Sabbath, which God had instituted in Eden, was as precious to John on the lonely isle as when he was with his companions in the cities and towns. The precious promises that Christ had given regarding this day he repeated and claimed as his own. It was the sign to him that God was his.... On the Sabbath day the risen Savior made His presence known to John [Revelation 1:10-13, 17, 18 quoted]

"The persecution of John became a means of grace. Patmos was made resplendent with the glory of a risen Savior. John had seen Christ in human form, with the marks of the nails, which will ever be His glory, in His hands and His feet. Now he was permitted again to behold his risen Lord, clothed with as much glory as a human being could behold, and live. What a Sabbath was that to the lonely exile, always precious in the sight of Christ, but now more than ever exalted!" (*The SDA Bible Commentary*, vol. 7, p. 955).

Revelation 1:17-20

"And when I saw him, I fell at his feet as dead. And he laid his right hand upon me, saying unto me, Fear not; I am the first and the last: I am he that liveth, and was dead; and, behold, I am alive for evermore, Amen; and have the keys of hell and of death. Write the things which thou hast seen, and the things which are, and the things which shall be hereafter; The mystery of the seven stars which thou sawest in my right hand, and the seven golden candlesticks. The seven stars are the angels of the seven churches: and the seven candlesticks which thou sawest are the seven churches."

The Revelation of Jesus Christ

John was surprised at what he saw and witnessed. Here he was permitted to see his Master, Jesus Christ, his risen Savior in His splendor and glory. This was a different form as compared to when Jesus was with them on earth preaching to the multitudes and walking from place to place preaching the good news to the people. John was so amazed and afraid that he fell down as a dead man. But Jesus in His mercy touched him and reassured him that he did not need to be afraid. He had a job for him to do; he must write everything that he saw and heard in a book.

This was a fulfillment of what Jesus told His disciples that some of them "standing here who shall not taste death till they see the kingdom of God" (Luke 9:27, NKJV; see also Matt. 16:28, Mark 9:1, Rev. 19:11).

Jesus came down to meet John and explain to him the mysteries of the stars that were in His right hand and the seven candlesticks/lampstands. This shows us that Jesus is interested in our affairs. The lampstands represent the churches. So here we see Jesus walking among the churches—this tells us that Jesus is with us, among us, and ready to help us. He has appointed a special angel to each church to guide them and report back to Him how their specific church is doing. Jesus cares for us too much to leave us alone in this sin-sick world.

This is to fulfill His promise "lo, I am with you always, even to the end of the age" (Matt 28:20).

The Holy Spirit is also the seven spirits in front of God's throne and the one involved in the affairs of humanity. Jesus told His disciples that He would send the Helper, which is the Holy Spirit to be with them and guide them (John 16:7-14). So, we need to listen to the Holy Spirit. And that's exactly why throughout the messages to the churches Jesus is repeating the importance for those who have an ear to listen to what the Spirit says to the churches because we can't understand without the Holy Spirit's illuminating power (Rev. 2:7, 11, 17, 29).

Don't be afraid to read the book of Revelation; God is ready to bless you if you read it, listen to Jesus' voice, and do the things written in it. Once you decide to read it and apply it to your life, God will send His Holy Spirit to help you. But it is up to you to take the first step. God never forces us to do anything. He always gives us choices, but once we choose Him, God will do the rest.

Have you decided what you are going to do with what you've read so far? Are you willing to follow Jesus and keep all of His commandments?

Chapter 2

Jesus's Messages to You and His Church Part 1

Revelation 2:1-7

"Unto the angel of the church of Ephesus write; These things saith he that holdeth the seven stars in his right hand, who walketh in the midst of the seven golden candlesticks; I know thy works, and thy labour, and thy patience, and how thou canst not bear them which are evil: and thou hast tried them which say they are apostles, and are not, and hast found them liars: And hast borne, and hast patience, and for my name's sake hast laboured, and hast not fainted.

"Nevertheless I have somewhat against thee, because thou hast left thy first love. Remember therefore from whence thou art fallen, and repent, and do the first works; or else I will come unto thee quickly, and will remove thy candlestick out of his place, except thou repent. But this thou hast, that thou hatest the deeds of the Nicolaitanes, which I also hate. He that hath an ear, let him hear what the Spirit saith unto the churches; To him that overcometh will I give to eat of the tree of life, which is in the midst of the paradise of God."

Jesus gave John seven messages for the seven Christian churches in Asia Minor. But just as the whole Bible is written for all of God's children, even though He chose a special group of people, the Israelites, to share the message to others, God sent seven messages to seven churches with the intention that all of us would benefit from the messages. I believe that the messages are applied to the seven continents of this world; therefore, it's for *all* human beings. They are seven letters with seven counsels from Jesus to the Christians in the world.

These seven messages are just as important for us today as the rest of the Bible is (2 Tim. 3:16, 17).

The picture of Jesus holding the seven stars, which are angels, in His right hand and walking among the seven golden menorahs, which represents the seven churches, tells us that Jesus and His Father are totally engaged in the affairs of humanity and His churches. Jesus is the one who keeps the light of each church going. If it were left for humans the lights on the candlesticks would fail and go out. God entrusted His Son to look after His churches and His people. It is comforting to know that God goes from church to church, heart to heart, house to house, board meeting to board meeting to check on His people.

He knows exactly what everyone is doing. He knows who is working for Him and who is working against Him. He knows who is patient and persevering and who is not. Who is weary of doing good and who is not. Who is pretending to be a Christian and who is not. Who is going through trials and persecution for His name and who is not. Who is associating with evil and wicked people and who is not. God has an interest in the affairs of His people. He is in our midst keeping a vigilant eye on His creation and has assigned His angel to guide and be the messenger for each church. So here you have it; God sees and knows us better than we know ourselves. We can fool other people, but we can never fool God.

Based on my research, I believe that the era of the church in Ephesus was the time of the apostles who received the gospel from Jesus Himself. They were zealous about the gospel, and because of their love for Jesus and His message, they worked hard and were willing to die for their faith. But as time went on some of them started to grow cold and sluggish in their work, and finally they lost their first love.

So here Jesus is saying to the Ephesian church and to us today after He has seen it all, "I know what you have been doing, how hard you have worked, how you have persevered, and how you can't stand wicked people; so you tested those who called themselves apostles but aren't – and you found them to be liars. You are persevering, and you have suffered for my sake without growing weary. But I have this against you: you have lost the love you had at first" (Rev. 2:2-4, *Complete Jewish Bible*).

The greatest sin that the church in Ephesus and some of us are guilty of is that we've lost our first love. That means that we have stopped caring. Whenever people stop caring, everything else is brought to a full stop. All their labor for Jesus is gone. They are no longer patient with each other; they no longer study the Bible. Their trials and persecution have made them weary, and they have stopped caring and ultimately lost their first love.

How about you? Have you lost your first love for Jesus Christ? Have you become weary and discouraged? Are you giving up on Jesus? Have you stopped caring? God knew that these things would happen, and that's why He asked John to write them down in a book so that when it did happen His people would know what to do. So, my friend, Jesus in His mercy is giving you and me the example of the church of Ephesus and admonishing us today. He's asking for all who have an ear to repent and turn from the sin of giving up on their first love for Him and to start doing what they used to do before for Jesus Christ.

If you have lost your first love for Jesus Christ, this is what you need to do:

Repent and turn from your sin. Ask God for forgiveness and the strength to resist temptation and the courage to serve Him all the way.

Do the first works that you used to do before. Share with others what God has done for you and will continue to do for you. Study your Bible, share with others what you've learned.

Pray without ceasing; pray at home, at work, in your car, on your bed, while you are walking, driving, talking, eating or resting.

The one commendation that God had for the Ephesians was that they hated the deeds of the Nicolaitanes, which He also hated. They promoted sexual immorality and worshiping of idols, which God will not stand for.

According to Revelation Seminar, "Ephesus was the church of the apostles. It represents God's church for the first century. During this century the church grew with incredible speed. Historian Gibbon says that there were up to six million Christians in the empire when the century ended. And Paul said that they had taken the gospel to the entire world, Colossians 1:5, 6, 23" (RS-005, p. 3).

Today, Jesus wants you to remember how you felt when you first received the message of Jesus Christ. Now, think about what caused you to lose that first love. What was it that distracted you to go astray? How did you end up where you are now without God in your life? What are you going to do about it? God knows all about you. You can't hide from Him or deceive Him. Jesus is willing and ready to forgive you and help you through your trials and difficult times. Jesus is ready to send His Holy Spirit to illuminate your mind and guide you. You just need to listen to Him and obey His voice. Therefore, the best thing for you to do is to: repent and turn from your sin. Ask God for forgiveness and the strength to resist temptation and the courage to serve Him all the way, and do the first works that you used to do before. Share with others what God has done for you.

The Revelation of Jesus Christ

The reward for those who repent is that they will have the right to eat from the tree of life, which is in the midst of Paradise. This tree is similar to the one that was placed in the Garden of Eden. As long as Adam and Eve ate from that tree, they had perpetual life and wouldn't die.

"He that hath an ear, let him hear what the Spirit saith unto the churches" (Rev. 2:7). This sentence gives us proof that this message is not only for the Ephesians. It applies to everyone who has an ear.

Let's bring it home. How many of us when we first heard the good news of Jesus Christ became so excited that we fell in love with Jesus? We were ready to change the whole world by proclaiming God's love to others. We shared the message with everyone we came in contact with. We couldn't stand those who were evil or who spread false doctrines. We studied the Bible to check what they were saying and verified things for ourselves. We would search the Scriptures to prove our point. But then the cares of this world took our attention away. We no longer had time to read the Bible; we became too tired or too busy to have devotions or pray in the morning and evening. We lost our first love. If people were doing evil, we just didn't want to get involved. If people were spreading false doctrines, we didn't have time to correct them.

The message to the Ephesians is a message to us, too. God is asking us to repent and start doing the first work that we did before (Isa. 43:25; Matt. 11:28; Acts 2:38; 3:19; 1 John 1:9). "But be doers of the word, and not hearers only, deceiving yourselves. For if anyone is a hearer of the word and not a doer, he is like a man observing his natural face in a mirror; for he observes himself, goes away, and immediately forgets what kind of man he was. But he who looks into the perfect law of liberty and continues in it, and is not a forgetful hearer but a doer of the work, this one will be blessed in what he does" (James 1:22-25, NKJV).

According to Ellen White, "In view of the many virtues enumerated, how striking is the charge brought against the church at Ephesus: 'Nevertheless I have somewhat against thee, because thou hast left thy first love.' This church had been highly favored. It was planted by the apostle Paul. In the same city was the temple of Diana, which, in point of grandeur, was one of the marvels of the world. The Ephesians church met with great opposition, and some of the early Christians suffered persecution; and yet some of these very ones turned from the truths that had united them with Christ's followers, and adopted, in their stead, the specious errors devised by Satan.

"This change is represented as a spiritual fall. 'Remember therefore from whence thou art fallen, and repent, and do the first works'—as outlined in the preceding verses. The believers did not sense their spiritual fall. They knew not that a change had taken place in their hearts, and that they would have to repent because of the noncontinuance of their first works. But God in His mercy called for repentance, for a return to their first love and to the works that are always the result of true, Christlike love" (*The SDA Bible Commentary*, vol. 7, pl 957).

Let us examine a quote from God Cares. "But who are the Nicolaitans? Iranaeus, a second-century minister who grew up near Ephesus, referred to them in one of his writings. The Nicolaitans claimed to be Christians, he said, but they considered it 'a matter of indifference to practise adultery, and to eat things sacrificed to idols.' It appears then that the Nicolaitans were Christians who felt that faith in Jesus released them from obedience to some of the Ten Commandments. In 1 John 2:4, John wrote against similar people who were saying, 'I know him [Jesus],' but those same people were breaking the commandments. Anyone who talks this way, John said, is a 'liar.'

"Calling a commandment-flouting Christian a 'liar' is strong language. Jesus used strong language when He said He 'hated' the teachings of the Nicolaitans. We remember that in the Sermon on the Mount Jesus said, 'Not every one who ways to me, "Lord, Lord," shall enter the kingdom of heaven, but he who does the will of my Father who is in heaven.' Matthew 7:21. Such language sobers us, especially when we consider that many people *today* say that faith releases Christians from keeping one or more of the Ten Commandments. Usually these Christians treat lightly the seventh commandment, about adultery, or the fourth, about keeping the seventh-day Sabbath.

"*The rebuke*. We are glad to learn that the Ephesian Christians rejected the misleading ideas of the Nicolaitans. In doing so, they followed Paul's counsel about not associating with deceivers. Apparently, however, they had not done so well in regard to another piece of Paul's advice. In Ephesians 5:2 Paul had urged them to 'walk in love, as Christ loved us.' But in Revelation 2:4 Jesus had to say, '**I have this against you, that you have abandoned the love you had at first.**' The Ephesian Christians had lost the keen edge of their first love for God. They had also lost the warmth of their first affection for one another.

"Jesus considered this loss of love as a sin of the first magnitude. '**Remember then from what you have fallen, repent and do the works you did at first,**' He pleaded. '**If not,**' said He, '**I will come to you and remove your lampstand from its place, unless you repent**'" (*God Cares,* vol. 2, pp. 99, 100).

Uriah Smith wrote the following regarding the church of Ephesus: "The first church named is Ephesus. According to the application here made, this would cover the first, or apostolic, age of the church.... Those early Christians had received the doctrine of Christ in its purity. They enjoyed the benefits and blessings of the gifts of the Holy Spirit. They were noted for their works, labor, and patience. In faithfulness to the pure principles taught by Christ, they could not bear those that were evil, and they tested false apostles, searched out their true characters, and found them liars" (*Daniel and the Revelation*, vol. 2, p. 24).

Today, God has a special blessing for those who repent. Why don't you claim your special blessing today? He's waiting on you right now. Just bow your head and talk to Him as you would talk to a friend. You will be blessed if you do.

Revelation 2:8-11

"And unto the angel of the church in Smyrna write; These things saith the first and the last, which was dead, and is alive; I know thy works, and tribulation, and poverty, (but thou art rich) and I know the blasphemy of them which say they are Jews, and are not, but are the synagogue of Satan. Fear none of those things which thou shalt suffer: behold, the devil shall cast some of you into prison, that ye may be tried; and ye shall have tribulation ten days: be thou faithful unto death, and I will give thee a crown of life. He that hath an ear, let him hear what the Spirit saith unto the churches; He that overcometh shall not be hurt of the second death."

Jesus said, "I am Alpha and Omega, the beginning and the ending," (Rev. 1:8). He is the first because He was present with His Father from the beginning of creation of this world, and He is the last because He will be there to the end of this world. He was dead because He died for our sins and came to life because His Father raised Him back to life. He knows everything that we're going through. It is comforting to know that Jesus knows how we are suffering and how poor we became as we try to serve Him by forsaking everything. But guess what? Being poor in this world and having Jesus is a recipe for being rich. A lot of time when we're down and out and feel like no one cares, Jesus is there to pick us up and comfort us because He's the only one that truly cares. Jesus promised us in Mathew 5:1-12 that when we're going through persecution for His name's sake (just because we want to serve Him and keep His commandments) that's when we are blessed. So don't be afraid of the trials, persecution, and threats of death that the devil brings your way—God is in control, and He has your back as long as you remain faithful to him.

Are you being persecuted today because of your faith in Jesus Christ and the true Sabbath? Are you being forced to work on God's Sabbath day? You are not alone. God knows about your suffering and persecution; others have gone through it before you did, so don't give up. Jesus said in Revelation 2:10, "Be thou faithful unto death, and I will give thee a crown of life," just as I was faithful unto death and received the crown from my Father. Jesus Christ went through similar trials and tribulation and proved that if we trust God He will see us through and make us conquerors, so hang in there and don't give up. "All things work together for good to those who love God," (Rom. 8:28).

When you live among wolves, sooner or later they will bite you when you cross their paths. Let's stay away from the devil and his evil angels. It's important to note that those who are poor because of their faith are rich because of their reward. And those who are rich now in serving the enemy, the devil, will be poor when they receive their reward of final destruction (Matt. 5:1-12). Following are some promises that Jesus gave us to help us and strengthened us as we go through the difficult time that the devil will throw our way:

"Do not fear any of those things which you are about to suffer. Indeed, the devil is about to throw some of you into prison, that you may be tested, and you will have tribulation ten days. Be faithful until death, and I will give you the crown of life" (Rev. 2:10, NKJV).

"Blessed is the man who endures temptation; for when he has been approved, he will receive the crown of life which the Lord has promised to those who love Him. Let no one say when he is tempted, 'I am tempted by God'; for God cannot be tempted by evil, nor does He Himself tempt anyone. But each one is tempted when he is drawn away by his own desires and enticed" (James 1:12-14, NKJV).

"So then, my beloved brethren, let every man be swift to hear, slow to speak, slow to wrath; for the wrath of man does not produce the righteous of God. Therefore lay aside all filthiness and overflow of wickedness, and receive with meekness the implanted word, which is able to save your souls" (James 1:19-21, NKJV).

"My brethren, count it all joy when you fall into various trials, knowing that the testing of your faith produces patience. But let patience have its perfect work, that you may be perfect and complete, lacking nothing. If any of you lacks wisdom, let him ask of God, who gives to all liberally and without reproach, and it will be given to him. But let him ask in faith, with no doubting, for he who doubt is like a wave of the sea driven and tossed by the wind" (James 1:2-6, NKJV).

What beauty and reassurance regarding persecution that God will give us the knowledge and wisdom to persevere (James 1:12-14).

I want to challenge everyone who has an ear, which includes you, to not be afraid of what you are about to suffer for the sake of Jesus and His commandments. As we are heading into the "new world order," the last days of this world as it is coming to its end, people will start getting crazy and will hate you for no apparent reason. Crime will increase to the point that the government will have no control. People will become desperate and do desperate things. This world is changing rapidly—the economy is changing things for everyone—but God is still in charge and in control. This is the time that we need to practice our faith and trust Him. The time will come when the world will blame all their problems on those that keep God's Ten Commandments and His true seventh-day Sabbath. But remember, Jesus said that they will hate you because they hated Him first. Everyone who follows Jesus and keep His commandments will be hated.

According to Revelation 2:10 the devil will throw some of Jesus' followers in prison to test them, and they will have tribulation and hard times for ten days; so don't give up. Remain faithful even to the point of death. This is where you will have to exercise your faith in God and claim His promises that He will never leave you or forsake you. Matthew 28:20 says, "Lo, I am with you always, even to the end of the age" (NKJV). This is the promise that God gave us to claim when we are going through persecution. He's always with us; we should not be afraid of those who can kill the body because they can't kill the soul (Matt. 10:28).

And we mustn't forget that our reward is a crown of life. We will not be hurt by the second death, which, according to the Bible, is the eternal death that Jesus is ready to spare His followers from. Please accept this free gift from Him and be prepared for the coming crisis.

Following is more in-depth information about the Smyrna church from a number of other authors. "Smyrna covers the church from about 100 A.D. through 313 A.D., and was a period of fearful persecution and martyrdom for the church. The Roman empire considered Christianity illegal and attempted to stamp it out. Only God knows how many of His children were decapitated, burned, fed to lions and slain with the sword. The church in this era lived so close to Jesus that He gave them no reproof. He did, however, give them blessed words of encouragement. What were these words?" (Revelation Seminar, RS-005, p. 3). "Fear none of these things which thou shalt suffer … be thou faithful unto death and I will give thee a crown of life" (Rev. 2:10).

Ellen White wrote, "Christ speaks of the church over which Satan presides as the synagogue of Satan. Its members are the children of disobedience. They are those who choose to sin, who labor to make void the holy law of God. It is Satan's work to mingle evil with good, and to remove the distinction between good and evil. Christ would have a church that labors to separate the evil from the good, whose members will not willingly tolerate wrong-doing, but will expel it from the heart and life" (*The SDA Bible Commentary*, vol. 7, p. 958).

According to Uriah Smith, "To the Smyrna church, about to pass through the fiery ordeal of persecution, He reveals Himself as one who was dead, but is now alive. If they should be called to seal their testimony with their blood, they were to remember that the eyes of One were upon them who had shared the same fate, but had triumphed over death, and was able to bring them up from a martyr's grave" (*Daniel and Revelation,* vol. 2, p. 28).

Even today Christians worldwide are being persecuted and thrown into jail because of their faith in Jesus Christ. God knew that all these things would happen; therefore, He revealed them to us beforehand to prepare us.

Revelation 2:12-17

"And to the angel of the church in Pergamos write; These things saith he which hath the sharp sword with two edges; I know thy works, and where thou dwellest, even where Satan's seat is: and thou holdest fast my name, and hast not denied my faith, even in those days wherein Antipas was my faithful martyr, who was slain among you, where Satan dwelleth. But I have a few things against thee, because thou hast there them that hold the doctrine of Balaam, who taught Balac to cast a stumblingblock before the children of Israel, to eat things sacrificed unto idols, and to commit fornication.

"So hast thou also them that hold the doctrine of the Nicolaitanes, which thing I hate. Repent; or else I will come unto thee quickly, and will fight against them with the sword of my mouth. He that hath an ear, let him hear what the Spirit saith unto the churches; To him that overcometh will I give to eat of the hidden manna, and will give him a white stone, and in the stone a new name written, which no man knoweth saving he that receiveth it."

The Bible, which is the Word of God, is represented as a sword (Isa. 49:2; Eph. 6:17; Heb. 4:12; Rev. 2:16). God's Word pierces through our hearts, and He judges us by His Word. God knows the most secret thoughts and desires of our heart. We can't hide anything from God. He knows where we live and what's going on in our lives. He knows it all and sees all. He will find you. King David said it best in Psalm 139 when he writes that even when we go down or up God is there. Jesus knows that we live in the enemy's territory, but He commends those who hold fast to His name and do not deny trusting in Him.

This period in earth's history appears to be the "everybody does it" era; therefore, it must be right! How wrong! It's not because of the majority that makes it right. The majority could be wrong and not know it. But here in Revelation Jesus is pleased to know that even though the majority are doing the wrong thing some of his faithful people stood firm for Him.

Jesus knows where you and I live, and He knows where Satan is. He knows where we work and what we do who and who we worship. Even though we might be surrounded by people who worship the enemy and disregard God's commandments, God will give us strength to hold fast to His name. Do not listen to the ones who will lead you astray, claiming to know better but who are doing what's wrong in God's eyes. Do not follow them. You may be living or working among evil people who worship Satan, but you're not alone. Jesus is with you and will strengthen you. Just keep your relationship with Him strong, and He will keep you safe.

"Pergamos covers the church during the 4th, 5th, and the first decades of the 6th centuries. It is the era of state supported religion and compromise. Christianity had grown so rapidly that Roman leaders felt insecure. In some places, Christians were outnumbering pagans. The Roman Emperor, Constantine, and his entire army were baptized and joined the Christian faith" (Revelation Seminar, RS-005, p. 4).

When the early Christian church started, Satan tried to destroy it by persecution. But that didn't work, so he sought to corrupt the church by popularity, compromise, and worldly alliance. Pagan beliefs and practices came into the church, and these heathen influences so changed the church that it lost its spiritual power. Pergamos was called Satan's seat (verse 13) because it was the capital of the Roman province, and thus, also, the headquarters of its heathen religion. The Lord rebuked the church living in this period for permitting false teachings to flourish in their churches.

God made it clear to church in Pergamos, and to us, that they needed to repent and turn away from their sins, which included teaching false doctrines and sexual sin.

God chastised them for beings as Balaam, who was a prophet of God who compromised his Christianity and became a traitor to gain favor of the king. Balaam told the children of Israel that it was acceptable to eat food sacrificed to idols.

The church was also guilty of sexual sins, including such things as fornication, pre-marital sex, pedifile, prostitution, sexual abuse, sex slaves, rape, adultery, incest, gay marriage, and bestiality. God did not institute these behaviors, and let's not kid ourselves by justifying our bad behaviors. God did not institute gay marriages—He blessed the marriage of Adam and Eve and told them to go and multiply (Gen. 1:28). Now ask yourself, how can a gay couple multiply biologically and naturally? Also in Genesis 2:24 and Matthew 19:5 God said, "A *man* shall leave his father and mother and be joined to his *wife*, and they shall become one flesh" (NKJV). The Bible is clear on this matter.

This is the time to pray, repent, and ask God to give us wisdom, knowledge, and courage to follow His mandates and not what other people say to do. He's waiting for you to come to Him. He does not force Himself on anyone. If you are living in any kind of sexual sin, this is your time to repent. Between you and God bring your burden to Him and leave it at His cross. He'll take care of it for you. Nothing is impossible for God. If you aren't keeping His laws and commands, repent and make things right. You'll be glad you did.

Now let's look at the last part of the section of scripture we are examining. What is the teaching of the Nicolaitanes? The Nicolaitanes advocated the practice of idolatry and sexual immorality. According to their teachings it was OK to practice idolatry and sexual immorality because everyone is covered under grace. But they were wrong. It's like telling your son it is OK to go steal, kill, and do whatever evil thing you can imagine because he's under your grace as his parent who will understand and forgive. What chaos this would create in the world. God is a God of order, and that's why He gave us the Ten Commandments to teach us how we need to act and live. His law is our guide in life to keep us safe and to love God and our neighbors. We must follow God's mandates and His mandates only. According to Jude, those who do these evil things are called "ungodly men" (verse 4).

Uriah Smith provides some additional historical information in *Daniel and Revelation*: "During this period, the doctrine of Christ was being corrupted, the mystery of iniquity was working, and Satan was laying the foundation of a stupendous system of apostasy, the papacy. Here was the falling away foretold by Paul in 2 Thessalonians 2:3" (vol. 2, p. 30).

The doctrines complained of in the church of Pergamos were of course similar in their tendency, leading to spiritual idolatry and an unlawful connection between the church and the world. Out of this spirit was finally produced the union of civil and ecclesiastical powers that culminated in the

The Revelation of Jesus Christ

formation of the papacy. If the period covered by the Pergamos church has been correctly located, it terminated with the setting up of the papacy in AD 538. The most natural division to be assigned to the church of Thyatira would be the time of the continuance of this power through the 1260 years of its supremacy, or from AD 538 to AD 1798. This well describes the state of the church of Jesus Christ during the long period of papal triumph and persecution. This age of dreadful tribulation for the church was such as never had been seen before (Matt. 24:21).

In this time and at the end of this world, we will be persecuted, tried, lied to, and beaten, but Jesus' promise is sure—He will never leave us or forsake us.

Uriah Smith also wrote, "It is interesting to note that the city of Pergamos became the seat of ancient Babylonian sun worship.... 'It is supposed that Antipas was not an individual, but a class of men who opposed the power of the bishops, or popes, in that day, being a combination of two words, 'Anti,' opposed, and 'Papas,' father, or pope; and many of them suffered martyrdom at that time in Constantinople and Rome, where the bishops and popes began to exercise the power which soon after brought into subjection the kings of the earth, and trampled on the rights of the church of Christ.... The doctrines complained of in the church of Pergamos were of course similar in their tendency, leading to spiritual idolatry and an unlawful connection between the church and the world. Out of this spirit was finally produced the union of civil and ecclesiastical powers which culminated in the formation of the papacy" (*Daniel and Revelation,* vol. 2, pp. 31, 32).

In spite of the persecution that Christ's followers experienced and will experience, Jesus will give those who persevere some of the hidden manna. Jesus has some hidden manna for those who repent and keep His commandments. Oh how I long to taste that hidden manna. What about you? Jesus will also give those who stand in the end a white stone on which is written a new name that nobody knows except the one receiving it. Jesus also has a new name for us. A new beginning with a new name. Wow! I can hardly wait.

Revelation 2:18-29

"And unto the angel of the church in Thyatira write; These things saith the Son of God, who hath his eyes like unto a flame of fire, and his feet are like fine brass; I know thy works, and charity, and service, and faith, and thy patience, and thy works; and the last to be more than the first. Notwithstanding I have a few things against thee, because thou sufferest that woman Jezebel, which calleth herself a prophetess, to teach and to seduce my servants to commit fornication, and to eat things sacrificed unto idols. And I gave her space to repent of her fornication; and she repented not. Behold, I will cast her into a bed, and them that commit adultery with her into great tribulation, except they repent of their deeds. And I will kill her children with death; and all the churches shall know that I am he which searcheth the reins and hearts: and I will give unto every one of you according to your works.

But unto you I say, and unto the rest in Thyatira, as many as have not this doctrine, and which have not known the depths of Satan, as they speak; I will put upon you none other burden. But that which ye have already hold fast till I come. And he that overcometh, and keepeth my works unto the end, to him will I give power over the nations: And he shall rule them with a rod of iron; as the vessels of a potter shall they be broken to shivers: even as I received of my Father. And I will give him the morning star. He that hath an ear, let him hear what the Spirit saith unto the churches."

Here God is telling us in plain language that Jesus is His Son. He has eyes as a flame of fire. He sees and knows it all. God says, "I know thy works, and charity, and service, and faith, and thy patience" (Rev. 2:19). The Thyatirans were hard working Christians who loved to serve the Lord, had great faith, and were patient. However, some of that patience caused them to allow the teachings of Jezebel in their churches, which caused its members to eat things sacrificed to idols and to commit sexual immorality. So here they were repeating the same sins that their sister church Pergamum was doing. (Please don't forget, mistakes should be learned from and not repeated.) It is a sin to tolerate pagan beliefs and practices in our churches no matter who's doing it or who's approving it. As church members we all need to stand alone as Daniel did, trusting fully in God. If we are going to stand firm, we must use the Bible, the Ten Commandments, and the testimonies of Jesus Christ as our guide.

"Thyatira covers a time period of about 1,000 years, from the sixth through the fifteenth centuries—the longest period of any of the seven churches. This period is sometimes called the Dark Ages. It was a time of fearful apostasy. The Lord rebuked the church of this era for opening its doors to an evil woman who corrupted the church. What was this woman's name? Revelation 2:20" (Revelation Seminar, RS-005, p. 4). I've learned that according to Revelation 2:20-23 this evil woman was Jezebel.

Now we'll examine a quote from *God Cares*, "We recognize that in Thyatira the Jezebel problem – immorality and eating food sacrificed to idols – was the same compromise with pagan culture that was advocated by the Nicolaitanes and the Balamites. The degree of compromise, however, was devastatingly worse. Jezebel had ripened her rebellion. Granted time for repentance, she had stubbornly refused to change her ways. As a result, she was to suffer from a dread disease, presumably brought on by her own excesses" (vol. 2, p. 106).

How about your church? Are you allowing the teachings of Balaam, Jezebel, and the Nicoliatanes in your church?

From this passage in Revelation, we learn that we must:

1. Turn from the sins of Jezebel and Balaam, which is eating items sacrificed to idols and sexual immorality.

2. Turn from the teachings of the Nicoliatanes—idolatry and sexual immorality.

3. Hold fast to our relationship and faith in Jesus until He comes.

4. Keep doing God's works and obey the Ten Commandments.

5. Not involve ourselves with the occult, whichcraft, palm readers, psychics, horoscope, spirits, and mediums. No one can reveal your future except God. Cards, psychics, the church of Satan, palm readers, etc., cannot predict their own destiny so how can they predict yours? It's all lies that Satan uses to confuse people and keep them in the dark.

In this world there are only two choices: good or evil. The good choice is God, Jesus Christ, and His plan of salvation. The evil choice is Satan, his evil angels, and their plan to destroy the human race forever. Satan can only succeed if *you* allow him. The choice is yours; whose side are you going to be on? I pray that you'll choose God and Jesus' side so that you will have eternal life. Remember, whatever you do in life, if it is not for God, it is for Satan, so you need to make up your mind. God made us with a free will to choose who we want to serve—Jesus or Satan.

Uriah Smith provides further insight regarding Thyatira: "This church is the only one that is commended for an improvement in spiritual things. But as in the church of Pergamos unfavorable circumstances were no apology for false doctrines in the church, so in this church, no amount of labor, charity, service, faith, or patience could compensate for a like sin. A rebuke is therefore given them for suffering an agent of Satan to remain in their midst" (*Daniel and Revelation,* vol. 2, p. 34).

The church of Thyatira's problem was "Jezebel." She led her husband into idolatry and fed the prophets of Baal at her own table. God's pleading to His people is to "hold fast till I come" (Rev. 2:25). Again this message is for everyone who has an ear to hear.

As we read about the churches of Revelation and think about today, we can see many similarities. Thyatira struggled with same-sex marriages, murder, spiritualism, Satan worship in their community and church. Let's compare this with today: There is no prayer in school, but there are same-sex marriages, Satan worship, spiritualism in government and people's homes, palm readers, psychics, killings, drive by shootings, and school shootings, to name just a few of the evil we face today.

So how are we doing today? Are we committing the same mistakes as the church of Thyatira? Are we tolerating devil worship and pagan practices in our churches, homes, schools, and work places? Ask yourself why you aren't opposing spiritualism, same-sex marriages, Satan worship, no prayers in school, guns, hate crimes, etc. The list can go on and on. What are you doing about these evils? Are you partaking with them or opposing them? Jesus needs people to stand up for what is right. Are you willing to stand up for Jesus today?

Remember, if you stand firm, your reward will be sure. Once Jesus returns, you will be on the victorious side and will obtain power over the nations. There will be no more burdens, and Jesus will give us the morning star. But if you want to stand, you must stay connected with Jesus.

Chapter 3

Jesus's Messages to You and His Church Part 2

Revelation 3:1-6

"And unto the angel of the church in Sardis write; These things saith he that hath the seven Spirits of God, and the seven stars; I know thy works, that thou hast a name that thou livest, and art dead. Be watchful, and strengthen the things which remain, that are ready to die: for I have not found thy works perfect before God. Remember therefore how thou hast received and heard, and hold fast, and repent. If therefore thou shalt not watch, I will come on thee as a thief, and thou shalt not know what hour I will come upon thee. Thou hast a few names even in Sardis which have not defiled their garments; and they shall walk with me in white: for they are worthy. He that overcometh, the same shall be clothed in white raiment; and I will not blot out his name out of the book of life, but I will confess his name before my Father, and before his angels. He that hath an ear, let him hear what the Spirit saith unto the churches."

Here God is revealing to us that Jesus is not only God but He also has the seven Spirits of God. As you know, the number seven is God's complete number; therefore, Jesus is complete in God the Father. He's also in charge of the angels; they follow His commands. Here Jesus is counseling the church of Sardis regarding how they are living and their dead works. To be a dead church means to go through the motion but not actually do the work.

James 2: 20-26 says, "But do you want to know, O foolish man, that faith without works is dead? Was not Abraham our father justified by works when he offered Isaac his son on the altar? Do you see that faith was working together

Jesus's Messages to You and His Church Part 2

with his works, and by works faith was made perfect? And the Scripture was fulfilled which says, 'Abraham believed God, and it was accounted to him for righteousness.' And he was called the friend of God. You see then that a man is justified by works, and not by faith only. Likewise, was not Rahab the harlot also justified by works when she received the messengers and sent them out another way? For as the body without the spirit is dead, so faith without works is dead also" (NKJV).

Let's bring it home now. In our daily lives we go to church, sing, pray, praise God, shout hallelujah, and lift our hands, but inside our hearts, we have somebody that we can't stand or even hate. And at times we make sure we get even with our enemies. We want to show them who's the boss; we gossip; we don't study the Bible as we should; we do not have worship in our homes; we do not participate in communion; we do not do any evangelistic work; we do not visit the sick, widows, or orphans. The list goes on and on. So we are similar to the Christians of the church of Sardis.

Sardis was the dead church that pretended to live up to its name by having a reputation of being alive. But in reality and in Jesus' eyes, it was a dead church that did not work or produce fruit. God told them and is telling us today that He knows our work. As we learned from the previous churches, we cannot run or hide from God. He sees everything and knows what we're doing, thinking, and planning to do, so we might as well give it up and give in to God. He's the only way, truth, and life.

A lot of people have to live a certain way because of who they are or the name they have to live up to—think about what we expect from presidents, pastors, pastors' wives, queens, teachers, judges, actors, etc. But when you compare them to what's really important, you'll realize that it's just a name, and a name without fruits is dead. I know you can think of some names that people would die for, but is it the name that one should live for? Is it the ideal way of living? Is it God's standards? Now you may ask, what type of religion and works is perfect in God's eyes? Or what type of works does He approve?

Let's look for the answers in James 1:27: "Pure and undefiled religion before God and the Father is this: to visit orphans and widows in their trouble, and to keep oneself unspotted from the world" (NKJV). James 2:10-12 says, "For whoever shall keep the whole law, and yet stumble in one point, he is guilty of all. For He who said, 'Do not commit adultery,' also said, 'Do not murder.' Now if you do not commit adultery, but you do murder, you have become a transgressor of the law" (NKJV) So, to live up to the name that will bring glory to God, we must follow His commandments and the testimonies

The Revelation of Jesus Christ

of Jesus Christ. And we cannot keep only one or two of the commandments; we must keep all of the Ten Commandments because if we break one we have broken all of them. Let's strive to keep all of God's Ten Commandments so that He can bless us.

Let's turn to the book of James and examine a number of other things he says regarding living a righteous life according to God's design. James 3:13-18 says, "Who is a wise man and endued with knowledge among you? let him shew out of a good conversation his works with meekness of wisdom. But if ye have bitter envying and strife in your hearts, glory not, and lie not against the truth. This wisdom descendeth not from above, but is earthly, sensual, devilish. For where envying and strife is, there is confusion and every evil work. But the wisdom that is from above is first pure, then peaceable, gentle, and easy to be intreated, full of mercy and good fruits, without partiality, and without hypocrisy. And the fruit of righteousness is sown in peace of them that make peace."

James 4:4 says, "Ye adulterers and adulteresses, know ye not that the friendship of the world is enmity with God? whosoever therefore will be a friend of the world is the enemy of God

Finally, James 5:7-12 says, "Be patient therefore, brethren, unto the coming of the Lord. Behold, the husbandman waiteth for the precious fruit of the earth, and hath long patience for it, until he receive the early and latter rain. Be ye also patient; establish your hearts: for the coming of the Lord draweth nigh. Grudge not one against another, brethren, lest ye be condemned: behold, the judge standeth before the door. Take, my brethren, the prophets, who have spoken in the name of the Lord, for an example of suffering affliction, and of patience. Behold, we count them happy which endure. Ye have heard of the patience of Job, and have seen the end of the Lord; that the Lord is very pitiful, and of tender mercy. But above all things, my brethren, swear not, neither by heaven, neither by the earth, neither by any other oath: but let your yea be yea; and your nay, nay; lest ye fall into condemnation."

Now let's read what the Revelation Seminar says about Sardis: "Sardis embraces Christianity in the 16th, 17th and the first part of the 18th centuries. It covers the crucial period of reformation, when spirit-filled men of God shook the world with their messages. The Bible, God's book, was once again brought back into favor, and Christian beliefs were tested by it. Some of these men founded great church denominations that still exist today. But, alas, when these men died, their followers, instead of prayerfully seeking for more truth, abandoned part of what they already possessed, and the church went backwards

Jesus's Messages to You and His Church Part 2

with astounding rapidity" (Revelation Seminar, RS-005, p. 5).

After Jesus' rebuke, He gave the church of Sardis a commendation. He indicated that there were a few people in Sardis who had not soiled their clothes, and He promises that they will walk with Him, clothed in white, because they are worthy. Sardis had some faithful believers who were living up to its name and brought glory to God's name; therefore, they will be clothed in white and walk with God.

When John wrote Revelation, God used the illustration from the seven churches in Asia Minor to reflect different types of Christians who exhibit those types of characteristics of the churches or who will display them until He comes. That's why God made it plain that the messages that He gave to the seven churches apply to and is for everyone who has an ear. That means it is for you and me.

God featured seven different Christian characteristics throughout the earth's history. You and I, at one time or another, will see ourselves in the behaviors of the members of the churches of Ephesus, Smyrna, Pergamos, Thyatira, Sardis, Philadelphia, and the Laodiceans. Why? Because these seven messages were not only for those people but for all those who have an ear. So these messages and blessings are for you, too, provided that you read, listen, and do what the Bible says for you to do.

Let's review a few additional thoughts pertaining to the church of Sardis. "The church of Sardis is represented as having in it a few faithful ones among the many who had become, as it were, careless and insensible of their obligations to God. 'Thou hast a few names even in Sardis which have not defiled their garments; and they shall walk with me in white: for they are worthy.' Who is so favored as to be numbered among these few in Sardis? Are you? Am I? Who are among this number? Is it not best for us to inquire into this matter, in order that we may learn to whom the Lord refers when He says that a few have not stained their white robes of character?" (*The SDA Bible Commentary,* vol. 7, p. 959).

God calls upon this church to make a change. They had a name to live by, but their works were destitute of the love of Jesus. Oh how many have fallen because they trusted in their profession for salvation! How many are lost by their effort to keep up a name! If one has the reputation of being a successful evangelist, a gifted preacher, a man of prayer, a man of faith, a woman of special devotion, there is positive danger that he or she will shipwreck their faith when tried by the little tests that God allows to come. Often they will crumble in an effort to maintain their reputation. People who live in fear that others do not appreciate their value lose sight of Him who alone makes us worthy of glorifying God. Let us be faithful stewards. Let us look away from self to Christ. Then there will be no trouble at all.

God Cares says the following: "The situation in Sardis was serious, but it was not hopeless. Christ's concern for everyone then as now was as warm and attentive as if each individual were the only person for whom He gave His life. So even in this self-satisfied 'smoky' congregation, Jesus knew **'a few names'** of people who had not 'soiled their garments'" (vol. 2, p. 110).

Uriah Smith offers the following commentary regarding the church of Sardis: "The great fault found with Sardis is that it has a name to live, but is dead… This church was to hear the proclamation of the doctrine of the second advent. 'If therefore thou shalt not watch, I will come on thee as a thief.' Verse 3. This implies that the doctrine of the advent would be proclaimed, and the duty of watching would be enjoined upon the church. The coming spoken of is unconditional; the manner only in which it would come upon them is conditional. Their not watching would not prevent the coming of the Lord; but by watching they could avoid being overtaken as by a thief.… James says: 'Pure religion and undefiled before God and the Father is this, To visit the fatherless and widows in their affliction, and to keep himself unspotted from the world. James 1:27" (*Daniel and Revelation*, vol. 2, pp. 383, 384).

What about you? Are you watching and living up to the name that God wants you to live by? Are you prepared and ready for His Second Coming? If you live your life as God requests, the rewards will be yours when Jesus returns. He promises to dress us in white clothing, place our name in the book of life, and acknowledge us before God the Father and the angels.

Now let's learn about the church of Philadelphia.

Revelation 3:7-13

"And to the angel of the church in Philadelphia write; These things saith he that is holy, he that is true, he that hath the key of David, he that openeth, and no man shutteth; and shutteth, and no man openeth; I know thy works: behold, I have set before thee an open door, and no man can shut it: for thou hast a little strength, and hast kept my word, and hast not denied my name. Behold, I will make them of the synagogue of Satan, which say they are Jews, and are not, but do lie; behold, I will make them to come and worship before thy feet, and to know that I have loved thee.

"Because thou hast kept the word of my patience, I also will keep thee from the hour of temptation, which shall come upon all the world, to try them that dwell upon the earth. Behold, I come quickly: hold that fast which thou hast, that no man take thy crown. Him that overcometh will I make a pillar in the temple of my God, and he shall go no more out: and I will write upon him the name of my God, and the name of the city of my God, which is new Jerusalem, which cometh down out of heaven from my God: and I will write upon him my new name. He that hath an ear, let him hear what the Spirit saith unto the churches."

Only one person is holy and true and has the key of David, and what He opens no one can shut and what He shuts no one can open. The one person with this authority is the Creator of the universe. Only Jesus can fit in this category. No angel can do this. As with the other churches, again, God is telling the Christians in the Philadelphia church, "I know your works." God is always in charge and knows what's going on. The Philadelpian's story reminds me of the story of the ten virgins (Matt. 25:1-13). Five were wise because they had enough oil in their lamps, and although they slept a little, they were still able to use their remaining oil (their little strength) to go in with the bridegroom. The other five foolish ones did not have enough oil to carry them through. For you and I, now is the time to buy our oil from the Holy Spirit while we are waiting for our Lord and Savior's Second Coming. How can we buy the oil? By studying the Word of God, praying, and daily communing with God. Keep the Ten Commandments and the testimonies of Jesus Christ.

In all of the messages to the churches, God placed His stamp of approval on them to let everyone who has an ear know where the message is coming from. This is not John's message; it is from God Himself. Therefore, we must pay close attention and obey. The work of the faithful ones in Philadelphia is known to God. He commends them for obeying His message about persevering and holding on to the truth. As a result of their faithfulness, God places an open door that no one can shut. It is an open door to partake of God's glory and riches, a chance to follow Jesus and receive eternal life.

An open door from God means the universe and eternity are the limit. Therefore, it is something big and great that "eye has not seen, nor ear heard, nor have entered into heart of man the things which God has prepared for those who love Him" (1 Cor. 2:9). Here Jesus is telling His faithful ones that He knows that they have but little power, but yet they have obeyed His message and have not disowned Him. Jesus loves it when we stand for Him even when we are not strong enough. He's ready to pick up the missing pieces to help us through. Read the example of the three Hebrew boys who stood for God even to death (Dan. 3).

If we are going to be prepared, we must hold on to God and not let anyone take our crown away. We are not strong enough to do it on our own; we must trust God, make a stand for Him, and let Him take care of the rest.

If you keep oil in your lamp, Jesus will help you in the time of trial that will come upon the whole world. The last test that will come upon the world is the "Sunday law," where everyone will be forced to worship on Sunday. And if they refuse, they will not be able to buy or sell. They'll be ostracized, persecuted, and killed.

As we've learned in our previous chapters, God's day of worship is on His holy Sabbath, which is the seventh-day Saturday according to His Ten Commandments. Sunday worship, according to history, is a pagan day of worshiping the sun. Here is where we need to choose and show our true allegiance. Will you follow God and worship on His true Sabbath or Satan and his evil angels and worship on the man-made pagan day of worship, which is Sunday? This is the test that you and I will have to go through at the end time of this world. Who will it be? Jesus or Satan? The choice is always yours. God does not force people to do anything, because He loves us too much to force us to choose Him.

Satan, through his human agent, is the one who will be forcing people to follow the Sunday law and worship him on Sunday. They will formulate laws to kill everyone who refuses to worship him on Sunday, the day he instituted and even attempted to change God's laws regarding worshiping on Sabbath. Don't let him stand in your way of salvation. Ask Jesus to help you make the right decision for eternal life. (Further on we will cover the big trial that's coming upon the whole earth).

According to Acts 5:27-29 we must follow what God says and not what man says. The Bible tells us that God will allow some to fall asleep who are unable to withstand the enemy's test. Jesus knows our strengths and weaknesses. He knows who's able to withstand this trial and the time of trouble and who's not. Therefore, in His mercy He won't allow those who are unable to endure go through this hard and difficult time. Revelation 14:13 says, "Then I heard a voice from heaven saying to me, 'Write: "Blessed are the dead who die in the Lord from now on."' 'Yes,' says the Spirit, 'that they may rest from their labors, and their works follow them'" (NKJV; see also James 5:7-11).

Let's look at the history surrounding the church of Philadelphia. "The Philadelphia era of the church covers the second half of the 18th century and the first half of the 19th century. It is the era of the birth and expansion of foreign missions. Both the American and British Bible Societies were organized during this time, and missionaries began encircling the world. Great revival preachers like Wesley and Whitefield helped spark a global revival. World-wide study of the books of Daniel and Revelation expanded the revival into the greatest since Pentecost. The name 'Philadelphia' or 'brotherly love' is, indeed, fitting for this time period. As Jesus looked at His church in this period He offered no reproof. This church, however, had difficulties with the same group as did the church of Smyrna" (Revelation Seminar, RS-005, p. 6).

Uriah Smith wrote, "The word 'Philadelphia' signifies 'brotherly love,' and expresses the position and spirit of those who received the Advent message up to the autumn of 1844. The great religious awakening in the early part of the nineteenth century which resulted from a study of the prophecies, culminated in this advent movement. Men from all denominations were convinced that the coming of Christ was near. As they came out of the various churches, they left sectarian names and feelings behind, and every heart beat in unison as all joined to give the alarm to the churches and to the world, and pointed to the coming of the Son of man as the believer's true hope" (*Daniel and Revelation*, vol. 2, p. 386).

Here is another thought to consider: "It is good to want to be a Christian; but evidently wanting to be one isn't enough. Many people will be lost while hoping and desiring to be saved. We must decide to be Christians. We must choose to live faith when we feel like grumbling; to live love when we feel like being bitter; to do good when we feel like doing nothing or being mean. And we must choose to do so in the only way possible, through a vital personal relationship with Jesus Christ. We must open the door and let Him in. If we want ours to be a Christian family, we must exert ourselves to bring Christ into it" (*God Cares,* vol. 2, p. 115).

John says in Revelation 14:12: "here is the patience of the saints; here *are they that keep the commandments of God, and the faith of Jesus.*" Those who now live in patient, faithful obedience to the commandments of God and the faith of Jesus, will be kept in the hour of temptation and peril (Rev. 13:13-17).

Once again, Jesus promises a reward for the members of the church of Philadelphia and those of us in these last days. He promises to make all individuals who follow Him and obey His commands a pillar in God's temple. And Jesus will write on us God the Father's name and the name of the city of God.

Later on in Revelation 14:12 Jesus reiterates the importance of obeying His commands: "Here is the patience of the saints; here are those who keep the commandments of God and the faith of Jesus." We will learn about those who went through a great time of trouble and pleased God by keeping His commandments even when they were at risk of losing their lives.

Now let's learn about the last of the seven churches—Laodecia.

Revelation 3:14-22

"And unto the angel of the church of the Laodiceans write; These things saith the Amen, the faithful and true witness, the beginning of the creation of God; I know thy works, that thou art neither cold nor hot: I would thou wert cold or hot. So then because thou art lukewarm, and neither cold nor hot, I will spue thee out of my mouth. Because thou sayest, I am rich, and increased with goods, and have need of nothing; and knowest not that thou art wretched, and miserable, and poor, and blind, and naked: I counsel thee to buy of me gold tried in the fire, that thou mayest be rich; and white raiment, that thou mayest be clothed, and that the shame of thy nakedness do not appear; and anoint thine eyes with eyesalve, that thou mayest see.

"As many as I love, I rebuke and chasten: be zealous therefore, and repent. Behold, I stand at the door, and knock: if any man hear my voice, and open the door, I will come in to him, and will sup with him, and he with me. To him that overcometh will I grant to sit with me in my throne, even as I also overcame, and am set down with my Father in his throne. He that hath an ear, let him hear what the Spirit saith unto the churches."

Jesus is the Amen, the Faithful and True Witness. Likewise, He said, "I am the Alpha and the Omega, the Beginning and the End" (Rev. 1:8, NKJV). Jesus is the same from Genesis to Revelation in letting us know who He is and what He stands for. Laodicea Christians are the lukewarm church that's wretched, miserable, poor, blind, naked, and doesn't even know it. Many times we think we are strong, rich, healthy, well-dressed, pretty, smart, and know it all, but in God's eyes we are the opposite. Paul counsels us, "Therefore let him who thinks he stands take heed lest he fall" (1 Cor. 10:12, NKJV).

You've heard the saying that people can be sincere in doing what's wrong, but that does not make them right. Saul's experience is a perfect example of this. He had perfect 20/20 vision as he sought out the followers of Jesus in an attempt to throw them in prison; he thought that he was doing good work for God. God saw his sincerity and potential to work for Him; therefore, he made him blind so that he could see what he was doing. He did not realize that by persecuting the Christians he was actually persecuting Jesus (Acts 9:1-5).

Jesus told His disciples that if an individual harms someone it is as if they are harming Him. Jesus gave us the example that whenever someone is sick and you visit him/her you are actually visiting Jesus. Whenever you visit someone in prision, feed the poor, or do good for someone in need, you are actually doing it to Jesus. So let's practice doing good to everyone that we come in contact with because by doing good or helping someone we are doing it to Jesus (Matt. 25:31-46).

The Laodicean church, similar to many of us today, was in a precarious condition of lukewarm feelings. As was their condition, we feel too comfortable because we know the truth and we are on our way to heaven. We do not see the need to change our ways or correct our mistakes because in our own eyes we are doing the right things. But in reality we are deceiving ourselves (Matt. 7:21).

"Laodicea – the heart beats a bit faster when we consider this era of the seven churches, because Laodicea represents the church today. The words to Laodicea are Jesus' direct counsel and reproof for Christians living now. He knows what our Spiritual problems are, and what the solutions are. He knows what we need, and He lovingly offers His assistance" (Revelation Seminar, RS-005, p. 7).

As we learned before the messages to the seven churches are for the churches from the period of the apostles to the end of the world. So this last message to the Laodicean church applies to the time we are living in now. The end time that is the last church before Jesus' return.

Jesus is saying to you today, "Buy of me gold tried in the fire, that thou mayest be rich; and white raiment, that thou mayest be clothed, and that the shame of thy nakedness do not appear; and anoint thine eyes with eyesalve, that thou mayest see" (Rev. 3:18). We can only buy these things from Jesus. If we want the true riches that only God can give us then we need to go to Jesus to get them.

Let's examine this verse more closely to understand the meaning of the symbols. Gold represents the true riches of heaven, which are manifested in a golden character and will stand up under the fire of persecution and adversity. It includes God's Word (Ps. 19:7-10) and faith which works by love (Job 23:10; Gal. 5:6; James 2:5).

White raiment represents Jesus' robe of righteousness (Isa. 61:10; Rev. 19:8). Jesus is willing to take our filthy rags away and clothe us with His robe of righteousness. It is a free gift. We do nothing to earn it. We receive it by faith in Jesus alone (Zech. 3:1-5). And it is retained only by faith in Jesus (Rom. 1:17).

Eyesalve represents discernment to understand God's Word (Ps. 119:18;

1 John 2:20, 27). It also represents the Holy Spirit helping us to see our true condition and make proper choices (John 14:26; Eph. 1:17-19).

Listen to God's voice and let Him come into your heart. He's standing at the door knocking. Won't you let Him in? If you do, Jesus will come in and eat with you and you will be granted the right to sit with Jesus on His throne, just as Jesus also won the victory and sits with His Father on His throne.

It is interesting to note that Jesus does not give any commendations to the church of Laodicea. How sad that God did not have any commendation for this last church or these types of Christians. According to King Solomon, "Pride goes before destruction" (Prov. 16:18, NKJV). Anytime we feel proud and say that we do not need anything, we are doomed for destruction. It is only when we recognize our need of a Savior and salvation that we can be blessed.

If you have ears, don't cover them with your hands or stick your head in the sand as an ostrich does. Hear what the Spirit is saying to the churches. Obey so that you too will receive the blessings God is ready to give you provided you do what He says in His Word.

Uriah Smith provides the following insight, "'Laodicea' signifies 'the judging of the people,' or, according to Cruden 'a just people.' The message to this church brings to view the closing scenes of probation. It reveals a period of judgment. It is the last stage of the church. Consequently it applies to believers under the third angel's message, the last message of mercy before the coming of Christ. (Revelation 14:9-14).... 'These Things Saith the Amen.' This is, then, the final message to the churches before the close of probation.... The charge He brings against the Laodiceans is that they are lukewarm, neither hot nor cold. They lack that religious fervor and devotion which is demanded by their position in the world's closing history with the light of prophecy beaming upon their pathway. This lukewarmness is shown by a lack of good works, for it is from knowledge of their works that the faithful and true Witness brings this fearful charge against them" (*Daniel and Revelation*, vol. 2, p. 391).

"The Laodicean message is applicable to the church at this time. Do you believe this message? Have you hearts that feel? Or are you constantly saying, We are rich and increased in goods, and have need of nothing? Is it in vain that the declaration of eternal truth has been given to this nation to be carried to all the nations of the world?... The Laodicean message applies to all who profess to keep the law of God, and yet are not doers of it. We are not to be selfish in anything. Every phase of the Christian life is to be a representation of the life of Christ. If it is not, we shall hear the terrible words, 'I know you not'" (*The SDA Bible Commentary*, vol. 7, pp. 961, 962).

Jesus's Messages to You and His Church Part 2

So what should the Laodicean people do? "I counsel thee to buy of me gold tried in the fire, that thou mayest be rich; and white raiment, that thou mayest be clothed, and that the shame of thy nakedness do not appear; and anoint thine eyes with eyesalve, that thou mayest see'" (*The SDA Bible Commentary,* vol. 7, p. 966). "The Lord knocks at the door of your heart, desiring to enter, that He may impart spiritual riches to your soul. He would anoint the blind eyes, that they may discover the holy character of God in His law, and understand the love of Christ, which is indeed gold tried in the fire" (*The Review and Herald*, Febraruy 25, 1890).

Jesus is going from door to door, standing in front of every soul, proclaiming, "I stand at the door and knock." As a heavenly merchant, He opens His treasures and cries, "Buy of me gold tried in the fire, that thou mayest be rich; and white raiment, that thou mayest be clothed, and that the shame of thy nakedness do not appear." The gold that He offers is without alloy, more precious than that of Ophir, for it is faith and love. The white raiment He invites the soul to wear is His own robe of righteousness, and the oil for anointing is the oil of His grace, which will give spiritual eyesight to the soul in blindness and darkness that he may distinguish between the workings of the Spirit of God and the spirit of the enemy. "Open your doors, says the great Merchantman, the possessor of spiritual riches, and transact your business with me. It is I, your Redeemer, who counsels you to buy of me" (*The Review and Herald,* August 7, 1894).

Now that you know what God wants you to do, check on yourself weekly to see how you're doing. Our spiritual journey is just that, a journey and a learning process; however, it is good to check where you are and keep your eyes focused on what you hope to accomplish and where you want to see yourself with God's help.

So, where do you see yourself? If you're like me, you probably saw yourself in all of the seven churches' characteristics one way or another. There was a time that I lost my first love; I stopped caring and did not want to do anything. I grumbled while I was going through some trials and hard times, asking God, why me? Other times I carried the name of being a Christian but did not live as a Christian should. I had several idols in my life, such as television, school work, sleep, shopping, and time on the computer. God had to show me my errors and talk to me so that I could turn away from these sins.

Other times I felt that I was a better Christian than a whole lot of other folks in the church. I started to elevate myself because I worship only God in heaven, I don't worship idols, I don't take God's name in vain, I keep God's holy Sabbath day, I honor my elders and everybody else, I don't steal, I don't kill, I don't commit adultery, I try not to lie, I don't covet anybody's things, and I don't drink, go to the movies, eat pork, go to clubs, wear jewelry, etc. I felt as if I was ready for translation. But oh how mistaken I was. I forgot that the Christian life is a journey and that we are constantly growing in God's grace. So don't be discouraged; God is still working with me and you. He will never give up on us.

After thinking about where you are on your spiritual journey and where you stand, ask Jesus to strengthen your walk with Him, so that where you are weak, He can make you strong. Keep working on your walk with Christ because that's the only way you can persevere.

The book of Revelation is not a closed book, rather it's an open book. Some prophecies were given to Daniel but with the instruction to close the book until the time of the end (Dan. 12:4-9; Rev. 10:1-7). Revelation has been opened because the end is *NOW*.

Some people argue that the messages that Jesus gave John for the seven churches do not apply to us today. That is a wrong assumption because if that's the case then the whole Bible does not apply to us either, and we know that that's not true. The Bible is God's way to communicate with us. God made us and gave us His instructions in the Bible of how to live upright lives so that someday we can be reunited with Him again.

I grew up in a family of fifteen children—I was number fourteen. I was not even born when my parents laid the ground rules for our household, yet all those rules that were instituted before my time applied to me as well. I couldn't tell my parents that I wasn't going to follow their rules because when they implemented it I was not there and it was for my older brothers and sisters and not for me and my younger sister. Oh no, I had to abide by all their rules regardless if I was present or not when they were created.

The same thing is true for the messages that God gave to the seven churches—Ephesus, Smyrna, Pergamos, Thyatira, Sardis, Philadelphia, and Laodicea. All of the messages to these churches apply to everyone who has an ear. Just in case you missed it in the message to the first church, Jesus repeated the plea again and again after each message given to the seven churches: "He that hath an ear, let him hear what the Spirit saith unto the churches" (Rev. 3:22).

So even though you and I were not present when John sent these messages to the seven churches, guess what, they apply just the same to us. Therefore, let's read, hear, and do what Jesus wants us to do so that we can receive His blessings and be able to go home with Him when He comes again.

Chapter 4

God's Throne

Revelation 4:1-11

"After this I looked, and, behold, a door was opened in heaven: and the first voice which I heard was as it were of a trumpet talking with me; which said, Come up hither, and I will shew thee things which must be hereafter. And immediately I was in the spirit: and, behold, a throne was set in heaven, and one sat on the throne. And he that sat was to look upon like a jasper and a sardine stone: and there was a rainbow round about the throne, in sight like unto an emerald. And round about the throne were four and twenty seats: and upon the seats I saw four and twenty elders sitting, clothed in white raiment; and they had on their heads crowns of gold. And out of the throne proceeded lightnings and thunderings and voices: and there were seven lamps of fire burning before the throne, which are the seven Spirits of God.

"And before the throne there was a sea of glass like unto crystal: and in the midst of the throne, and round about the throne, were four beasts full of eyes before and behind. And the first beast was like a lion, and the second beast like a calf, and the third beast had a face as a man, and the fourth beast was like a flying eagle. And the four beasts had each of them six wings about him; and they were full of eyes within: and they rest not day and night, saying, Holy, holy, holy, LORD God Almighty, which was, and is, and is to come. And when those beasts give glory and honour and thanks to him that sat on the throne, who liveth for ever and ever, The four and twenty elders fall down before him that sat on the throne, and worship him that liveth for ever and ever, and cast their crowns before the throne, saying, Thou art worthy, O Lord, to receive glory and honour and power: for thou hast created all things, and for thy pleasure they are and were created."

The next vision that John saw was heaven and God's throne. John said that immediately he was in the Spirit, or in vision, and he saw a throne set in heaven and Sinless One sat on the throne. And He who sat there was as a jasper and a sardius stone in appearance, and there was a rainbow around the throne that appeared as an emerald. Can you picture that in your mind?

The one sitting on the throne was God the Father. John described specifically how God's throne looks in heaven. It was as if John was given an "open house" tour so that he could explain to us what he saw, heard, and experienced. When I was in my teens, I always wondered about heaven—what it looks like, how it is set up, what things are there, what the angels do, etc. God, knowing that there are many people like me who wonder about the same things about heaven, in His mercy gave us a glimpse/picture of what heaven looks like. John tried his best to describe the indescribable, because no human being can describe God. There is no humanly vocabulary that's able to describe God.

The picture that I got from John's description is that of a beauty you can't describe. John used the most precious stones that human beings consider to be beautiful to describe God, jasper and sardine and a beautiful rainbow surrounding His throne. He couldn't describe God's face and form because of the bright and beautiful light surrounding Him. But we have an idea of what God looks like because He told us back in Genesis that we were made in His own image. God said, "Let Us make man in Our image" (Gen. 1:26, NKJV).

When Jesus returns and transforms our sinful bodies, we will be able to see God face to face. I can hardly wait! God is all light and the most beautiful light. No wonder Jesus said that He is the Light of the world.

This open house that John was permitted to see gives me the reassurance that God is in charge of His universe. God is in charge of our world. We are not left destitute; God's eye is watching and documenting everything that's going on in this world, and one day He will say, "Enough!" And then He will take it all back. Satan and his evil angels will pay for all the evil they caused this world and humanity.

It is comforting to me to know that God has a rainbow around His throne in appearance as an emerald. To me rainbows signify many things. It first reminds me that God created heaven and earth, and when man became so evil that He had to destroy the earth with a flood, He gave His word that He would never again destroy the earth with a flood (Gen. 9:12-17). Instead, God will destroy the earth with fire at the end of this world (Rev. 20:9, 10, 14). Secondly, it gives me the assurance that if we trust and believe Jesus and choose to be on His side He will save us from this fire and we will live with Him forever.

God's Throne

Third, it reminds me that God loves colors—red, yellow, orange, blue, black, white, pink, brown, etc. It does not matter what the color is; He loves them all. So the color of your skin does not matter in God's eyes because God loves you just the way you are. We are all His rainbow colors.

John went on saying that around the throne are twenty-four thrones. On the thrones he saw twenty-four elders sitting clothed in white robes with crowns of gold on their heads. According to Matthew 27:50-54 when Jesus Christ died and was resurrected, "the graves were opened; and many bodies of the saints who had fallen asleep were raised; coming out of the graves after His resurrection, they went into the holy city and appeared to many."

When Jesus went to heaven, He took these saints with Him (Eph. 4:8; Ps. 68:18). This is just to prove to us that when Jesus comes again the second time, He is able to raise the rest of the saints that are dead and sleeping in the dust. So I believe that the twenty-four elders are some of those saints that rose at Jesus' resurrection.

John went on to describe that from the throne proceeded lightning, thunder, and voices. Seven lamps of fire were burning before the throne, which are the seven Spirits of God. The lightening and thunder are angels as they move around God's throne (Ezek. 1:14; 10:5; Heb. 1:7). The seven Spirits is, of course, the Holy Spirit.

Every time the four living beings gave glory and honor to God, the twenty-four elders would bow down and worship God by saying, "Thou art worthy, O Lord, to receive glory and honour and power: for thou hast created all things, and for thy pleasure they are and were created" (Rev. 4:11). Here is a clear testimony that there is a God; He created heaven and earth and all that therein is.

For the people who do not believe in God and call themselves atheist, I want to tell you that God is real, and if it was not for God, you would not have even existed to say that there's no God. God knew that the enemy Satan would confuse people's mind and their way of thinking, so that's why He has given us several proofs of His existence. First and foremost is the air we breathe, the rain He sends to water the earth, the ocean that never fills up even though it constantly receives more water, the rainbow that comes out to remind us of His promise, the sun that shines on the good and bad, and the stars and the moon that we see in the sky at night. God is also evident in the fact that our conscious speaks to us and steers us in the right direction if we chose to listen to it.

But even with all the above, God knew that some people would still reject Him and propose in their hearts that there's no God. That's why He said in

The Revelation of Jesus Christ

Psalm 14:1 that "the fool has said in his heart, 'There is no God.'" It is so true that only a fool will say that there is no God because after all the evidence that's around in this world and they still believe that there's no God then they are fools. The admonition goes to you today; don't be a fool. God gave us a brain to process information and to understand, and He's ready to help us understand if we so desire. Let's trust in God because there's no other way (Prov. 24:7; 28:26).

John went on, saying that before the throne was a sea of glass, like crystal. And in the midst of the throne, and around the throne, were four living creatures full of eyes in front and in back. The first living creature looked like a lion, the second like a calf, the third had a face like a man, and the fourth was like a flying eagle. The four living creatures, each having six wings, were full of eyes around and within. "And they rest not day and night, saying, 'Holy, holy, holy, LORD God Almighty, which was, and is, and is to come" (Rev. 4:8).

And whenever the living creatures give glory and honor and thanks to Him who sits on the throne, who lives forever and ever, the twenty-four elders fall down before Him and worship Him, casting their crowns before the throne and saying: "Thou art worthy, O Lord, to receive glory and honour and power: for thou hast created all things, and for thy pleasure they are and were created" (Rev. 4:11).

The description of these four living creatures full of eyes with four different faces sounds a bit scary. But you know what? After we decode the symbols they are not scary at all. John used figurative speech to help us break it down so that we can understand. These living creatures are cherubim or seraphim, which are powerful angels that have Jesus' characteristics, and they are round about God's throne: "The LORD reigns; let the peoples tremble! He dwells between the cherubim; let the earth be moved!" (Ps. 99:1, NKJV; see also Ezek. 1). Again we can see parallels in the Old Testament and the New Testament.

John was not the only prophet that saw God's throne and the four living creatures. Isaiah and Ezekiel also saw them in their visions. Isaiah called these living creatures seraphim (Isa. 6). And Ezekiel called them cherubim (Ezek. 10). So these living creatures are powerfull angels that carry God's throne wherever the Spirit leads them to. That tells me that God's throne is mobile and He can go anywhere He wants to while sitting on His throne. Wow, that's awesome. Can you picture that in your mind?

Again, as we've learned before, the book of Revelation is full of symbols that have real meanings and a message for our learning. All the characteristics

God's Throne

in the four living beings represent Jesus. The first living being was like a lion, which represents strength and kingship. Jesus is the Lion of the tribe of Judah, the King of kings. One day at the appointed time, Jesus Christ will take over His throne and kingdom that His Father has given Him, and He will begin to reign (Rev. 11:15-18).

The second living being was like a calf, which represents humility, service, and meekness. Jesus is the sacrificial Lamb of God who was led to the slaughter as a lamb in order to save us. He came to this world to serve, not be served. He humbled Himself and left heaven and His beautiful abode to come to this dark world to die on the cross just to save us from our sins and the claws of Satan. Instead of letting us die for our sins, He came and died for us. And the only reason why He did it is because He loves us (John 3:16).

The third living being had a face like a man, which represents intelligence and wisdom. Jesus is all-powerful and all-knowing. Wisdom only comes from God. Jesus Christ became human and died on the cross for our sins. He suffered and was tempted just as we are. He understands our feelings and sufferings because He went through it too.

The fourth living being was like a flying eagle, which represents keenness, agility, power, and the divinity of Jesus Christ. Now, if we put the above descriptions into our human terms, we can say that the lion is the king of the beast, the calf grows to be head of the cattle, man is the head of the animal kingdom, and the eagle is the head of all birds. All these symbols tell us that Jesus is the head of it all. He's the King of kings, Lord of lords, and there is no one like Him.

Again, all these symbols were used in these four living creatures to help us understand Jesus' characteristics and how powerful these four angels that work around God's throne are. So there is nothing scary about them; it's just to give us the true picture so that we can understand who Jesus is, was, and is to come.

Going back to the Old Testament, I learned that the twelve tribes of Israel were divided into groups of four around God's tabernacle. Each group represented one of these four symbols of Jesus Christ—Judah was the lion; Reuben was the man, Ephraim the ox or calf; and Dan the eagle. As with the cherubim/seraphim, these four symbols of Jesus Christ dwell round about God's throne. Likewise the chosen tribes of Israel with these four symbols encamped around the sanctuary where God was dwelling among the people of Israel (Exod. 25:8).

All the living creatures had six wings full of eyes, which means omniscient, all seeing or able to see and discern everything. One of the duties of these

The Revelation of Jesus Christ

four living creatures is to praise God day and night, giving Him glory. Here we learn that sinless angels are praising God day and night. This causes me to ask myself, how about you and me who were born in sin and should be praising God every second of our lives for His love and mercy toward us. What about us sinners? We should be the first ones thanking God, praising Him day and night for His love and mercy bestowed on us for dying in our place and redeeming us back to His Father and blessing us with LOVE. This is true love.

So how do you show your gratitude to God and His Son, Jesus? Are you praising Him day and night? Or are you too busy with the cares of this world that makes you so tired that you can't even stay up to pray? Are you so tired when you come home from school or work that you only want to spend time watching television, robbing God from His worship? Guess what? There is hope! Now is the time to change and make amends with God. Now is the time to buy oil, which represents God's Holy Spirit to guide you and help you to see your sinful self. Why don't you ask God and His Son, Jesus, for forgiveness now and ask the Holy Spirit to guide you going forward with your life. He is ready to help you; you just need to ask.

My brothers and sisters, heaven is real. God has proved it to us again and again in His Word. And He even gave John an open house of heaven to prove it. John saw it with his own eyes. God is preparing mansions for us in heaven (John 14:1-3). He longs for the day when we will be with Him forever and ever. He wants to love us and shower us with His wonderful gifts. But it's up to us to accept His invitation and His gifts. He has done everything on His part, so now it is up to you and me to believe and accept His offer or reject it. Today, He's pleading with you to believe and accept Him and His gift of eternal life. I don't know about you, but I definitely believe in Jesus Christ and accept His gifts and invitation to be with Him. He's the only way, truth, and life, and He is the only one who truly loves us.

What about you? Do you want to accept His free gift today? If you accept His free gift of salvation why don't you bow your head right now and let Him know that you've accepted His gift of salvation and have opened the door of your heart to Him. Invite Him to come in. He's ready to enter and sup with you. You can do it right now. It does not matter how sinful you've been or how many bad things you've done in your life. You just need to confess your sins and ask Jesus for forgiveness (1 John 1:9). He can wash you clean in His blood that He shed on the cross. You just need to ask Him. Just bow your head right now and ask Him to forgive you and to enter your heart. This will be the best thing that you've ever done in your life, and you will never regret it.

Chapter 5

Jesus the Lamb of God

Revelation 5:1-5

"And I saw in the right hand of him that sat on the throne a book written within and on the backside, sealed with seven seals. And I saw a strong angel proclaiming with a loud voice, Who is worthy to open the book, and to loose the seals thereof? And no man in heaven, nor in earth, neither under the earth, was able to open the book, neither to look thereon. And I wept much, because no man was found worthy to open and to read the book, neither to look thereon. And one of the elders saith unto me, Weep not: behold, the Lion of the tribe of Judah, the Root of David, hath prevailed to open the book, and to loose the seven seals thereof."

In Revelation 4 the emphasis was on God the Father and His throne. Now chapter 5 goes back to God's Son Jesus Christ.

John felt very bad to the point that he wept because no one was able to take the scroll from the Father's hand, open it, and break its seals. No one in heaven—no cherubim, no angels, no birds, no one on the earth, no human being, no animals, no one under the earth, no evil angel—was able to open the scroll and loosen its seals. No one was found worthy. But one of the elders comforted John and said, "Weep not: behold, the Lion of the tribe of Judah, the Root of David, hath prevailed to open the book, and to loose the seven seals thereof" (Rev. 5:5). Only Jesus was found worthy because He was the only one worthy to die on the cross to redeem us from our sins. He prevailed against Satan, thus He earned the right and authority to be the one to open the scroll and loosen its seals. I'm sure that John felt relieved, and I do too.

Revelation 5:6

"And I behold, and lo, in the midst of the throne and of the four beasts, and in the midst of the elders, stood a Lamb as it had been slain, having seven horns and seven eyes, which are the seven Spirits of God sent forth into all the earth."

In the midst of the throne and the four living creatures and the elders, John saw a "Lamb as it had been slain, having seven horns and seven eyes, which are the seven Spirits of God sent forth into all the earth" (Rev. 5:6). The Lamb came and took the book out of the right hand of His Father that was sitting upon the throne. So who is the Lamb with seven horns and seven eyes? Remember, Revelation was written in signs and symbols, so let's decode it and learn the message from God. I've learned that the Lamb is Jesus Christ, the Lamb of God who takes away our sins. Jesus spoke to Moses and instructed him to sacrifice a lamb to take away the sins of the people. This sacrificial lamb was a symbol of Jesus' own sacrificial death to save man and take their sins away. Jesus' death covers everyone who has committed sin but has asked for forgiveness (Isa. 53:5; Zech 3:9; 4:10; John 1:29; 1 Pet. 2:24).

Remember when our forefathers Adam and Eve sinned and thus infected and contaminated the whole world with sin and darkness? They gave Satan entrance into this world to cause people to sin. Therefore, their children were born in sin. But God promised them that Jesus Christ, His only Son, would be the Lamb of God that would ransom them from their sins and ours. Jesus Christ, the seed of the woman, would bruise Satan, the serpent's head, and Satan would bruise Christ's heel (Gen. 3:15). This was God's plan of salvation for humanity, and He kept His promise when Jesus came to this earth and died on the cross for our sins. The Lamb is no other than Jesus Christ our Savior.

The seven horns are synonymous with authority, power, and strength. Only God the Father, God the Son, and God the Holy Spirit have the authority and power to save us from Satan, the devil, dragon, adversary, enemy, old serpent, and liar (Deut. 33:17; Ps. 112:9; Rev. 12:9). The seven eyes is the Spirit of God that is sent throughout the earth. The eyes are God's eyes, which see everything in the universe (Job 34:21; Ps. 33:13-15, 18, 19; Prov. 15:3; Heb. 4:13).

Revelation 5:7-14

"And he came and took the book out of the right hand of him that sat upon the throne. And when he had taken the book, the four beasts and four

Jesus the Lamb of God

and twenty elders fell down before the Lamb, having every one of them harps, and golden vials full of odours, which are the prayers of saints. And they sung a new song, saying, Thou art worthy to take the book, and to open the seals thereof: for thou wast slain, and hast redeemed us to God by thy blood out of every kindred, and tongue, and people, and nation; And hast made us unto our God kings and priests: and we shall reign on the earth. And I beheld, and I heard the voice of many angels round about the throne and the beasts and the elders: and the number of them was ten thousand times ten thousand, and thousands of thousands; Saying with a loud voice, Worthy is the Lamb that was slain to receive power, and riches, and wisdom, and strength, and honour, and glory, and blessing. And every creature which is in heaven, and on the earth, and under the earth, and such as are in the sea, and all that are in them, heard I saying, Blessing, and honour, and glory, and power, be unto him that sitteth upon the throne, and unto the Lamb for ever and ever. And the four beasts said, Amen. And the four and twenty elders fell down and worshipped him that liveth for ever and ever."

After Jesus took the scroll from His Father's right hand, the four living creatures and the twenty-four elders holding the bowls of incense containing the prayers of the saints started to worship and praise Jesus. Then the angels joined in worshiping and praising Jesus. But more than that, every creature in heaven, in earth, under the earth, and in the sea gave glory to Jesus. I've learned that "at the name of Jesus every knee should bow" (Phil. 2:10, NKJV; see also Rom. 14:11). Isaiah 45:23 predicted this a long time ago. Again, we see the harmony in the Old and New Testaments.

Now please note carefully that John said that every creature worshiped and praised Jesus Christ. That means that all the angels, including Satan and his evil angels (that just goes to tell you that you don't need to waste your time on Satan's side and his evil angels because they are all losers), every human being in this world and the other worlds, and all animals shall bow to Jesus and confess to God.

We can't confess to any man or priest here on earth to receive forgiveness of our sins, only Jesus and Him only can forgive our sins (Isa. 45:21-24). So my brothers and sisters, don't waste time confessing your sins to your priest or pastor for forgiveness. Only Jesus can forgive your sins. What you should do is to go directly to the person(s) who you've hurt, ask him or her to forgive you, and then go to Jesus on your knees with a broken and contrite heart and ask Him to save you and forgive the sins that you've committed (Matt. 5:23, 24). That's all you have to do, and you'll be forgiven. Jesus is telling you and

The Revelation of Jesus Christ

I today, just as He told the prostitute women after her accusers brought her to Him, to "go and sin no more" (John 8:11, NKJV). Once Jesus forgives us from our sins, He asks us not to commit the same mistakes or sins again. He's ready to help us if we stay close to Him. So my brothers and sisters, don't be fooled. Only Jesus can save you and forgive you from your sins. Nobody else can do that.

Let's go back to the scroll. No one except Jesus was able to open the scroll and loosen its seals. This is a crucial revelation about Jesus that the Father wanted us to know. Jesus is the Man; there is no other besides Him. For this reason, every knee shall bow to Jesus. Isaiah 45:18-24 tells us this very thing, once again documenting that the Old and New Testaments go hand in hand. Everything that was said in the Old Testament is repeated in the New Testament because the God of yesterday is the same God today. Again, this shows us that the revelation was given to Jesus because He has earned the right to sit at the right hand of His Father's throne. Jesus, through His redeeming blood, was able to take the scroll and open it.

Praise God; give glory to God in the highest. Jesus is the Lamb of God. Some people dispute the fact that Jesus is God. They see Him as a good man and prophet but not as God. Well, Jesus is the Son of God, and therefore, He's also God—the "Mighty God" (Isa. 9:6, 7). Jesus and the Father are one (John 2:22, 23). In Hebrews 1:8, 9 God the Father is telling Jesus, His Son, that "Your throne, *O God*, is forever and ever; A scepter of righteousness is the scepter of Your kingdom. You have loved righteousness and hated lawlessness; Therefore God, Your God, has anointed You with the oil of gladness more than Your companions" (NKJV).

Before these words were written, David wrote, "Your throne, O God, is forever and ever" (Ps. 45:6, NKJV). Therefore, I have no doubts about Jesus' divinity and that He is God. Jesus is our God. We've learned in Revelation 1 that Jesus is the Word of God. "In the beginning was the Word and the Word was with God, and the Word was God" (John 1:1, NKJV). Jesus is the Word, and Jesus is God.

Revelation 5:9, 10 makes it plain as to why Jesus is the only one worthy to take the scroll and open the seals. "For thou wast slain, and hast redeemed us to God by thy blood out of every kindred, and tongue, and people, and nation; and hast made us unto our God kings and priests: and we shall reign on the earth."

My brothers and sisters, here is the proof again that salvation and the messages given to the seven churches apply to everyone (every tribe, tongue, people, and nation) who has an ear, and that includes you and me. Jesus died for everyone who has an ear. He already paid the price for you and wants to save you. He wants to protect you from the calamities that are about to come on the earth. He wants you to have eternal life and live forever with Him. He's only asking you to read His word, listen to His calling, repent, and do what He's asking you to do. That's all. How hard or difficult is that? But first you have to believe Him and accept Him in your heart. God does not force us to do anything. He leaves it for us to decide and choose. But the admonition comes to you today, just as Joshua asked the people of Israel in the Old Testament, "Choose you this day whom ye will serve" (Josh. 24:15; see also Heb. 3:15; 4:7).

Jesus is asking you today to choose Him and choose life. Although Jesus wants us to choose Him, He's not going to force us. Anytime people force you to do things you should run away because it's not from God. God always gives us the choice after He's given us all the facts, truth, and information for us to make an informed consent. What a God! What love! Praise God; give glory to God in the highest forever and ever. Now what about you? Who are you choosing today? You alone can answer that question. You can't continue to put this off any longer. Jesus is ready to save you. I encourage you to once again pray and ask Jesus to guide you and to come into your heart. You will be glad you did. If you die tonight, where are you going to spend eternity? When Jesus comes again, will you be with the saints or with the sinners? You need to choose where you want to go or whom you want to serve. If you hear the Lords' voice calling you, do not harden your heart (Heb. 3:15).

God speaks to us today through His Son, Jesus (Heb. 1:1). Therefore, we need to listen and believe Him. This is our only chance to be saved. God is light and not darkness (John 1:5). So, if you choose God, you also choose light. If you refuse light, you automatically accept darkness and will be condemned (John 3:18, 19).

The other point that I want to emphasize again because it made an impact in my life and made me happy is that Jesus died for everyone who has an ear, which is people from every tribe, language, people, and nation. How many languages, people, and nations do we have in this world? There are many different languages in China, Africa, the Middle East, Australia, India, Europe, the Caribbean, etc. But the good news is that Jesus had you and me in mind when He died on the cross to redeem us. If you have an ear, listen to the word of God. Forsake your sins and do what He wants you to do and you will be truly blessed.

Chapter 6

Jesus Opening the Seals

Revelation 6:1, 2

"And I saw when the Lamb opened one of the seals, and I heard, as it were the noise of thunder, one of the four beasts saying, Come and see. And I saw, and behold a white horse: and he that sat on him had a bow; and a crown was given unto him: and he went forth conquering, and to conquer."

I think that the rider on the white horse is Jesus Christ our Messiah. He went forth conquering and to conquer. Satan, the enemy in the form of a serpent, lied to our first parents, Adam and Eve, causing them to sin just as he's doing to us now. He continues to destroy Adam's family. But thank God for His Son, Jesus Christ, who died on the cross for our sins and reconnected us with His Father again. Thank you, Jesus. He went forth conquering and to conquer. Through the story of the sower, Jesus showed us that He is spreading the message to everyone who has an ear, but then the enemy, which is Satan, came in and choked some (Mark 4).

I've also learned that winds and horses in prophetic language of the Bible mean strife, wars, and conflict. So here God is using the symbol of a horse in four of these seals to depict the strife and conflicts or wars in each era (Rev 7:1-3; see also Jer. 25:31-34; 49:36-39; 51:1, 2; Dan. 7:2; Zech. 1:8-10; 6:2-5). Through these symbols God is showing us the different timetables that His people would have to go through starting with the time of the apostles all the way to the end of the world, which will culminate with Jesus' Second Coming. I've learned that these seven seals cover the same time period as the seven churches that we learned about in Revelation 2 and 3. Let's examine each of these symbols to be able to understand what God is telling us.

After Jesus took the scroll from His Father's right hand, He opened the first seal and saw a white horse. White represents purity, which is synonymous

Jesus Opening the Seals

to Jesus' character. Before Jesus reached to heaven after His resurrection, He gave His disciples the commission to go and preach the gospel to the whole earth (Mark 16:15; Matt. 28:18-20). According to Paul the gospel had been preached to the entire world at the time that he was writing to the Colossians (Col. 1:5, 6, 23).

But what about today? Now that the world has a population of more than six billion people, are we preaching the gospel to the entire world? How about you and me? Are we telling others what God and His Son, Jesus, have done for us? Now that we are living in the end time it is crucial for us to preach and tell others of Jesus' Second Coming. We are living in borrowed and extended time because God does not want anyone to perish but to receive eternal life. He's being patient so that everyone can have a chance to hear His message and decide for themselves who they want to follow. Now is the time to share Jesus with your family, friends, brothers, sisters, husband, wife, children, supervisor, neighbors, in-laws, acquaintances, etc. You don't want anyone to blame you for not telling them about the good news of Jesus and salvation through His death on the cross for our sins. Don't be afraid or shy to talk to others about Jesus. He has promised to give us the right words to say. You don't have anything to lose, but you have much to gain.

Now let's look at the meaning of the crown. In James 1:12 we learn that a crown is synonymous with victory (see also 1 Cor 9:25; 2 Tim. 4:7, 8). Jesus, by defeating Satan, received His crown. Now it is up to us to trust Jesus, resist the devil, and persevere in our difficult times so that we can receive our crown.

Finally, we will examine the bow. In Psalm 45:4, 5 we learn that the bow is synonymous to success in battle. During the era of the apostolic church of Ephesus, the church was very successful and grew mightily, just as fast as an arrow flies in the air. Thousands and thousands were added to the church daily. I wish this was happening now, too.

Revelation 6:3, 4

And when he had opened the second seal, I heard the second beast say, Come and see. And there went out another horse that was red: and power was given to him that sat thereon to take peace from the earth, and that they should kill one another: and there was given unto him a great sword."

When Jesus opened the second seal, John saw a fiery red horse going out and a sword was given to the rider. The red color of the second horse according to history represents the bloody destruction and persecution of God's people by pagan Rome (Jer. 46:10; Ezek. 32:6, 11; Nah. 2:3). By this persecution, the peace of God's people was destroyed. The sword is associated with war and bloodshed (1 Chron. 22:8; Isa. 3:25; Jer. 46:10, 13, 14; Ezek. 32:11, 12). It is also associated with persecution (Acts 12:1, 2). Many Bible scholars believe that the red horse covers the same time period as the church of Smyrna.

Let's review a few quotes: "Red represents blood and persecution. This time period corresponds to the church of Smyrna, the period of pagan persecution of the Christian church. Literally millions died as the pagan Roman emperors tried to wipe out Christianity" (*Revelation Speaks Messages of Hope for a World in Turmoil,* p. 50)

"Tragically, in course of time the world turned the church upside down. Pagan Rome adopted some of the doctrines, customs, and the name of the Christians. But Christians adopted the authoritarianism, the political intrigue, much of the philosophy, and even the name of pagan Rome....

"There were changes. Christian Rome did not crucify people as pagan Rome had done. No. Christian Rome burned them alive. Pagan Rome tortured criminals for stealing. Christian Rome tortured Christians for reading the Bible their own way" (*God Cares,* vol. 2, p. 183).

God's people will go through great tribulation, trials, hard times, wars, strife, and persecution before the end of this world. But the greatest thing that will motivate them is that the battle is already won. The enemy, Satan, was defeated when Jesus died on the cross. Satan's destiny of death was sealed forever. So we don't have to worry about him; he's a loser. But because he's a loser, he causes people to fight, hate, and kill each other just to give him his evil satisfaction and cause God sadness and pain to see His children suffer by his hand. Don't forget, this battle is not yours or mine; we're caught in the middle. The battle is the Lord's—God against Satan; good against evil. Ephesians 6:12 reminds us that we are not wrestling "against flesh and blood, but against principalities, against powers, against the rulers of the darkness of this age, against spiritual wickedness in high places" (NKJV). So don't even try to do this on your own. Only through Jesus Christ are we able to go through this hard time.

Revelation 6:5-8

"And when he had opened the third seal, I heard the third beast say, Come and see. And I beheld, and lo a black horse; and he that sat on him had a pair of balances in his hand. And I heard a voice in the midst of the four beasts say, A measure of wheat for a penny, and three measures of barley for a penny; and see thou hurt not the oil and the wine. And when he had opened the fourth seal, I heard the voice of the fourth beast say, Come and see. And I looked, and behold a pale horse: and his name that sat on him was Death, and Hell followed with him. And power was given unto them over the fourth part of the earth, to kill with sword, and with hunger, and with death, and with the beasts of the earth."

The command went out to spare the oil and the wine. The oil represents the Holy Spirit and the wine Jesus' precious blood that He shed for us on the cross; therefore, in all the darkness and moral decay the command was given not to remove the oil, which symbolizes the Holy Spirit, because by removing the Holy Spirit this would cause the people to forget God all together. Therefore, the Holy Spirit had to stay to illuminate the few remaining Christians' minds to continue to hold on and not to forget the blood of Jesus to the point that they let Christianity die among the darkness.

According to *Revelation Speaks Messages of Hope for a World in Turmoil*, "Here we discover that, indeed, the black horse-symbol of apostasy and corruption and subjection to the powers of darkness-is a fitting description of the church of Pergamos" (p. 5).

"Repeatedly, in the Scripture, darkness or blackness symbolizes moral darkness, sin, apostasy and error – the very opposite of the light of the gospel. The symbol is very fitting for the church during the 4th, 5th and half of the 6th centuries (the Pergamos church period) when Christianity became the state religion. Millions of unconverted people crowed into the church. Popularity and compromise brought Pagan errors into the church, which virtually crowded out the gospel" (Revelation Seminar, RS-009, p. 3).

The Pergamus church was where the seat of the devil was. This seat symbolizes darkness, witchcraft, mediums, spirits, psychics, palm readers, sorcery, sacrifices of children, spells, and magic. According to the Bible, darkness symbolizes moral darkness. Anytime we choose darkness, we leave Jesus, which is the Light, and therefore, we commit sin. The church of Pergamus tolerated and accepted pagan beliefs and rituals into their church.

When Jesus opened the fourth seal, John saw a pale horse. The pale or gray horse, according to Bible scholars, parallels with the church of Thyatira. In the early centuries, God's people went through terrible persecution where millions were killed by sword, starvation, wild beast, cruelty, and other barbarian forms of torture. I can remember wathing some documentary stories about Rome and the type of cruelties they inflicted on people. I could not believe my eyes. I asked myself how fellow human beings could treat others like that. Then I remembered that it is Satan who's behind all this. He wants to cause God pain by bringing suffering upon His children. But God has Satan's number, and he will pay for all the evil schemes that he has made God's children go through. Until the end of this world the eternal death will be for the devil, his evil angels, and those humans who choose to be on Satan's side.

"The pale horse with the rider Death, followed closely by the grave ('Hades' in Greek), is perfect symbolism of the devastating persecution of God's people and the multiplied millions who were destroyed by sword, starvation, wild beasts and other cruel methods. This is the same period covered by the Thyatira church—from the sixth through the 15th centuries, the period known as the Dark Ages. Jesus said this period of tribulation was the worst ever to be, Matthew 24:21. And even more tragic, it was the Church, now in apostasy, which was persecuting and killing those who differed with her. This terrible period of tribulation is mentioned other times in the Bible, Daniel 7:21,25; 12:7; Revelation 13:5; 12:6,14;17:6, because it almost destroyed God's true people from the earth. Jesus plans for these martyrs to be closest to Him in His new kingdom (Revelation 7:13-17)" (Revelation Seminar, RS-009, p. 4).

Revelation 6:9-11

"And when he had opened the fifth seal, I saw under the altar the souls of them that were slain for the word of God, and for the testimony which they held: And they cried with a loud voice, saying, How long, O Lord, holy and true, dost thou not judge and avenge our blood on them that dwell on the earth? And white robes were given unto every one of them; and it was said unto them, that they should rest yet for a little season, until their fellowservants also and their brethren, that should be killed as they were, should be fulfilled."

When Jesus opened the fifth seal, John saw the souls of the maryrs under the altar. They were martyred because of the Word of God and the testimonies of Jesus. In the last days, we too may be killed because of the Word of God, His Ten Commandments, and the testimonies of Jesus Christ. God did something very wonderful for His martyrs. He invited them to rest a little longer, leaving their cases entirely in His hands until the number of their fellow servants and their brethren should be complete. And God saw to it that each one of the victims received a white robe. Sometimes we want God to act right away and give people and Satan what they deserve, but God is a just God, and He does things in His own time. We must learn to be patient because He will never fail us.

"Here is symbolism from Moses' altar of burnt offerings. The sacrifice was offered and the blood poured out at the base of the altar, Leviticus 4:7. In the

Jesus Opening the Seals

5th seal, the blood of the martyred saints cried out symbolically to God, like the blood of Abel did after he was slain by his brother, Genesis 4:10. The word 'soul' also means 'life', Job 12:10, and the 'blood' is the 'life,' Deuteronomy 12:23, so, soul here refers to the blood or lives of those who had been slain" (Revelation Seminar, RS-009, p. 4).

"Jesus taught in one of His parables (Matthew 22:1-14) that all that God requires of us for admission to His heavenly banquet is possession of the wedding garment, His own white robe. Receiving the white robe is akin to receiving the rider on the white horse. The garment represents His own purity and righteousness, which we accept and make our own through faith" (*God Cares*, vol. 2, p. 187).

The fifth seal discusses the souls of the martyrs. I've learned about another parallel found in Genesis 4:10 where God is talking to Cain about the 'voice of thy brother's blood crieth unto me from the ground.' So here, the souls of the martyrs are crying to God asking Him 'how long before he avenges their blood.'

"During the Middle Ages millions of faithful Christians who dared to prefer death to the sacrifice of a good conscience were martyred. God's church had to go underground.... No longer were pagans persecuting Christians, or Christians persecuting pagans. Now 'Christians' were killing other Christians! Only priests were allowed to own and interpret the Bible. Those who should have been ministers of life actually became ministers of death during this time" (*Revelation Speaks Messages of Hope for a World in Turmoil*, p. 52).

J. A. Wylie stated it well when he said, "The noon of the papacy was the midnight of the world" (*The History of Protestantism*, book 1, p. 16).

Before finishing our examination of the four horses, I want to share with you what I learned from Zechariah. He too saw four different horses in vision. But his vision was different from John's in Revelation 6. However, I just want to add it here because God used the same or similar symbols to get His message across in the Old and New Testments, and that's another way we can tell that the Word of God is true.

New Tesatment	**Old Testament**
Rev. 6 – White Horse, Red Horse, Black Horse, Pale Horse	Zech. 6 – Red Horses, Black Horses, White Horses, Dappled Gray Horses
Rev. 7 – Four Angels Holding Four Winds	Jer. 25:31-34; 49:36; 51:1, 2, 11; Dan. 7:2 – Four Winds

The Revelation of Jesus Christ

Revelation 6:12-17

"And I beheld when he had opened the sixth seal, and, lo, there was a great earthquake; and the sun became black as sackcloth of hair, and the moon became as blood; And the stars of heaven fell unto the earth, even as a fig tree casteth her untimely figs, when she is shaken of a mighty wind. And the heaven departed as a scroll when it is rolled together; and every mountain and island were moved out of their places. And the kings of the earth, and the great men, and the rich men, and the chief captains, and the mighty men, and every bondman, and every free man, hid themselves in the dens and in the rocks of the mountains; And said to the mountains and rocks, Fall on us, and hide us from the face of him that sitteth on the throne, and from the wrath of the Lamb: For the great day of his wrath is come; and who shall be able to stand?

The opening of the sixth seal caused a great earthquake and other signs in heaven. History has shown us that some of these things have already happened. For example, on November 1, 1755, the earth experienced a huge, devastating earthquake sometimes referred to the Lisbon earthquake because the majority of causalities occurred in that part of the city. I wonder if this was one of the first recorded tsunamis.

Twenty-five years later on May 19, 1780, the sun did not shine and the moon was red as blood. This is recorded as the dark day. On November 13, 1833, the stars were recorded as falling. But according to the Bible, at the end of this world these earthquakes will be of greater magnitude. The elements of nature will be shaken (Matt. 24).

Can you imagine what it will be like when the elements of this world are shaken? We get scared whenever it thunders or whenever we see the power of lightning. Can you imagine when the other elements are shaken? The natural disasters currently taking place are to prepare us before the great one comes. This is just a forewarning to help us trust in God even more because He's the only one that can see us through these hard and difficult times. We just need to thank God for giving us the heads up and the assurance that His words are true. Therefore, we must believe Him because He has opened our eyes to the things that are about to happen in this world. The clock is ticking for this earth to come to its end and for God to take His redeemed home to live with Him.

Those who refuse to believe in Jesus and choose His side will cry for the rocks and mountains to fall on them and cover them from God the Father who sits on the throne and from the wrath of the Lamb, which is Jesus Christ. Revelation 6:16 is the text that my mother used to share with her Bible students

Jesus Opening the Seals

and plead with them to choose Jesus, get on God's side, and be safe. If you're on God's side, you'll lift up your hands when He comes and say, "This is our Lord; we've waited for Him." You'll be happy to see Him because you are ready (Isa. 25:9). But if you're on Satan's side, you'll try to hide from God's face by asking the rocks and mountains to cover you.

Whose side are you on? There are only two sides, and everyone must choose. If you don't choose, that means you're automatically on Satan's side because God does not force anyone to follow Him. He tells you what's coming before it happens but you have to decide which side you want to be on. Satan has polluted some people's mind to think that he (Satan) does not exist. Some people I work with told me, as I was sharing the Bible with them, that they do not believe that there is a devil. It's only a "force." I assured them that Satan is real and that "force" they believe in is Satan in person. He rejoices when he causes people to be confused.

Today if you will hear Jesus' voice, do not harden your heart in rebellion (Ps. 95:7). Choose Jesus Christ and live. Don't let Satan deceive you. He's a liar and a loser.

Before the wicked cry out for the rocks to fall on them, the sky recedes as a scroll and every mountain and island are moved out of its place. Through my studies I've learned that this prophecy has not been fulfilled yet. Since I was born on the beautiful Island of Curacao, this text caught my attention because it mentioned that every mountain and island will be moved out of its place. I believe that this is when the earth becomes one. All islands will unite to the closest continent to make the world one in preparation for the battle of Armageddon. We will discuss this battle later on, so stay tuned.

As we close this chapter, I want to look at the symbolism of the horses and discuss two of the seals. The black horse signifies apostasy from the light of God to the darkness of Satans' teachings. The era of the church of Pergamos is when Satan started with his church, the synagogue of Satan. Again Jesus started His church (seed), but the enemy came and destroyed what God started. False teachings started to come into the churches.

But what about now? When we start a new church, everyone loves each other and studies the Word of God and helps each other. But soon after, the enemy, Satan, comes in and starts his destructive work by sowing discontent, distrust, gossip, and strife to take our minds off of Jesus, and people start fighting with each other. No wonder we have so many different wars going on in the world and even in our churches today.

The pale horse represents the time for some of the Christians of the church of Sardis. They were the church that thought it was alive but in reality was dead. Now in our days some of us still think that we are better than some of the non-Christians, but in reality we are dead and deceiving ourselves. During times of strife and war, we often suffer the consequences of turmoil such as famines, biological germs that cause diseases, and murder.

After the fourth seal, that of the pale horse, was opened, Jesus showed John the fifth seal, which was that of the martyrs. Many martyrs were killed because they held on to the Word of God and the testimonies of Jesus Christ. The Spirit of Prophecy is the testimony of Jesus Christ. But the martyrs did not die in vain, because the sixth seal reveals the reward for our faithfulness—eternal life upon Jesus' return.

Matthew 24:29-31 talks about how Jesus will come back again. The only part that's not fulfilled yet is the heaven rolling back as a scroll, which will occur when Christ is at the door of His Second Coming.

"When the fifth seal was opened, John the Revelator in vision saw beneath the altar the company that was slain for the Word of God and the testimony of Jesus Christ. After this came the scenes described in the eighteenth [chapter] of Revelation, when those who are faithful and true are called out from Babylon [Revelation 18:1-5]" (*The SDA Bible Commentary,* vol. 7, p. 968).

Chapter 7

Sealing of God's people

Revelation 7:1-3

"And after these things I saw four angels standing on the four corners of the earth, holding the four winds of the earth, that the wind should not blow on the earth, nor on the sea, nor on any tree. And I saw another angel ascending from the east, having the seal of the living God: and he cried with a loud voice to the four angels, to whom it was given to hurt the earth and the sea, Saying, Hurt not the earth, neither the sea, nor the trees, till we have sealed the servants of our God in their foreheads."

As I studied and researched this chapter of the book of Revelation, it made me aware that this is one of the most important chapters of Revelation. Not that the others are not important, but this chapter is extremely important and holy because it deals with the character of God, His name, and His seal. Although this is a short chapter, I spent more time researching, praying, and putting it together because of the need to keep it reverent, holy, and sacred.

This chapter showed me that God is in control of this world and the whole universe. God and His Son, Jesus Christ, created this world and everything that is in it, and He has full control of what's going on. Nothing will happen if it is not Their will.

As we have already discussed, wind in Bible prophecy represents disaster, strife, destruction, war, violence, and bloodshed (Jer. 4:11-13; 25:31, 32; 49:36-37; Zech. 7:14). Daniel also tells us about the time of trouble that will come on this earth in the last days. He indicates that it will be one such as never was since there was a nation (Dan. 12:1; see also Jer. 30:7). So this is why God commissioned His angels to prevent it until after the sealing of His people. If God did not keep these destructions in check, the devil would have a field day with us humans before the appointed time. But thank God that He's

The Revelation of Jesus Christ

always in control and looking out for His servants. Therefore, He stationed His four angels on the four corners, which in our terms are the compass of the world—north, south, east, west—to hold back the strife and destruction until His servants are sealed on their foreheads. God never leaves His people in the dark. He always gives us a warning before it happens. Therefore, no one should say, "I did not know." God speaks to us through His holy Word, but He does not force us to do anything. He allows us to choose what we want to do, although He would love for us to read His Word, learn of Him, study about what's going to happen at the end of this world, and seek protection from Him. But again He never forces us. He wants us to serve Him because we love Him and not because of fear or by force. This is true love.

What is a seal? Well, according to the American Heritage Dictionary, a seal is "the impression made; the design or emblem itself, belonging exclusively to the user; the king's seal." So a seal is a stamp of authority, approval, or law. A government usually places its seal on important documents to make it official and thus incorporate the information into law. A seal usually consist of three parts: name, title, and territory or dominion.

The question that I've asked, and I am sure many other people have asked, is what is the seal of God? And who can read it? Through study I've learned that the seal of God is found in His holy law, which is the Ten Commandments. And if you read it carefully, the fourth commandments contains all the components of the seal of God. Let's read it in Exodus 20:8-11: "Remember the Sabbath day, to keep it holy. Six days you shall labor and do all your work, but the seventh day is the Sabbath of the LORD your God. In it you shall do no work: you, nor your son, nor your daughter, nor your male servant, nor your female servant, nor your cattle, nor your stranger who is within your gates. For in six days the LORD made the heavens and the earth, the sea, and all that is in them, and rested the seventh day. Therefore the LORD blessed the Sabbath day and hallowed it" (NKJV). So, in the fourth commandment we have the name, which is God—"the seventh day is the Sabbath of the LORD your God."

The fourth commandment also lists God's title, which is Creator of the world—"For in six days the LORD made the heavens and the earth, the sea, and all that is in them."

And we also know that God rules the territory or dominion of heaven and earth. God sits on His throne and sees everything in the universe. Nothing escapes His eyes.

The Sabbath is the only day that God blessed and sanctified and made holy. To sanctify is to set it aside for sacred use. Thus God blessed the Sabbath

Sealing of God's people

day and placed it aside for His sacred use. The Sabbath is the only holy and special day that bears God's seal and character. Therefore, the Sabbath is God's holy day (Exod. 20:12, 20; 1 Chron. 17:27). Some people believe that they can choose any day they want to worship God on. Oh how mistaken they are. If God specifically blessed His special day, sanctified it, and asked us to "remember" to keep it holy, then who are we to change His day and worship Him on any other day? Think about it.

Consider this scenario. If you want to throw a party, you pick a specific day that you want to have your party on. You then send your invitation to everyone to come to your party on the specified day that you told them to. How would you feel if some of your guests did not show up on the specific day of your party but came by the next day after your party. What would you do or tell them? I would tell them that they missed the party. So it is with God's special day, too. He specifically chose the Sabbath as His special day to meet with His people and receive their prayers, worship, and adoration, so if they do not show up on His special day, they miss out.

It is striking to learn that the fourth commandment is the only one that God placed the emphasis to "remember." This commandment is so special that God did not want anyone to forget His sacred day. He wants us to keep His special day holy. But a lot of people don't know that God's holy day is the Sabbath. Some people believe that Sunday is God's holy day or that the Sabbath is only for the Jews. But the Bible tells us that God's Sabbath is made for man. God chose the Jewish nation as a special nation to teach the Gentiles the way of the Lord and His Ten Commandments. But that does not mean that the Sabbath is only for the Jews. If that was true then the whole Bible should be only for the Jews and the rest of us Gentiles would be lost forever. And that's not the God that loves us and wants all of His children to be saved.

I've learned that God always placed a mark or seal on His faithful people/servants to protect them from danger. Let us go back to the beginning in Genesis and learn how God, because of His love, placed a mark on Cain although he killed his brother so that no one would kill him when they saw him (Gen. 4:15).

Next, let's go to Exodus and learn how God protected His people from the plagues in Egypt, and see how God used the same type of mark or sealing of His people before (Exod. 12:7, 12, 13). In order to protect the Israelites from the plaque that He was about to put on the Egyptians, they had to act on faith and mark the top frame of the door of their house with the blood of a perfect lamb without any blemish so that when the angel of death saw the blood he would pass over and thus protect their firstborns.

Now notice that they had to use the blood of a lamb without blemish. The reason why this lamb had to be perfect, clean, and without blemish is because it had to represent the real Lamb of God, which is Jesus Christ. Again the Israelites had to listen and obey to be able to receive God's blessings and protection.

Next, let us go to Jerusalem to the ancient house of Israel and Judah when God was ready to destroy those who had committed sin and abomination and protect those who had remained faithful to Him. "And the LORD said to him, 'Go through the midst of the city, through the midst of Jerusalem, and put a mark on the foreheads of the men who sigh and cry over all the abominations that are done within it.' To the others He said in my hearing, 'Go after him through the city and kill; do not let your eye spare, nor have any pity" (Ezek. 9:4, 5, NKJV; see also verses 6-11).

I asked myself what the abomination was that had been committed. I've learned that God showed Ezekiel in a vision what the abominations were. He showed Ezekiel what the elders of Israel did in the dark. How the elders who where supposed to be the religious leaders of the church were the ones committing abominations by worshiping idols. Ezekiel saw every sort of creeping thing, abominable beasts, and all the idols of the house of Israel portrayed all around on the walls and the elders, along with Jaazaniah the son of Shaphan, each had a censer in their hand, and a thick cloud of incense was rising up.

Then He told Ezekiel to turn again and see greater abominations that they were doing. And he showed Ezekiel the north gate of the Lord's house where women were sitting weeping for Tammuz. Tammuz was a false god. Ezekiel was dismayed at what he saw. But then he was told that there was an even greater abomination that he would see. God took Ezekiel into the inner court of the Lord's house, and there at the door of the temple of the lord, between the porch and the altar, were about twenty-five men with their backs toward the temple of the Lord and their faces toward the east, and they were worshiping the sun toward the east (Ezek. 8).

This was too much. Here the people of Israel, the chosen ones that God had given His Torah and teachings to and instructed to teach the Gentiles, were themselves committing abominations by worshiping idols and the sun instead of God, the Creator of the sun. Ironically, even today people worship the sun without knowing it and some knowingly are doing it. But God was against these abominations and was ready to destroy them all except those who did not participate in these abominations. Those who remained faithful to Him, He

Sealing of God's people

placed a mark on their foreheads so that they would not be destroyed.

Similarly, He will place a mark on His servants who refuse to worship idols and refuse to worship the false sabbath, which is Sunday, so that they will be protected from the disasters and plagues that will follow before the end of the world. The question we have to ask ourselves is which group am I in? Are you on the side that will stand fast on the principles and commandments of God and receive the mark on your forehead, or will you be on the side that worships idols, worships the sun, and experiences the plagues and calamities. The choice is yours and mine. But as for me, I chose Jesus and His Ten Commandments, including the seventh-day Sabbath. I hope and pray that you do the same and are saved from the coming disasters.

In Revelation 7:3 the command went forth, "Do not harm the earth ... until we have sealed the servants of our God on their foreheads." The forehead is where our mind is. We think and make all decisions in our mind. We learn, choose, and decide in our mind. So when we decide to follow Jesus Christ and keep His Sabbath holy, we are accepting God's seal on our forehead (Rom. 7:25).

Many people believe that salvation and the Sabbath are only for the Jews. This is not true. Salvation and the Sabbath are for all of God's children. If salvation and the Sabbath are only for the Jews, than we don't need to read the Bible because the Bible advises and teaches us to obey God's Ten Commandments and keep His Sabbath holy. Therefore, if the Bible is for us, too, then so is salvation and the Sabbath. It is for everyone who accepts Jesus Christ as their personal Savior and keeps His commandments.

To prove this concept, Jesus showed John the great multitude consisting of people from every nation, tribe, people, and languages standing in front of God's throne and serving God in His temple. These people consisted of all the nations of the world, not only the Jews.

At this point you may be wondering, but what is the seal of God? Ellen White addresses the mark of distinction in the *The SDA Bible Commentary*: "Those who would have the seal of God is their foreheads must keep the Sabbath of the fourth commandment. This is what distinguishes them from the disloyal, who have accepted a man-made institution in the place of the true Sabbath. The observance of God's rest day is the mark of distinction between him that serveth God and him that serveth Him not.... Many will not receive the seal of God because they do not keep His commandments or bear the fruits of righteousness" (vol. 7, p. 970).

The Revelation of Jesus Christ

Revelation 7:4-17

"And I heard the number of them which were sealed: and there were sealed an hundred and forty and four thousand of all the tribes of the children of Israel. Of the tribe of Juda were sealed twelve thousand. Of the tribe of Reuben were sealed twelve thousand. Of the tribe of Gad were sealed twelve thousand. Of the tribe of Aser were sealed twelve thousand. Of the tribe of Nephthalim were sealed twelve thousand. Of the tribe of Manasses were sealed twelve thousand. Of the tribe of Simeon were sealed twelve thousand. Of the tribe of Levi were sealed twelve thousand. Of the tribe of Issachar were sealed twelve thousand. Of the tribe of Zabulon were sealed twelve thousand. Of the tribe of Joseph were sealed twelve thousand. Of the tribe of Benjamin were sealed twelve thousand.

"After this I beheld, and, lo, a great multitude, which no man could number, of all nations, and kindreds, and people, and tongues, stood before the throne, and before the Lamb, clothed with white robes, and palms in their hands; And cried with a loud voice, saying, Salvation to our God which sitteth upon the throne, and unto the Lamb. And all the angels stood round about the throne, and about the elders and the four beasts, and fell before the throne on their faces, and worshipped God, Saying, Amen: Blessing, and glory, and wisdom, and thanksgiving, and honour, and power, and might, be unto our God for ever and ever. Amen.

And one of the elders answered, saying unto me, What are these which are arrayed in white robes? and whence came they? And I said unto him, Sir, thou knowest. And he said to me, These are they which came out of great tribulation, and have washed their robes, and made them white in the blood of the Lamb. Therefore are they before the throne of God, and serve him day and night in his temple: and he that sitteth on the throne shall dwell among them. They shall hunger no more, neither thirst any more; neither shall the sun light on them, nor any heat. For the Lamb which is in the midst of the throne shall feed them, and shall lead them unto living fountains of waters: and God shall wipe away all tears from their eyes."

John saw a great multitude that no one could number, consisting of all nations, tribes, people, and tongues. I personally thank God for showing John this great multitude because it proves to me and the rest of the world that the Sabbath and salvation are not only for the Jews but for everyone who accepts Jesus as their personal Savior and keeps His Ten Commandments and His holy Sabbath.

Sealing of God's people

If you listen to the daily news you will notice that what God revealed to us is already being fulfilled. Therefore, this should make our faith stronger and we should become obedient to the Word of God. "Already kingdom is rising against kingdom. There is not now a determined engagement. As yet the four winds are held until the servants of God shall be sealed in their foreheads. Then the powers of earth will marshal their forces for the last great battle. How carefully we should improve the little remaining period of our probation" (*The SDA Bible Commentary,* vol. 7, p. 968).

Prophecies are being fulfilled as God said they would. The news and history prove it. Now is the time to seek God before it is too late. Now is the time to choose God so that you can be protected from what's ahead. This is the time to make your choice so you will be sealed with God's seal.

The following quote is written by Ellen White and is taken from the *The SDA Bible Commentary.* It provides additional insight on the important subject of the sealing of God's followers. "Just before we entered it [the time of trouble], we all received the seal of the living God. Then I saw the four angels cease to hold the four winds. And I saw famine, pestilence and sword, nation rose against nation, and the whole world was in confusion (*Day-Star*, March 14, 1846).

"Everything in the world is in an unsettled state. The nations are angry, and great preparations for war are being made. Nation is plotting against nation, and kingdom against kingdom. The great day of God is hasting greatly. But although the nations are mustering their forces for war and bloodshed, the command to the angels is still in force, that they hold the four winds until the servants of God are sealed in their foreheads (The Review and Herald, January 28, 1909)....

"What is the seal of the living God, which is placed in the foreheads of His people? It is a mark which angels, but not human eyes, can read; for the destroying angel must see this mark of redemption. The intelligent mind has seen the sign of the cross of Calvary in the Lord's adopted sons and daughters. The sin of the transgression of the law of God is taken away. They have on the wedding garment, and are obedient and faithful to all God's commands (Letter 126, 1898).

"The Israelites placed over their doors a signature of blood, to show that they were God's property. So the children of God in this age will bear the signature God has appointed. They will place themselves in harmony with God's holy law. A mark is placed upon every one of God's people just as verily as a mark was placed over the doors of the Hebrew dwellings, to preserve the

The Revelation of Jesus Christ

people from the general ruin. God declares, 'I gave them my Sabbaths, to be a sign between me and them, that they might know that I am the Lord that sanctify them' (The Review and Herald, February 6, 1900)....

"Every soul in our world is the Lord's property, by creation and by redemption. Each individual soul is on trial for his life. Has he given to God that which belongs to Him? Has he surrendered to God all that is His as His purchased possession? All who cherish the Lord as their portion in this life will be under His control, and will receive the sign, the mark of God, which shows them to be God's special possession. Christ's righteousness will go before them, and the glory of the Lord will be their rereward. The Lord protects every human being who bears His sign [Exodus 31:12-17 quoted]....

"The Lord has a work for us all to do. And if the truth is not rooted in the heart, if the natural traits of character are not transformed by the Holy Spirit, we can never be colaborers with Jesus Christ. Self will constantly appear, and the character of Christ will not be manifested in our lives (Letter 80, 1898)....

"God can use the human agent just to the extent that he will be worked by the Holy Spirit. To men who accept positions of responsibility as presidents, ministers, physicians, or workers in any line, I am bidden to say: God will test every man who enters His service. He does not ask, Do they possess learning and eloquence? Have they ability to command and control and manage? He asks, Will they represent My character? Will they walk in humility, that I may teach them My way? The soul temple must not be defiled by any loose or unclean practice. Those whom I will acknowledge in the courts of heaven must be without spot and wrinkle.

"The Lord will use humble men to do a great and good work. Through them He will represent to the world the ineffaceable characteristics of the divine nature (Letter 270, 1907)....

"In a little while every one who is a child of God will have His seal placed upon him. O that it may be placed upon our foreheads! Who can endure the thought of being passed by when the angel goes forth to seal the servants of God in their foreheads (The Review and Herald, May 28, 1889)?...

"Only those who receive the seal of the living God will have the passport through the gates of the Holy City. But there are many who take upon themselves responsibilities in connection with the work of God who are not wholehearted believers, and while they remain thus cannot receive the seal of the living God. They trust in their own righteousness, which the Lord accounts as foolishness (Letter 164, 1909)....

"Those who would have the seal of God in their foreheads must keep the

Sealing of God's people

Sabbath of the fourth commandment. This is what distinguishes them from the disloyal, who have accepted a man-made institution in the place of the true Sabbath. The observance of God's rest day is the mark of distinction between him that serveth God and him that serveth Him not (MS 27, 1899)" (vol. 7, pp. 968-970).

Growing up, I always wanted to be picked by the best team. Well, this is the best of the best team of all. You can't afford to be left behind. I've learned that Sabbath observance plays a vital role in being picked and sealed. We must recognize God's holy Sabbath as the seventh-day Sabbath and keep it holy in order to be sealed with God's seal.

My brothers and sisters, don't follow the majority. Follow the Bible. That's the only way to be saved. God wants us to keep His commandments in order to be sealed. We must follow God's mandates and not what our pastor, priest, pope, neighbor, or teacher says. Jesus is the Word of God. God revealed Him to us so let us do what He says.

I'm going to repeat this quote again because it is very important: "Many will not receive the seal of God because they do not keep His commandments or bear the fruits of righteousness (Letter 76, 1900)....

"The great mass of professing Christians will meet with bitter disappointment in the day of God. They have not upon their foreheads the seal of the living God. Lukewarm and halfhearted, they dishonor God far more than the avowed unbeliever. They grope in darkness, when they might be walking in the noonday light of the Word, under the guidance of One who never errs (Letter 121, 1903)....

"Those whom the Lamb shall lead by the fountains of living waters, and from whose eyes He shall wipe away all tears, will be those now receiving the knowledge and understanding revealed in the Bible, the Word of God....

"We are to copy no human being. There is no human being wise enough to be our criterion. We are to look to the man Christ Jesus, who is complete in the perfection of righteousness and holiness. He is the author and finisher of our faith. He is the pattern man. His experience is the measure of the experience that we are to gain. His character is our model. Let us, then, take our minds off the perplexities and the difficulties of this life, and fix them on Him, that by beholding we may be changed into His likeness. We may behold Christ to good purpose. We may safely look to Him; for He is all-wise. As we look to Him and think of Him, He will be formed within, the hope of glory. Let us strive with all the power that God has given us to be among the hundred and forty-four thousand (The Review and Herald, March 9, 1905)" (*The SDA Bible*

The Revelation of Jesus Christ

Commentary, p. 970).

God does not want us to look up to any person and compare ourselves to him/her or to trust him/her. God wants us to trust Him only because that's the best thing to do. He will never fail us. "It is better to trust in the Lord than to put confidence in man" (Ps. 118:8, NKJV).

"The palms [in the hands] signify that they have gained the victory, and the white robes that they have been clothed with the righteousness of Christ. Thank God that a fountain has been opened to wash our robes of character, and make them as white as snow (Und. MS 23)" (*The SDA Bible Commentary*, vol. 7, p. 970; see also Matt. 22:11, 12; Rom 11:33).

God repeats these messages and others throughout the Bible several times to help us understand what He is saying. Jesus and His Father have done everything they can for us. Now we must choose to believe, trust, and accept Their free gift. I pray that you will make the right decision. As proof of God's character and His eternal message, compare the following texts:

Old Testament: "He will swallow up death forever, and the Lord GOD will wipe away tears from all faces; the rebuke of His people He will take away from all the earth; for the LORD has spoken" (Isa 25:8, NKJV).

New Testament: "Then Death and Hades were cast into the lake of fire. This is the second death" (Rev. 20:14, NKJV).

Old Testament: "The LORD is my shepherd; I shall not want. He makes me to lie down in green pastures; He leads me beside the still waters. He restores my soul; He leads me in the paths of righteousness for His name's sake" (Ps. 23:1-3, NKJV). "They shall neither hunger nor thirst, neither heat nor sun shall strike them; For He who has mercy on them will lead them, even by the springs of water He will guide them" (Isa. 49:10, NKJV).

New Testament: "And God will wipe away every tear from their eyes; there shall be no more death, nor sorrow, nor crying. There shall be no more pain, for the former things have passed away" (Rev. 21:4, NKJV).

Chapter 8

The Trumpets' Warning of Catastrophes Part 1

Revelation 8:1, 2

"And when he had opened the seventh seal, there was silence in heaven about the space of half an hour. And I saw the seven angels which stood before God; and to them were given seven trumpets."

I've learned that the number seven is God's number of completion. According to the Bible when God does things it usually is in sevens

From the previous chapters we have already learned that it was Jesus, the Lamb of God, who was worthy to open or break the seals. Here again it is Jesus who opens the seventh seal. At that time John saw that there was silence for about half an hour. This could be due to expectation of what's coming next. I can imagine the angels looking in amazement; no one was singing or playing any music. All was quiet as if they were expecting to see what would happen next. And then John saw the seven angels who stand before God receive seven trumpets.

According to Matthew 18:10 and Luke 1:19, these angels are the ministering spirits who are commissioned to guard, protect, and warn God's children. Trumpets in Bible prophecy symbolize warnings; a sign to assemble or move; announcement of destruction, calamities, wars; or any adverse event that is coming. In our human terms, I believe that it is God's way of raising His voice to let His people know what's ahead and for them to get prepared. God is trying to get our attention. His trumpets give us a chance to repent (Jer. 4:5-9, 19, 20). Therefore, we should listen and put our house in order. Pray and reason with God for forgiveness (Isa. 1:18). Also, we will learn later on that the sounding of the seventh trumpet is linked with the finishing of the "mystery of God" (Rev. 10:7). The mystery of God is the proclamation of the gospel (Rom. 16:25, 26; Eph. 3:4; 6:19; Col. 4:3). We can also say that it is the closing up of the gospel (Eph. 3:2-7).

God takes our prayers seriously. Although at times we feel as if we pray and pray and pray but nothing happens, God is listening. He hears our sincere prayers, but we need to be careful how we pray. We need to have a sincere heart, be respectful to God by hallowing His sacred name, believe in His Son, Jesus Christ, ask for our needs, and thank Him for answering our prayers (Glenn Coon, *ABC's of Bible Prayer*, pp. 13-17).

How many warnings have you received about the coming destruction and the end of this world? This goes to show you God's mercy toward us. He gives us so many warnings and time to prepare, and He waits until we put our house in order, but it's up to us to respond and obey His warnings. All these warnings are because of His love for us. He is patiently waiting on us. But He will not wait forever; we must decide who we will give our hearts to and worship.

Prayer is a powerful connection with heaven. Think about this: "As the high priest sprinkled the warm blood upon the mercy seat while the fragrant cloud of incense ascended before God, so while we confess our sins and plead the efficacy of Christ's atoning blood, our prayers are to ascend to heaven, fragrant with the merits of our Savior's character. Notwithstanding our unworthiness, we are to remember that there is One who can take away sin, and who is willing and anxious to save the sinner. With His own blood He paid the penalty for all wrongdoers. Every sin acknowledged before God with a contrite heart, He will remove. [Isaiah 1:18; Hebrews 9:13, 14] (RH Sept. 29, 1896)" (*The SDA Bible Commentary,* vol. 7, p. 970).

The power of prayer can be utilized in each household during evening worship and prayers. "Then let the evening prayers in every family rise steadily to heaven in the cool sunset hour, speaking before God in our behalf of the merits of the blood of a crucified and risen Savior. That blood alone is efficacious. It alone can make propitiation for our sins. It is the blood of the only-begotten Son of God that is of value for us that we may draw nigh unto God, His blood alone that taketh 'away the sin of the world.' Morning and evening the heavenly universe behold every household that prays, and the angel with the incense, representing the blood of the atonement, finds access to God (MS 15, 1897)" (*The SDA Bible Commentary,* vol. 7, p. 971).

Revelation 8:3, 4

"And another angel came and stood at the altar, having a golden censer; and there was given unto him much incense, that he should offer it with the prayers of all saints upon the golden altar which was before the throne. And the smoke of the incense, which came with the prayers of the saints, ascended up before God out of the angel's hand."

This other angel is Jesus Christ. Jesus is also referred to as the Archangel. But we know that He is God because He and His Father are one. So here John sees Jesus working as the High Priest on our behalf, mixing our prayers with His merit as a sweet-smelling incense. Jesus our High Priest is doing the intercessory work, which is to offer the incense with the prayers of the saints before His Father. So in essence, Jesus is our Mediator. He stands between us and His Father, mediating on our behalf through His merits (Rom. 8:26; Heb. 4:14; 7:25; 1 Tim. 2:5, 6; Rev. 5:8).

"People who learn the lessons the trumpets are designed to teach won't have to suffer the catastrophic judgments of the seven last plaques. But the seven trumpets are bad enough in their own right. They constitute *severe* judgment warnings. In many places in the Bible God talks to us quietly, but not here. In the trumpets He fairly shouts at us, 'Watch where you're going! Look out!'" (*God Cares,* vol. 2, p. 224).

Revelation 8:5-7

"And the angel took the censer, and filled it with fire of the altar, and cast it into the earth: and there were voices, and thunderings, and lightnings, and an earthquake. And the seven angels which had the seven trumpets prepared themselves to sound. The first angel sounded, and there followed hail and fire mingled with blood, and they were cast upon the earth: and the third part of trees was burnt up, and all green grass was burnt up."

I've learned that God sent similar judgments to Gog and Egypt (Exod. 7:17; Ezek. 38:22). According to Isaiah 44:3, 4 trees and grass symbolize people. And as the angels were moving around God's throne, John heard the noises, thundering, lightning, and earthquake (Ezek. 1:14, 24; 10:5; Rev. 4:5).

Some Bible scholars believe that this prophecy was fulfilled when the Roman empire was invaded by the Visigoths, and the destruction that they caused as a result of the warfare symbolized the hail, fire, and blood.

Revelation 8:8-11

"And the second angel sounded, and as it were a great mountain burning with fire was cast into the sea: and the third part of the sea became blood; And the third part of the creatures which were in the sea, and had life, died; and the third part of the ships were destroyed. And the third angel sounded, and there fell a great star from heaven, burning as it were a lamp, and it fell upon the third part of the rivers, and upon the fountains of waters; And the name of the star is called Wormwood: and the third part of the waters became wormwood; and many men died of the waters, because they were made bitter."

This star that fell from heaven according to Isaiah 14:12-17 is no other than Satan. Remember, star is decoded to be an angel; therefore, this fallen angel is Satan. He made all the waters bitter with his evil (evil equals bitterness) contamination, causing many people to die. Satan always pollutes what is pure, but Jesus always purifies what Satan pollutes with His blood on the cross.

So my friends, Wormwood is Satan polluting people with his false doctrines and lies, causing people to die in their sins without God.

Revelation 8:12

"And the fourth angel sounded, and the third part of the sun was smitten, and the third part of the moon, and the third part of the stars; so as the third part of them was darkened, and the day shone not for a third part of it, and the night likewise."

The Old and New Testaments as we have learned go hand in hand. God also predicted this prophecy in Isaiah 13:10, which says, "For the stars of heaven and their constellations will not give their light; the sun will be darkened in its going forth, and the moon will not cause its light to shine" (NKJV). God is consistent in what He says, and His words are true. This same prophecy was repeated again in Revelation 8.

Jesus is the Fountain of living water. Just as He said to the Samaritan woman, He is saying it to you and me today: "Whoever drinkgs of the water that I shall give him will never thirst" (John 7:14, NKJV). So let's ask and accept Jesus' living water today. He's ready to give it to you and me. On a spiritual level we could say that spiritual darkness rests on the earth. This spiritual darkness is the result of false teachings, distorted biblical principles, superstitions, witchcraft, and devil worship. But thank God that His Son, Jesus Christ, is the Light of the World (John 8:12; 9:5) and the "Sun of Righteousness" (Mal. 4:2, NKJV). He's able to penetrate through this darkness and give us the light from His Father.

Revelation 8:13

"And I beheld, and heard an angel flying through the midst of heaven, saying with a loud voice, Woe, woe, woe, to the inhabiters of the earth by reason of the other voices of the trumpet of the three angels, which are yet to sound!"

John sees an angel flying in the midst of heaven announcing that the last three trumpts that are yet to come will take the people of earth by surprise. You would think that the previous four trumpets were bad but the angel seems to be saying, wait until you see what's coming next. Oh boy, can you imagine? These calamities are fearful and terrible in their own right. But remember, God is revealing all these things to us so that we can escape them and be under His banner of protection if we believe in His Son, Jesus Christ, and accept and keep His Ten Commandments. He is ready to protect us, but we have to let Him know that we want His protection.

Why don't you bow your head right now and ask Him for His protection? Some people wear some type of emblem or charm on their neck and wrist, thinking that they are protected. My friend, don't be fooled; that's another tactic that Satan uses to keep you in the dark. The only true protection comes from God and His Son, Jesus Christ. No other source. He's the only one who does not slumber or sleep. So what better protection can we get? And guess what? His protection is free. We just need to accept Jesus Christ as our Savior and this protection is ours. So what are you waiting for? Now is the time to ask. You'll be glad you did.

Let's do a quick recap. So far we've learn about Jesus as:

1. The Lamb of God who taketh away our sins

2. Our High Priest, mediating on our behalf

3. The Great Judge and our Advocate, preparing us for God's judgment ahead

Chapter 9

The Trumpets' Warning of Catastrophes Part 2

Revelation 9:1-4

"And the fifth angel sounded, and I saw a star fall from heaven unto the earth: and to him was given the key of the bottomless pit. And he opened the bottomless pit; and there arose a smoke out of the pit, as the smoke of a great furnace; and the sun and the air were darkened by reason of the smoke of the pit. And there came out of the smoke locusts upon the earth: and unto them was given power, as the scorpions of the earth have power. And it was commanded them that they should not hurt the grass of the earth, neither any green thing, neither any tree; but only those men which have not the seal of God in their foreheads."

We learned in chapter 8 that Jesus is the Light of the world and He's the truth and life. The opposite of light is darkness; the opposite of truth is lies; and the opposite of life is death, which spells Satan. He's full of darkness and evil; he's the father of lies and death. So here again God is showing us another side of the devil. He's the fallen star that we learned about in Revelation 8. Now we learn that he was given the key to the bottomless pit. In other words, he's the one controlling the abyss, the darkness and the evil events that come out of this darkness (Prov. 4:19; Luke 11:34; John 3:19-21; 1 Pet. 2:9).

The smoke that came out represents Satan's false teachings, aliens, superstitions, lies, errors, and evil plans. As we have learned, beasts in Bible prophecy represent power, kingdoms, or rulers. These scorpions that came out of the smoke represent a kingdom. They were given power as a scorpion

The Trumpets' Warning of Catastrophes Part 2

to hurt everyone who does not have the seal of God. And guess who's their leader—Satan himself. Many times we allow Satan to control us and push us to commit evil things such as killing, lying, cheating, and hurting or hating others. But the best thing we can do is to control ourselves and ask Jesus to give us strength to resist the devil. We can't fight him on our own; we need Jesus to intervene for us.

Some historians parallel this prophecy with the Arabs who swept through eastern Rome and the Ottoman Turks' attack at the battle of Bapheum near Nicomedia, which ended in July 27, 1449.

Here we get a glimpse of how God's people will be protected during these difficult times. The locusts were permitted to torment only those who did not have the seal of God on their foreheads. My friends, it pays to have God's seal on your forehead. As we learned before, the seal of God is His seventh-day Sabbath. And having this seal on your forehead means that you will be protected from these locust. We learned that these locusts were given power as the scorpions. This power lied in their tails. According to Isaiah 9:15 a tail represents prophets who teach lies. Therefore, the source of their power was in their prophets who were liars. And we already know that all lies come from Satan because he is the father of lies.

So again, this fallen star is none other than Satan when he was thrown out of heaven. He came down with huge wrath and hatred for Jesus and His created human beings. He's no one's friend. His plan is to destroy all humans that God created. He was thrown out of heaven, so he's trying to trick everyone into listening to his lies and schemes and keep them from going to heaven. He's no friend of man; he hates all of God's servants who love His Son, Jesus Christ, and keep His testomonies.

The only reason Satan tries to befriend humanity is to give them power, fame, riches, and popularity for a time and lull them into his web. Then he destroys them with drugs, alcohol, sex, or he kills them before they have time to wake up and stretch out their hand to Jesus so that Jesus can pull them up out of their misery and save them. Remember, there are only two choices or two parties in this world—Jesus or Satan. You are either on Jesus' side or Satan's; there's no middle ground.

Many famous people have sold their souls to the devil just to be rich and famous. If only they knew that it is only through Jesus Christ that they can have eternal riches and fame. Perhaps many of them didn't or don't know better. No one told them the truth about Satan. I pray that through this book as many as possible will come to know Jesus for the first time and accept His free gift of eternal life, riches, and fame. I pray that after reading this book that their eyes will be open to the deceptions of Satan so that they can break loose from his grip of lies and accept Jesus Christ in their lives as their personal Savior and receive peace of mind.

After Satan was expelled from heaven, according to Revelation 12:7, he took up his abode on this earth or the "underworld" as some call it in modern terms. We have movies coming out about the underworld, which features nothing other than Satan and his evil angels.

It is striking to know that even after all these calamities the rest of the people who were not killed by these plaques will not turn from their idols that they have made with their own hands. They will not stop worshiping demons (Satan's church) and idols made of gold, silver, bronze, stone, and wood, which cannot see or hear or walk. Nor will they stop breaking God's holy commands such as not worshiping idols, murdering, killing, engaging in sexual immorality, dealing with the occult, doing drugs, stealing, etc.

Unfortunately, a lot of people worship idols without knowing it. An idol can be anything that takes your time away from God. If you spend more time with an item than you spend with God, then that thing or item becomes your idol. It can be your car; TV; carved images of Mary, Peter, or any of the apostles; work; music; pageants; Internet; computer; sports; soap operas; or any other items that drag you away from God. If you spend more time with these things or you worship them, then they become your idols and false gods. In Exodus 20:3-6 Jesus said, "You shall have no other gods before Me. You shall not make for yourself a carved image—any likeness of anything that is in heaven above, or that is in the earth beneath, or that is in the water under the earth; you shall not bow down to them nor serve them. For I, the LORD your God, am a jealous God, visiting the iniquity of the fathers upon the children to the third and fourth generations of those who hate Me, but showing mercy to thousands, to those who love Me and keep My commandments" (NKJV).

Going back to the locusts, we can see that at this time, when these locusts are torturing people, they can't touch God's people because God's people are protected by His angels. They have the seal of God, which means they can't be touched by the enemy, Satan.

According to Revelation 9:2 the sun and the air were darkened because of the smoke that came from the bottomless pit. Sun in Bible prophecy represents the glory of God revealed in the gospel. According to the Bible the gospel is the "good news of salvation" (Isa. 61:1, NKJV). So for the sun to be darkened with this smoke it is because Satan's false teachings are covering the good news of salvation. He tries to get rid of the Bible, and his false teachings take over, causing darkness to reign. People on earth breathed the dark smoke, which was the false teachings of Satan.

Revelation 9:5-9

"And to them it was given that they should not kill them, but that they should be tormented five months: and their torment was as the torment of a scorpion, when he striketh a man. And in those days shall men seek death, and shall not find it; and shall desire to die, and death shall flee from them. And the shapes of the locusts were like unto horses prepared unto battle; and on their heads were as it were crowns like gold, and their faces were as the faces of men. And they had hair as the hair of women, and their teeth were as the teeth of lions. And they had breastplates, as it were breastplates of iron; and the sound of their wings was as the sound of chariots of many horses running to battle."

They were given authority to torment those who did not have the seal of God in their foreheads for five months. This reminds me of some of the religious groups that we see today. They kill, torture, and burn people all in the name of their god. They are blinded to think that they are serving the real God, but in reality they are serving their god, Satan. The picture resembles men possessed by evil spirits. And their king is Satan himself. How many people today are being deceived by the snake just as Eve was? Are you being deceived by Satan? Are you participating in killing others in the name of your religion? If you are then today is the day that you can learn about the truth and know who's behind the lies. Today Jesus is ready to cut you loose from Satan's web of lies. You only need to pray and ask Jesus to help you and trust Him to do the job. That's all. You don't have to do anything else. Jesus is ready to save you if you ask Him. So go ahead, this is your chance to let Jesus enter your heart.

Revelation 9:10-19

"And they had tails like unto scorpions, and there were stings in their tails: and their power was to hurt men five months. And they had a king over them, which is the angel of the bottomless pit, whose name in the Hebrew tongue is Abaddon, but in the Greek tongue hath his name Apollyon. One woe is past; and, behold, there come two woes more hereafter. And the sixth angel sounded, and I heard a voice from the four horns of the golden altar which is before God, Saying to the sixth angel which had the trumpet, Loose the four angels which are bound in the great river Euphrates. And the four angels were loosed, which were prepared for an hour, and a day, and a month, and a year, for to slay the third part of men.

"And the number of the army of the horsemen were two hundred thousand thousand: and I heard the number of them. And thus I saw the horses in the vision, and them that sat on them, having breastplates of fire, and of jacinth, and brimstone: and the heads of the horses were as the heads of lions; and out of their mouths issued fire and smoke and brimstone. By these three was the third part of men killed, by the fire, and by the smoke, and by the brimstone, which issued out of their mouths. For their power is in their mouth, and in their tails: for their tails were like unto serpents, and had heads, and with them they do hurt."

After the sixth trumpet sounded, Jesus commanded the four angels to be released who were bound at the great river Euphrates. Back in chapter 7 these four angels were holding the wind until God's people were sealed. Now the time, hour, and year came when they were released. As long as the angels were holding the winds of strife, things were quiet in this world, but after they are released all kinds of warfare, battles, are started and one-third of the people are killed.

Revelation 9:20, 21

"And the rest of the men which were not killed by these plagues yet repented not of the works of their hands, that they should not worship devils, and idols of gold, and silver, and brass, and stone, and of wood: which neither can see, nor hear, nor walk: Neither repented they of their murders, nor of their sorceries, nor of their fornication, nor of their thefts."

Wow, even though people witnessed all this destruction, because of their disobedience to God's laws they still continued to be disobedient by killing others, practicing whitchcraft, worshipping the devil, engaging in sexual immorality, and stealing. They did not repent. That is scary. People saw, heard, and witnessed these events and still did not believe or repent from their sins. Don't let this happen to you. Today is your chance to repent and ask God for forgiveness. Believe in God's Son, Jesus Christ, who died for you and me and be saved. Don't let the devil steal your joy.

In summary, I've learned that those who accept Jesus' free gift of eternal life and keep His commandments and testimonies will receive His seal or mark in their foreheads and be protected from the plague of the locusts. But those who refuse Jesus' free gift or choose not to keep His Ten Commandments

The Trumpets' Warning of CatastrophesPart 2

and His testimonies will not receive His seal or mark in their foreheads, and thus, they will be tortured for five months. Again, God is showing us these things in advance so that we can decide whose side we will be on. The specific commandments that the people are breaking in this time period according to Exodus 20 and the New Testament are numbers 1, 2, 3, 4, 6, 7, and 8.

- "Thou shalt have no other gods before me" (verse 3).
- "Thou shalt not make unto thee any graven image, or any likeness of any thing that is in heaven above, or that is in the earth beneath, or that is in the water under the earth. Thou shalt not bow down thyself to them, nor serve them: for I the LORD thy God am a jealous God, visiting the iniquity of the fathers upon the children unto the third and fourth generation of them that hate me; and shewing mercy unto thousands of them that love me, and keep my commandments" (verses 4-6).
- "Thou shalt not take the name of the LORD thy God in vain; for the LORD will not hold him guiltless that taketh his name in vain" (verse 7).
- "Remember the sabbath day, to keep it holy. Six days shalt thou labour, and do all thy work: But the seventh day is the sabbath of the LORD thy God: in it thou shalt not do any work, thou, nor thy son, nor thy daughter, thy manservant, nor thy maidservant, nor thy cattle, nor thy stranger that is within thy gates: For in six days the LORD made heaven and earth, the sea, and all that in them is, and rested the seventh day: wherefore the LORD blessed the sabbath day, and hallowed it" (verses 8-11).
- "Thou shalt not kill" (verse 13; see also Rom. 13:9).
- "Thou shalt not commit adultery" (verse 14; see also Rom 13:9; James 2:11).
- "Thou shalt not steal" (verse 15; see also Ps. 115; 135:15-17; Dan. 5:23).

History has a way of repeating itself. Humanity commits the same sins again and again.

So therefore, by these words from the Ten Commandments they will be judged. Those who will receive God's wrath are those who do not obey God's commandments. And according to James 2:10, 11 if you break one of the commandments you have broken them all. Please review God's commands found in Exodus 20.

Are you willing to keep all of God's Ten Commandments as He requested?

Chapter 10

Jesus and the Little Open Book

Revelation 10:1

"And I saw another mighty angel come down from heaven, clothed with a cloud: and a rainbow was upon his head, and his face was as it were the sun, and his feet as pillars of fire:"

John saw a mighty angel coming down dressed with a cloud. Clouds in my opinion are angels. When Jesus comes again, He will be surrounded by angels dressed in white, and thus, He will look as if He is in a white cloud. White signifies purity. It is also important to note that this mighty angel had a rainbow over His head. Remember, back in Genesis God explained His promise of the rainbow. This rainbow is to remind us of His eternal promise that sin will never reign again. God never forgets.

This verse also depicts that His face was bright and shining as the brightness of the sun so that no one can look at. In addition, His legs are as columns of fire. In Malachi 4:2 we are told that Jesus Christ is the "Sun of Righteousness" (NKJV). Because of His glory and brightness, no one can look at it and live. His legs, which are as columns of fire, represent His power. In a similar manner, Jesus used a burning bush to demonstrate His power to Moses in the book of Exodus (Exod. 3:1-7).

At times Jesus is called an angel, yet He is given a greater distinction because He is also God, the Archangel (Jude 9).

Based on this description it sounds like this mighty angel parallels with the person mentioned in Revelation 1, which is Jesus Christ. So this tells me that this message was so important that God the Father had to send His own Son to tell it to us. What a God!

Jesus and the Little Open Book

Revelation 10:2

"And he had in his hand a little book open: and he set his right foot upon the sea, and his left foot on the earth,"

John saw that He had a little book open in His hand. This caused me to ask myself if this is an open book was there a time when it was closed? Where in the Bible does it say that it was closed before? Again, the Old Testament and the New Testament go hand in hand. Let's go back to Daniel to find out about this closed book. You need to keep in mind that Daniel and Revelation are a continuation of each other, and they also parallel each other. In Daniel 8 we learn of this closed book that Jesus opened for us in Revelation 10. Let's review it.

Daniel 8:19 says, "And he said, 'Look, I am making known to you what shall happen in the latter time of the indignation; for at the appointed time the end shall be" (NKJV; see also verses 20-26). A few chapters further, Daniel 12:1-4 says, "At that time Michael shall stand up, The great prince who stands watch over the sons of your people; And there shall be a time of trouble, such as never was since there was a nation, even to that time. And at that time your people shall be delivered, every one who is found written in the book. And many of those who sleep in the dust of the earth shall awake, some to everlasting life, some to shame and everlasting contempt. Those who are wise shall shine. Like the brightness of the firmament. And those who turn many to righteousness like the stars forever and ever. 'But you, Daniel, shut up the words, and seal the book until the time of the end; many shall run to and fro, and knowledge shall increase'" (NKJV).

So Jesus told Daniel to seal this book because these things will happen at the end time, the end of the world. There was no need to dwell on those prophecies during Daniel's lifetime, so the book was closed. But now that we are living in the end of time, God told John not to seal the message of Revelation because these prophecies will be fulfilling shortly. Here the sealed book was unsealed and given to John to share with the whole world. Please note, however, that not all of Daniel's messages were sealed, just the ones for the end time.

Let's review the parallels between Daniel 12 and Revelation 10.
- Daniel 12:4 - "shut up the words, and seal the book" until the time of the end
- Revelation 10:2 - He had a "little book "open" in His hand
- Daniel 12:5 Two men stood one on each side of the riverbank

The Revelation of Jesus Christ

- Revelation 10:2 - Angel standing on the land and sea
- Daniel 12:6 - Man clothed in linen
- Revelation 10:1 - Mighty angel clothed with a cloud
- Daniel 12:7 - Held up both hands and swore by Him who lives forever
- Revelation 10:5 - Lifted up hand and swore to Him who lives forever and ever
- Daniel 12:9 - seal the words until the time of the end
- Revelation 10:8 - take the little book that is open
- Daniel 12:10 - the wicked will remain wicked and not understand, but the wise understand
- Revelation 10:9 - eat the book (see also Revelation 22:11: "He that is unjust, let him be unjust still: and he which is filthy, let him be filthy still: and he that is righteous, let him be righteous still: and he that is holy, let him be holy still.")
- Daniel 12:11, 12 - 1290-day prophecy and 1335-day prophecy
- Revelation 10:11 - we must prophesy again to many people, nations, tongues, and kings

Here you can see that the same Jesus presented the same message to Daniel and John. To Daniel. He gave him a preview of what will happen in the end time, and He told him to seal it until the end time. But to John He told him to take the little book that is open and prophecy to many people, nations, tongues, and kings. Please note that John was not to tell it to one group of people or nationality. He was instructed to share it to many people, nations, tongues, and kings. In a nutshell that is everyone who has an ear. God wants everyone to be saved. But it is up to each individual to accept His free gift and be saved. God does not force anyone. You have the power of choice, and the choice will always be yours.

Jesus placed His right foot on the sea and His left foot on the land. This to me signifies two things:

That He was reclaiming what was His—the whole earth. Not just the water, but the land as well. He's taking back the sea that He made and the earth that He formed with His own hands (Gen. 1:9, 10; Ps. 95:5). Satan was defeated at the cross so now the world that he took from Jesus is being taken back from him.

That Jesus wanted this message to go to the whole world to all people, even those across the waters. Therefore, to every tribe, language, nation, king, and people—to everyone who has an ear to listen.

In Daniel 12:4, 9 Daniel was instructed to seal the book because the prophesies were for the end time and many years to come and were not for then. But here Jesus opened the book and told John to prophesy again about many people, nations, languages, and kings because the time has come for these prophecies to be fulfilled. So now that we are actually in the end time, John had to make sure that he shared with everyone—rich, poor, all languages and nations—about what was shown to him.

There's another harmony between the Old and New Testaments that we can read in Deuteronomy 8. The same God from yesterday is the same today and tomorrow. Chapter 8 parallel with the end time that we will be going through; a terrible time of trouble. But if we keep God's commandments and the testimonies of Jesus Christ, we will enjoy the mansions that He is preparing for us.

Revelation 10:3-5

"And cried with a loud voice, as when a lion roareth: and when he had cried, seven thunders uttered their voices. And when the seven thunders had uttered their voices, I was about to write: and I heard a voice from heaven saying unto me, Seal up those things which the seven thunders uttered, and write them not. And the angel which I saw stand upon the sea and upon the earth lifted up his hand to heaven, And sware by him that liveth for ever and ever, who created heaven, and the things that therein are, and the earth, and the things that therein are, and the sea, and the things which are therein, that there should be time no longer."

Here is God's message to everyone, including atheists, Darwinist, evolutionist, and all those who do not know better or believe that there is a God. There is a God who created heaven and earth and all that there is. Nothing came to be by chance. God created everything: the sea, earth, animal kingdom, heaven, people, mountains, etc. (see Gen. 1:31; 2:1; Exod. 20:11; Deut 10:14; 32:40; 2 Kings 19:15; Ps. 146:6; Neh. 9:6). Now is your chance to come to Him—hear His words, obey, and receive His blessings. Why don't you accept Him now before it is too late? Just ask Him to come into your heart. He's standing and knocking at your heart, why don't you let Him in? You'll be glad you did.

Next, God instructed John what he needed to do with the message that He had unsealed and opened to him. John is commanded to take the open book and prophecy or tell it to everyone who has an ear. Don't be fooled by Satan, and don't play the fool. God already knew that some people wouldn't believe in Him or His Father God. In Psalm 14:1 Jesus said, "The fool has said in his heart, 'There is no God'" (see also Isa. 45:18, 22). Don't be a fool. There's too much evidence that there is a God for you not to believe and thus be a fool. If you hear God's voice calling you today, don't harden your heart.

Revelation 10:7

"But in the days of the voice of the seventh angel, when he shall begin to sound, the mystery of God should be finished, as he hath declared to his servants the prophets."

Then the angel (Jesus) lifted up His right hand toward heaven and swore to God who created heaven and what is in it, the earth and what is in it, and the sea and what is in it that there will be no more delay and that when the seventh angel blows his trumpet the "mystery of God should be finished, as he hath declared to his servants the prophets" (Rev. 10:7).

This verse drove me to do some more research about the mystery that Jesus Christ declared to His servants the prophets. I found out that this mystery is the *good news of salvation* for you and me. It is the gospel that God gave to His prophets and servants. It is the good news that Jesus incarnate came to this world and died on the cross just to save us; this is the mystery. He wants to save us in His kingdom. His Father made Him the King of Kings, and He wants us to be part of His kingdom. The invitation is for you and me. That is the good news (Rev. 11:15). He created this world, but we sinned. He then died for our sins, and He wants us with Him again. This is the good news of the gospel! Aren't you excited? It gives me chills to know that God loves us so much that He sacrificed His only Son, Jesus Christ, just to save us. Wow! We should be praising His name day and night in thanksgiving.

So if you believe in God, this good news is for you, too. Jesus died for your sins to save you. He did His part of the job. Now you have to do yours. It is not hard; you just need to accept this free gift and obey Jesus' commandments and keep His testimonies. That's all. But the choice is yours.

Examine this truth: "The gospel dispensation is the last period of probation that will ever be granted to men. Those who live under this dispensation of test and trial and yet are not led to repent and obey will perish with the disloyal. There is no second trial. The gospel that is to be preached to all nations, kindred, tongues, and peoples presents the truth in clear lines, showing that obedience is the condition of gaining eternal life. Christ imparts His righteousness to those who consent to let Him take away their sins. We are indebted to Christ for the grace which makes us complete in Him" (*The SDA Bible Commentary*, vol. 7, pp. 971, 972).

So, as I understand it, based on what Jesus said above, that "in the days of the voice of the seventh angel, when he shall begin to sound, the mystery of God should be finished, as he hath declared to his servants the prophets" (Rev. 10:7). Please note that this time, according to Ellen White, "is not the end of this world's history, neither of probationary time, but of prophetic time, which should precede the advent of our Lord" (*The SDA Bible Commentary*, vol. 7, p. 971).

During the time when the seventh angel was about to sound his trumpet, God's mystery would be finished. The good news of redemption has been fulfilled. Then Jesus warned John that when the good news was received it would be sweet in his mouth but bitter in his stomach. This was fulfilled when Christians all over the world began to study the scriptures regarding Jesus' Second Coming and the prophecies of Daniel. They received the message with gladness; it was sweet in their mouth; but when Jesus did not return as expected, it was bitterness in their stomach because of the great disappointment.

Revelation 10:8, 9

"And the voice which I heard from heaven spake unto me again, and said, Go and take the little book which is open in the hand of the angel which standeth upon the sea and upon the earth. And I went unto the angel, and said unto him, Give me the little book. And he said unto me, Take it, and eat it up; and it shall make thy belly bitter, but it shall be in thy mouth sweet as honey."

We've learned again and again that the Old and the New Testaments go hand in hand. So again we learn from the Old Testament that God commanded Ezekiel to eat the scroll and prophecy to the people (Ezek. 3:3). To eat the scroll is to hear the message, understand it, digest it, study it, and share it with others. Don't keep what you've learned to yourself. Share it with others so that they too can receive God's blessings. This is the same thing that was commanded to John to do.

Revelation 10:10, 11

"And I took the little book out of the angel's hand, and ate it up; and it was in my mouth sweet as honey: and as soon as I had eaten it, my belly was bitter. And he said unto me, Thou must prophesy again before many peoples, and nations, and tongues, and kings."

This means that we must tell it to everyone who has an ear. Not only to the Jews or Christians but to everyone who has an ear—Jews, Gentiles, Christians, non-Christians, everyone!

Many nineteenth-century Bible scholars and Christians, after searching the scriptures, concluded that the end time of Bible prophecy began in 1798 and that the 2300 days would end in 1844, at which time Christ would return. Their calculations and understanding of Daniel's prophecies, the opening of the sealed message that was given to him, were correct and sweet like honey in their mouth, but their interpretation of Christ's Second Coming was wrong. So when Christ did not return as calculated, they experienced a bitter disappointment in their stomach. Thus this prophecy was fulfilled as it was told to John. Some of the believers left the church while others followed God's mandate to study, read, listen, and prophecy to the world—to every tongue, nation, and people.

"When did this bitter-sweet experience occur? In the early 1800s, independent of one another, Bible students around the world began a reviewed study of the prophecies of Daniel. This rekindled interest in prophecy led those honest-hearted men and women of God to believe that Jesus was coming very soon. They misunderstood the prophecies regarding the time of the end. They thought Jesus would come in 1844. The date was right, but the event was wrong! Like the first-century disciples, a misunderstanding of Bible prophecy led them to be bitterly disappointed" (*Revelation Speaks Messages of Hope for a World in Turmoil,* p. 76).

Ellen White said, "The mighty angel who instructed John was no less a personage than Jesus Christ. Setting His right foot on the sea, and His left upon the dry land, shows the part which He is acting in the closing scenes of the great controversy with Satan. This position denotes His supreme power and authority over the whole earth. The controversy has waxed stronger and more determined from age to age, and will continue to do so, to the concluding scenes when the masterly working of the powers of darkness shall reach their height. Satan, united with evil men, will deceive the whole world and the churches who receive not the love of the truth. But the mighty angel demands attention. He cries with a loud voice. He is to show the power and authority of His voice to those who have united with Satan to oppose the truth.

"After these seven thunders uttered their voices, the injunction comes to John as to Daniel in regard to the little book: 'Seal up those things which the seven thunders uttered.' These relate to future events which will be disclosed in their order. Daniel shall stand in his lot at the end of the days. John sees the little book unsealed. Then Daniel's prophecies have their proper place in the first, second, and third angels' messages to be given to the world. The unsealing of the little book was the message in relation to time.

"The books of Daniel and the Revelation are one. One is a prophecy, the other a revelation; one a book sealed, the other a book opened. John heard the mysteries which the thunders uttered, but he was commanded not to write them.

"The special light given to John which was expressed in the seven thunders was a delineation of events which would transpire under the first and second angels' messages. It was not best for the people to know these things, for their faith must necessarily be tested. In the order of God most wonderful and advanced truths would be proclaimed. The first and second angels' messages were to be proclaimed, but no further light was to be revealed before these messages had done their specific work. This is represented by the angel standing with one foot on the sea, proclaiming with a most solemn oath that time should be no longer....

"The gospel dispensation is the last period of probation that will ever be granted to men. Those who live under this dispensation of test and trial and yet are not led to repent and obey will perish with the disloyal. There is no second trial. The gospel that is to be preached to all nations, kindred, tongues, and peoples presents the truth in clear lines, showing that obedience is the condition of gaining eternal life. Christ imparts His righteousness to those who consent to let Him take away their sins. We are indebted to Christ for the grace which makes us complete in Him" (*The SDA Bible Commentary*, vol. 7, pp. 971, 972).

So, my friend, there is still more time for you to come to Jesus. The invitation still stands. Why don't you accept Him now before it is too late. Now is the time; Jesus is the answer to your problems. He's ready to help you if you allow Him to.

Chapter 11

Jesus' Two Witnesses—The Old and New Testament

Revelation 11:1, 2

"And there was given me a reed like unto a rod: and the angel stood, saying, Rise, and measure the temple of God, and the altar, and them that worship therein. But the court which is without the temple leave out, and measure it not; for it is given unto the Gentiles: and the holy city shall they tread under foot forty and two months."

I've learned that everyone will be measured to see if they have met God's standards, requirements, and have the appropriate garment on according to His law and the Ten Commandments. We all have to give an account to God about our deeds in this life, whether it is good or evil. We need to measure ourselves daily from top to bottom and side to side to see if we've defiled God's holy name and His Ten Commandments. Measure from head to toe. Our head and heart plan and control our actions and emotions. Our feet take us to places that we should or should not go. Our right hand plans or makes deals that's are or are not pleasing to God; and our left hand can or cannot do evil things that are not good in God's eyes.

We need to measure our life against God's holy law and His Ten Commandments. Have we taken other gods before our holy God? Have we taken His holy name in vain? Are we worshiping Satan the devil, spirits, or idols, such as cars, houses, TV, jobs, friendships, money, etc.? Are we keeping God's holy Sabbath? Some people say that it does not matter which day you choose to worship God on as long as you worship Him. To these same people God is saying today, "I do not want sacrifice; I want obedience." If God chose the seventh-day Sabbath as His holy day and blessed it and hallowed it and told us to "Remember the Sabbath day, to keep it holy" (Exod. 20:8, NKJV), then who are we to change it and worship on any other day? We must obey Him and do what He says without questioning Him.

Are we honoring our parents? Do we dump our parents in a nursing home when they are old and vulnerable without visiting them, and as soon as they die, we go searching for the things they left behind? Or are we caring for them while they are sick and old as God requires us to do. Do we kill other people, either physically or by hating them? Are we committing adultery against our spouses or against God? Do we take things that do not belong to us? Are we stealing from our job, neighbor, government, or friends? Do we lie or bear false testimony against our neighbors? Are we coveting our neighbor's house, wife, servant, car, or anything that belong to our neighbor?

If you are innocent, then you passed the test. If you answered no to most of these questions, then you are on the right path. You are keeping God's commandments as He asks you to. If you are not doing what God is requesting you to do, please be advised that you still have time to make things right with God. Now is the time for you to set your life and house in order. You have the guidelines by which to measure your life—God's Ten Commandments and the testimonies of Jesus Christ, which is the spirit of prophecy. If you follow these guidelines and ask Jesus to send the Holy Spirit into your life, you should not have any problem.

I pray that we will all measure up according to God's standards that He gave us. Many people think that God's Ten Commandments are either for the Jews or that they were done away with. How mistaken they are; God's commandments are for everyone and they are forever. They can never be done away with because they represent God's character, which will never be done away with.

After the great disappointment, God asked His servants to get up and search the scriptures again. By so doing they realized where they had gone wrong and why Christ did not return in 1844. Their first mistake was in setting a date for Jesus' return. When Jesus was on this earth, He said, "But of that day and hour no one knows, not even the angels in heaven, nor the Son, but only the Father" (Mark 13:32, NKJV). God is the only one who knows. By setting a date they set themselves up for failure. Even now people are setting dates for the coming of Jesus or for the end of this world. But no one knows the day and time. Only God knows; so don't waste your time in what they are saying. Search the scriptures, and God will guide you to the truth.

Today, God is asking you and me to research the scriptures again. At times

The Revelation of Jesus Christ

we might feel disappointed, discouraged, and want to give up. But God is telling us, don't give up, get up; read the scriptures to find out where you stand and correct what you need to correct in your life before it is too late. Measure your life to see where you're standing today. Ask yourself if you measure up to what God wants you to measure up to? Are you keeping God's commandments and the testimony of Jesus Christ? Are you loving your neighbors as yourself? Do you love your family, friends, neighbors, in-laws, and out-laws? How are you doing? How is your walk with Jesus? Are you safe in His arms or are you doubting? Come to Jesus today, and He will make it clear for you.

God permitted John to see the original Ten Commandments, which He wrote with His own fingers. This is to prove to everyone that His Ten Commandments are forever and He expects all those who love Him to keep them holy as well. For those who say that the Ten Commandments were done away with, God is giving them proof that it is not true. His original Ten Commandments are alive and well. God said in Mathhew 5:17 that He came "not ... to destroy but to fulfill" the law.

Let's see another parallel between Revelation and Zechariah.

Revelation	**Zechariah**
Chapter 11:1, 2 – Prophet given rod to measure with, measures the temple of God and worshipers	Chapter 2 – Man with measuring line measures Jerusalem
Chapter 11:3, 4 – Two olive trees, two candlesticks, and two witnesses (prophets)	Chapter 4 – Two olive trees, candlestick with seven lamps, two anointed ones that stand by the Lord

What does this all mean? Ellen White provides some insight into these verses. "The grand judgment is taking place, and has been going on for some time. Now the Lord says, Measure the temple and the worshipers thereof. Remember when you are walking the streets about your business, God is measuring you; when you are attending your household duties, when you engage in conversation, God is measuring you. Remember that your words and actions are being daguerreotyped [photographed] in the books of heaven, as the face is reproduced by the artist on the polished plate....

"Here is the work going on, measuring the temple and its worshipers to see who will stand in the last day. Those who stand fast shall have an abundant entrance into the kingdom of our Lord and Savior Jesus Christ. When we are doing our work remember there is One that is watching the spirit in which we are doing it. Shall we not bring the Saviour into our everyday lives, into our

Jesus' Two Witnesses—The Old and New Testament

secular work and domestic duties? Then in the name of God we want to leave behind everything that is not necessary, all gossiping or unprofitable visiting, and present ourselves as servants of the living God (MS 4, 1888)....

"When God's temple in heaven is opend, what a triumphant time that will be for all who have been faithful and true! In the temple will be seen the ark of the testament in which were placed the two tables of stone, on which are written God's law. These tables of stone will be brought forth from their hiding place, and on them will be seen the Ten Commandments engraved by the finger of God. These tables of stone now lying in the ark of the testament will be a convincing testimony to the truth and binding claims of God's law. (Letter 47, 1902)....

"Sacrilegious minds and hearts have thought they were mighty enough to change the times and laws of Jehovah; but, safe in the archives of heaven, in the ark of God, are the original commandments, written upon the two tables of stone. No potentate of earth has power to draw forth those tables from their sacred hiding place beneath the mercy seat" (*The SDA Bible Commentary,* vol. 7, p. 972).

For further study on measuring, read Ezekiel 40-44, Zechariah 2:1-4, and Revelation 21:15.

God took the time to write the Ten Commandments and give them to us; therefore, they are very important. The first four commandments address our loyalty to God, and the other six address our loyalty to our fellow human beings. According to the Bible, the Ten Commandments represent God's character. In Matthew 22:37-40 Jesus narrowed it down to two great commandments, to love God with all your heart and to love your neighbor as yourself.

Revelation 11:3-10

"And I will give power unto my two witnesses, and they shall prophesy a thousand two hundred and threescore days, clothed in sackcloth. These are the two olive trees, and the two candlesticks standing before the God of the earth. And if any man will hurt them, fire proceedeth out of their mouth, and devoureth their enemies: and if any man will hurt them, he must in this manner be killed. These have power to shut heaven, that it rain not in the days of their prophecy: and have power over waters to turn them to blood, and to smite the earth with all plagues, as often as they will.

"And when they shall have finished their testimony, the beast that ascendeth out of the bottomless pit shall make war against them, and shall overcome them, and kill them. And their dead bodies shall lie in the street of the great city, which spiritually is called Sodom and Egypt, where also our Lord was crucified. And they of the people and kindreds and tongues and nations shall see their dead bodies three days and an half, and shall not suffer their dead bodies to be put in graves. And they that dwell upon the earth shall rejoice over them, and make merry, and shall send gifts one to another; because these two prophets tormented them that dwelt on the earth."

Who are the two witnesses of God? I've learned that God's two witnesses, the two olive trees or the two menorahs standing before the Lord of the earth, are His Old Testament and New Testament. John 1:1-5 says, "In the beginning was the Word, and the Word was with God, and the Word was God. He was in the beginning with God. All things were made through Him, and without Him nothing was made that was made. In Him was life, and the life was the light of men. And the light shines in the darkness, and the darkness did not comprehend it" (NKJV). Verse 14 says, "And the Word became flesh and dwelt among us, and we beheld His glory, the glory as of the only begotten of the Father, full of grace and truth" (NKJV). I've learned that this Word of God was and is Jesus Christ the Son of God (1 John 5:5-12; Rev. 19:11-14).

The Old Testament and the New Testament bear witness to God's Word, which is His Son, Jesus Christ. The Old Testament prophesied of Jesus, the Son of God, who was to come, and the New Testament fulfilled that the Word, Jesus, came. So the only two witnesses are the Old and New Testaments, God's Word, the Bible.

According to God Cares, volume 2, page 300, "A witness is a person who bears a witness, someone who makes a testimony or testifies about something. The words witness, *bear witness*, and *testify* are closely related in meaning. When they occur in the New Testament, they are translated from Greek words related to *martureo*, from which comes our word *martyr*. A martyr is a person who in life and death testifies to or bears witness to his faith in God.

"In John 5:39, Jesus said of (1) the *Old Testament scriptures*, 'It is they that bear witness to me.' And during the Olivet Discourse He said, (2) 'This gospel of the kingdom will be preached throughout the whole world, as a testimony [or witness] to all nations' Matthew 24:14."

Revelation 11:11-14

"And after three days and an half the spirit of life from God entered into them, and they stood upon their feet; and great fear fell upon them which saw them. And they heard a great voice from heaven saying unto them, Come up hither. And they ascended up to heaven in a cloud; and their enemies beheld

Jesus' Two Witnesses—The Old and New Testament

them. And the same hour was there a great earthquake, and the tenth part of the city fell, and in the earthquake were slain of men seven thousand: and the remnant were affrighted, and gave glory to the God of heaven. The second woe is past; and, behold, the third woe cometh quickly."

Satan and his people tried to destroy the Bible. They kept it away from the people, prevented people from reading it, and even killed those who were caught with a Bible in their homes. According to history the Bible was removed for three and a half years in Europe during the French Revolution. The French Revolution was noted for its grosse opposition to Christianity. After the three and a half years, Christianity awakened again and flourished faster than before. God's Word, the Bible, can never be destroyed or suppressed because "the word of God stands forever" (Isa 40:7, 8).

People such as John Wesley, George Whitefield, Henry Martyn, David Livingstone, Martin Luther, Joseph Bates, Ellen White, William Miller, Dwight Moody, preached the Word of God with might and power. How about you? Are you willing to witness to others about Jesus? Are you ready to lose your life for Jesus today? If you are, then God will make it up to you with an eternal reward.

"We found that three and a half prophetic days represent three and a half literal years. The French assembly voted to ban the Bible in November, 1793. And three and a half years later, just as predicted, in June of 1797, it was restored. God's Word proves its accuracy again! When the French Revolution ended, the Bible enjoyed a greater circulation than it had had in centuries. The world's Bible societies were born. The Word of God was circulated by the tens of thousands of copies. The two witnesses have borne their testimony to the world" (*Revelation Speaks Messages of Hope for a World in Turmoil,* p. 83).

"During the Dark Ages, from A.D. 538 to A.D. 1798, church and state united in Europe. The two witnesses were clothed in sackcloth, a symbol of mourning. During much of this period, the Bible was not readily available to the people. For one thing, it was not translated into the common language of the people. Very few people understood the Hebrew, Greek, and Latin translations.

"Before the printing press in A.D. 1456, the few handwritten copies which existed were usually kept in monasteries. The medieval church taught that the common people could not understand the Bible. The church's view was that the Bible could only be understood by religious leaders, who would then interpret it for the people. In A.D. 1299, church leaders placed the Bible on the now infamous Index—a list of forbidden books for which the faithful were condemned if they read. God's witnesses, the Old and the New Testaments—His cherished Word—suffered a mortal blow" (*Revelation Speaks Messages of*

The Revelation of Jesus Christ

Hope for a World in Turmoil, p. 81).

Revelation 11:15-19

"And the seventh angel sounded; and there were great voices in heaven, saying, The kingdoms of this world are become the kingdoms of our Lord, and of his Christ; and he shall reign for ever and ever. And the four and twenty elders, which sat before God on their seats, fell upon their faces, and worshipped God, Saying, We give thee thanks, O LORD God Almighty, which art, and wast, and art to come; because thou hast taken to thee thy great power, and hast reigned. And the nations were angry, and thy wrath is come, and the time of the dead, that they should be judged, and that thou shouldest give reward unto thy servants the prophets, and to the saints, and them that fear thy name, small and great; and shouldest destroy them which destroy the earth. And the temple of God was opened in heaven, and there was seen in his temple the ark of his testament: and there were lightnings, and voices, and thunderings, and an earthquake, and great hail."

Here Christ is reclaiming His earth that the enemy has been ruling and destroying. He finally says, "That's enough! I want my earth and people back." Now is the time for revenge. Now the martyrs will be vindicated and see their recompense—their dying was not in vain.

When the seventh angel sounds his trumpet, God's mystery is revealed. Jesus is taking up His kingdom. Satan has been defeated. All those who refuse to hear His voice and choose to be in His party will miss out on His plan of salvation. Jesus can't force people to love Him and follow Him. He has shown His love to everyone by dying on the cross to save humanity, but the choice is ours whether we will accept His free gift of eternal life or not. How He wishes that everyone who reads about His love will accept Him, but because He loves us so much, He allows us to choose. Now is the time to choose Jesus and live. Please pray and ask Jesus to come into your heart so that you can make the right decision and live with Him in His kingdom.

In this passage we see that Jesus is ready to start His kingdom and His rulership, and when He does, He will destroy all those who have destroyed His earth that He has made. I do not believe that God is pleased with nuclear testings, bombs that destroy His creation, or chemicals and toxic waste that are dumped into the earth and sea.

As we close this chapter, let's recap what we have learned. Who are God's two witnesses? They are the Old and New Testaments. They both testify about Jesus Christ. Jesus would like for you and I to become His witnesses, too. He wants us to share with others what He did and is doing for us. Whenever we share Jesus with others, we are testifying about Him to others.

The time will come, and I believe that it is now, that we must tell people about Jesus and the crisis that is about to come to our world. We do not want them to blame us for not telling them about the things that we know are about to happen. If we love our family members, friends, and neighbors, then we must warn them about the time of trouble that is soon at hand so that they will be aware and make the right decision to follow Jesus Christ before it is too late. Are you willing to testify about Jesus Christ to your family, friends, and neighbors today?

Chapter 12

Woman Pregnant With Jesus

Revelation 12:1, 2

"And there appeared a great wonder in heaven; a woman clothed with the sun, and the moon under her feet, and upon her head a crown of twelve stars: And she being with child cried, travailing in birth, and pained to be delivered."

Let's decode the symbols here. The woman clothed with the sun represents God's true church; the male child represents Jesus Christ; and the red dragon represents Satan.

Revelation 12:3-6

"And there appeared another wonder in heaven; and behold a great red dragon, having seven heads and ten horns, and seven crowns upon his heads. And his tail drew the third part of the stars of heaven, and did cast them to the earth: and the dragon stood before the woman which was ready to be delivered, for to devour her child as soon as it was born. And she brought forth a man child, who was to rule all nations with a rod of iron: and her child was caught up unto God, and to his throne. And the woman fled into the wilderness, where she hath a place prepared of God, that they should feed her there a thousand two hundred and threescore days."

Please note that the great controversy between Jesus and Satan started in heaven and Satan's next step was to cause our first parents to sin (Gen. 3:15). Satan is described with the following symbols: serpent, dragon, and beast symbols; while Jesus is identified with the woman and her seed. Read Isaiah 27:1 and Psalm 74:14 for more information about the Leviathan, serpent-like figure.

In the book of Revelation God reveals to us the struggle between Jesus

Woman Pregnant With Jesus

and Satan. This struggle is about capturing the hearts of human beings. Jesus wants our heart so that He can save us. But Satan wants our heart so that he can destroy us. So you have to be careful who you give your heart to. Are you willing to give it to Jesus or Satan? The choice is yours.

Revelation 12 is one of my favorite chapters because here God gives us a picture of the earth's history in a symbolic way. Once we uncover the symbols, you'll realize that it is telling us about the story of Jesus redeeming the earth and His church. Let's start with describing and decoding each symbol so that it will be easy to understand.

According to the Bible, a woman represents the church or God's people. Read Ephesians 5:25-32 to get the whole picture of how this symbol of a woman represents God's church (see also Gen. 3:1; Rev. 12; 19:6-8).

The sun represents Jesus and His righteousness (Ps. 84:11; Mal. 4:2; John 9:5). The **moon** has no light except what is reflected from the sun. It represents the Old Testament sacrificial system, which had no light except what was reflected from the gospel (Heb. 10:1). The crown of twelve stars represents the work of the twelve disciples, which crowned the early years of the church (Matt. 10:1-4). Remember that stars, according to Revelation 1:20, represent angels. Therefore, Satan deceived one-third of the angels, and he and his angels were cast out of heaven.

God's church is pregnant with God's Son, Jesus. The Holy Spirit came to Mary and placed the seed of Jesus in her womb (Matt. 1:20; Luke 1:35). After Christ's death and resurrection, the Holy Spirit fell on men and women, and they all became pregnant with Jesus. People who have received the Holy Spirit will know God's laws and will keep His testimonies. Thus, Jesus will live in their heart and life. How I wish that everyone will learn of Jesus and become pregnant with Him.

Satan, by using King Herod, tried to kill Jesus at His birth by destroying all the babies of Bethlehem (Matt. 2:1-18). But Joseph and Mary were forewarned by an angel and fled to Egypt. These two events were predicted by Old Testament prophets (Jer. 31:15; Hosea 11:1). Though the dragon represents Satan, it also has a secondary application to pagan Rome. Herod was a Roman ruler, whom Satan used to try to kill Jesus at birth. A beast normally represents a kingdom or political power (Dan. 7:23).

The woman screaming in the agony of labor represents God's church and saints going through the time of Jacob's trouble for their faith in Jesus and His testimonies, and similar to the woman, they too will be screaming in agony because of the persecution, pain, and torture that Satan will put on them because they choose to follow Jesus Christ. But by persevering they will receive the crown of life that Jesus is preparing for them.

The red dragon represents the devil, Satan, the adversary, the old serpent (Rev. 12:9). The dragon's tail represents Satan deceiving one-third of the angels in heaven, and as a result, they were cast out of heaven to the earth (Rev. 12:7-9). The dragon in front of the pregnant woman is Satan standing in front of God's church ready to destroy all the saints that are pregnant with Jesus, meaning that they are filled with the Holy Spirit.

The seven heads represent a system of seven kingdoms; each one follows each other by keeping the same pagan practices that came from Satan. The ten horns are the ten European countries.

The male child obviously represents Jesus. Revelation 12:5 tells us that He will rule all nations with a staff of iron. In that same verse we learn that God took the child to His throne. God protected Baby Jesus from being killed by King Herod who was under the influence of Satan.

The woman fled to the desert to a place God had prepared for her. God's church, running away from persecuction, ran to the mountains, caves, deserts, and then the United States of America because of religious persecution.

History tells us that many Christians were persecuted, killed, and burned because of their belief and loyalty to Jesus Christ. Jesus said, "My sheep hear My voice, … and they follow Me" (John 10:27, NKJV). Those who are not His sheep will not hear His voice and will not follow Him. Thus they will hear Satan's voice and will follow him. Once again we are back to the two choices/ two parties again. This is the time that God's people must trust God to deliver and protect them from the evil one.

Revelation 12:7-17

"And there was war in heaven: Michael and his angels fought against the dragon; and the dragon fought and his angels, And prevailed not; neither was their place found any more in heaven. And the great dragon was cast out, that old serpent, called the Devil, and Satan, which deceiveth the whole world: he was cast out into the earth, and his angels were cast out with him. And I heard a loud voice saying in heaven, Now is come salvation, and strength, and the kingdom of our God, and the power of his Christ: for the accuser of our brethren is cast down, which accused them before our God day and night. And they overcame him by the blood of the Lamb, and by the word of their testimony; and they loved not their lives unto the death. Therefore rejoice, ye heavens, and ye that dwell in them. Woe to the inhabiters of the earth and of

Woman Pregnant With Jesus

the sea! for the devil is come down unto you, having great wrath, because he knoweth that he hath but a short time.

"And when the dragon saw that he was cast unto the earth, he persecuted the woman which brought forth the man child. And to the woman were given two wings of a great eagle, that she might fly into the wilderness, into her place, where she is nourished for a time, and times, and half a time, from the face of the serpent. And the serpent cast out of his mouth water as a flood after the woman, that he might cause her to be carried away of the flood. And the earth helped the woman, and the earth opened her mouth, and swallowed up the flood which the dragon cast out of his mouth. And the dragon was wroth with the woman, and went to make war with the remnant of her seed, which keep the commandments of God, and have the testimony of Jesus Christ."

Michael, which is Jesus, and His angels fought against the dragon, which is Satan and his angels. Jesus and His angels won, and God expelled Satan and his angels from heaven. Satan is a loser from the beginning. Anyone who aligns themselves with him and his witchcraft are loser just as he is.

In this passage God reveals a lot of information about Jesus, His church, and the devil. Let's review everything carefully and prayerfully so that we can understand the verses. Whenever the Bible speaks about a woman in prophetic language, it represents the church. Now, there is only two legitimate churches in this world. God's pure church, and Satan's harlot church. In this case this woman represents God's true church (Isa. 54:5, 6; Eph. 5:23-32; Rev. 19:6-8). The pregnancy and baby represents Jesus Christ. Here God is revealing to us Jesus' birth. He will rule with an iron rod (Ps. 2:7-9; Rev. 12:5).

The red fiery dragon standing in front of the woman ready to devour her child is none other than Satan. Let's go back to the prophecies of Genesis 3:15 and the birth of Jesus to learn how Satan used Herod to try to kill Jesus after he was born and how God protected Him by sending His angel to warn Joseph in the night to take the baby and hide in Egypt. The story of Jesus' birth paralleled this prophecy. In the Old Testament it was prophecied, and in the New Testament it was fulfilled. The woman escaping to Egypt parallels with the woman escaping to the desert. The man child protected from King Herod parallels with the male child taken to heaven.

Satan attempted to kill baby Jesus by influencing King Herod to kill all the babies two years and under (Matt. 2:12-20). But God protected His Son by sending an angel to warn Joseph in a dream to flee to Egypt until Herod died. Thus Satan was unable to kill the child, so Satan was wroth and went after the woman, which is the church of God, to persecute her, but God came to her rescue again. She was given two wings of an eagle to flee into the wilderness where a place of safety was prepared for her. In fulfillment of this prophecy, God's people who were under persecution had to flee to the mountains, caves, wilderness, and finally America to escape persecution. The symbol of the earth opening up its mouth to rescue the woman, which represents God's people and true church, once again symbolized God's protection and provision for His people.

The woman, or God's church, was clothed with the sun and the moon was under her feet and on her head she had a crown of twelve stars. We've learned in Malachi 4:2 that Jesus Christ is the Sun of righteousness. Therefore, His true church/servants will be clothed with the light of His righteousness. Jesus said to His disciples that "I am the light of the world" (John 8:12; see also John 1:4).

So His servants must carry this light, which represents the gospel, to those in darkness so that they can see the light, repent, and accept the good news of Jesus Christ as the source of their light. This is the garment that God's church or His people must wear to be saved—the light of Jesus Christ and His character or His righteousness (Isa. 52:1; 61:10; Rom. 1:16, 17; 2 Cor. 5:21; Rev. 19:7, 8).

The red dragon is Satan working through pagan Rome to destroy Jesus Christ. When the dragon realized that he couldn't kill Jesus Christ or the woman, which is God's church, he turns his wrath toward the remnant of the woman's children, the ones who are left.

The moon is a symbol of permanency (Ps. 89:37). Therefore, if God's church (woman) stands on the moon, it is an indication that the foundation of God's church's is permanent, and thus God's church will last forever. Satan tries to obliterate God's church, but he's a liar and a loser. God's church will last forever. Thank God.

The crown of twelve stars represent Jesus choosing twelve appostles to start His church. Thus the crown of twelve stars signifies that God's church was started by these twelve apostles who Jesus Himself instructed and trained.

The great controversy between Christ and Satan, which has raged ever since the inception of sin, is first portrayed symbolically in Genesis 3:15. This prophecy of promise introduces those symbols that the protagonists in the controversy have themselves selected, and these become their means of identification in Bible prophecy. Satan has chosen for himself serpent-dragon and beast symbols, and Christ has chosen to identify Himself with the woman and her seed. In Isaiah 27:1 and Psalm 74:14 we find additional indication

Woman Pregnant With Jesus

of the serpent-dragon-Leviathan figure, which, interestingly, is also found in many non-biblical sources such as the Ras Shamra texts that tell of a seven-headed serpent dragon that rules the "underworld." The book of Revelation pictures the intensity of the struggle between Christ and Satan beginning in chapter 12, and it goes on to depict the final defeat of the terrible beast and the red dragon and the establishment of a new heaven and a new earth where sin and Satan are no longer present.

Satan was cast out of heaven because iniquity had entered his heart (Ezek. 28). God created all beings with the power to choose. He does not force or coerce anyone. Just as the angels chose between Satan and Jesus so we humans must choose between Satan and Jesus as well. We can't stay neutral. We must choose whom we will follow. I pray that you will choose Jesus and live. Satan only offers destruction and sorrow.

When Satan was still in heaven he deceived one-third of the angels living in heaven and started a revolt against Jesus and His angels, but Jesus and His angels fought back and won. As a result, Satan and his angels were thrown out of heaven. From that time on, the distinction between the angels existed. In the beginning they were all holy angels, but after the rebellion in heaven, Satan and his angels became the evil angels, and the angels in heaven that stayed loyal to God's commandments remained holy and good angels. When Satan and his evil angels came down to earth, they were furious. They hated every human being and worked to deceive them so that they will not receive God's blessings of eternal life, which they lost.

My favorite author, Ellen White, describes the scene that took place: "He [Satan] declares he cannot submit to be under Christ's command, that God's commands alone will he obey. Good angels weep to hear the words of Satan, and to see how he despises to follow the direction of Christ, their exalted and loving Commander. The Father decides the case of Satan, and declares that he must be turned out of heaven for his daring rebellion, and that all those who united with him in his rebellion should be turned out with him. Then there was war in heaven. Christ and His angels fought against Satan and his angels, for they were determined to remain in heaven with all their rebellion. But they prevailed not. Christ and loyal angels triumphed, and drove Satan and his rebel sympathizers from heaven. (Spiritual Gifts 3:38)....

"When Satan rebelled, there was war in heaven, and he, with all his sympathizers, was cast out. He had held a high office in heaven, possessing a throne radiant with light. But he swerved from his allegiance to the blessed and only Potentate, and fell from his first estate. All who sympathized with him were driven from the presence of God, doomed to be no more acknowledged in the heavenly courts as having a right there. Satan became the avowed antagonist of Christ. On the earth he planted the standard of rebellion, and round it his sympathizers rallied (MS 78, 1905)" (*The SDA Bible Commentary,* vol. 7, p. 973).

So here we learn that Satan is the antichrist. He has hated Christ from the beginning, and now he is convincing humans to hate Christ as well. But don't let him fool you.

"Cast out of heaven, Satan set up his kingdom in this world, and ever since, he has been untiringly striving to seduce human beings from their allegiance to God. He uses the same power that he used in heaven—the influence of mind on mind. Men become tempters of their fellow men. The strong, corrupting sentiments of Satan are cherished, and they exert a masterly, compelling power. Under the influence of these sentiments, men bind up with one another in confederacies (Letter 114, 1903)" (*The SDA Bible Commentary,* vol. 7, p. 973)

My friends, please note again that this battle is not yours. It is the Lord's. Satan started this battle in heaven against Jesus, and he brought it down to our world. But he's a loser from the beginning, and he will be defeated in the end, but this time it will be forever. Therefore, you need to make up your mind and choose whose side you are on. If you choose Jesus Christ, you will be blessed with eternal life; if you choose Satan, you will be lost forever in the eternal death. The choice is yours. There are only two choices to choose from. The purpose of our lives is to choose which side we want to be on before we die. Because by choosing we will decide how we are going to spend eternity. If we choose Jesus, we will live with Him forever. If we choose Satan, we will die with him forever. The choice is yours.

I pray that you will make the right choice and get on the side of Jesus Christ, our Redeemer and Savior. Our world is considered the lost sheep. Christ left the ninety-nine sheep behind to go and search for the one that was lost. He died on the cross to save you and me.

All the violence, wars, killing, stealing, and destroying of God's earth is all Satan's doing. He works through governments, kings, rulers, and people to enact his evil ways. Many times we humans get upset with each other because we've been hurt, but one thing we have to remember is that Satan is the one behind it all. That's why I like the song that talks about the battle not being ours but the Lord's. Truly, this is not our battle. We had nothing to do with it; Satan and his evil angels started this battle in heaven way before we were even born. He was cast out of heaven so now Satan is taking all his vengeance out on us humans who Jesus created so that he can get back at God and His Son, Jesus Christ.

Let me say it again, this battle is not ours, it's the Lord's. We are caught in the middle, but thankfully Jesus promises to fight it for us just as He fought Satan before. We have nothing to worry about as long as we are under Jesus' protection. This is a spiritual battle, and there's no way that we, as humans, can fight it. Just as He fought Satan in heaven and won, He can do the same for us here on earth. We just have to trust Jesus. Our forefathers, Adam and Eve, were deceived by Satan. When they sinned, they caused all of us to be born in sin. And as you know, we must die under the law. But Jesus paid the price for us! Instead of us dying for our sins, Jesus died for us and redeemed us back to His Father. Praise God! This is what grace is all about—Jesus paying the price of death for us.

According to Ellen White, "Opposition to the law of God had its beginning in the courts of heaven, with Lucifer, the covering cherub. Satan determined to be first in the councils of heaven, and equal with God. He began his work of rebellion with the angels under his command, seeking to diffuse among them the spirit of discontent. And he worked in so deceptive a way that many of the angels were won to his allegiance before his purposes were fully known. Even the loyal angels could not fully discern his character, nor see to what his work was leading. When Satan had succeeded in winning many angels to his side, he took his cause to God, representing that it was the desire of the angels that he occupy the position that Christ held.

"The evil continued to work until the spirit of disaffection ripened into active revolt. Then there was war in heaven, and Satan, with all who sympathized with him, was cast out. Satan had warred for the mastery in heaven, and had lost the battle. God could no longer trust him with honor and supremacy, and these, with the part he had taken in the government of heaven, were taken from him.

"Since that time Satan and his army of confederates have been the avowed enemies of God in our world, continually warring against the cause of truth and righteousness. Satan has continued to present to men, as he presented to the angels, his false representations of Christ and of God, and he has won the world to his side. Even the professedly Christian churches have taken sides with the first great apostate" (*The Review and Herald*, January 28, 1909).

Prophecy has predicted and history has taught us that Satan has been persecuting God's church even up to now. We've learned about the Pilgrims, the persecution of our European brothers who had to flee to America because of religious persecution. We hear about persecution in China. Our Christian brothers and sisters can't proclaim the gospel as they desire in that country. Pastors are being thrown into jail for the Word of God. In many other parts of the world persecution is going on in one form or the other. And according to history, the Waldensians and other religious groups had to hide in the mountains to escape religious percecution.

"Under the symbols of a great red dragon, a leopard-like beast, and a beast with lamblike horns, the earthly governments which would especially engage in trampling upon God's law and persecuting His people, were presented to John. The war is carried on till the close of time. The people of God, symbolized by a holy woman and her children, were represented as greatly in the minority. In the last days only a remnant still existed. Of these John speaks as they 'which keep the commandments of God, and have the testimony of Jesus Christ'" (*The Signs of the Times,* November 1, 1899).

According to Ellen White, "The casting down of Satan as an accuser of the brethren in heaven was accomplished by the great work of Christ in giving up His life. Notwithstanding Satan's persistent opposition, the plan of redemption was being carried out. Man was esteemed of sufficient value for Christ to sacrifice His life for him. Satan, knowing that the empire he had usurped would in the end be wrested from him, determined to spare no pains to destroy as many as possible of the creatures whom God had created in His image. He hated man because Christ had manifested for him such forgiving love and pity, and he now prepared to practice upon him every species of deception by which he might be lost; he pursued his course with more energy because of his own hopeless condition" (*The Spirit of Prophecy*, vol. 3, pp. 194, 195).

Listen, Satan is no match for us. We can only resist him by the power of God. And now I have finally learned and understand why we are a peculiar and special people. It is because God loved us so much that He sent His only begotten Son to die on our behalf. He left His throne, luxury, adoration, and the other worlds behind to come to our dark sinful world just to save you and me. What a love. We are a peculiar and chosen people (1 Pet. 2:9; Titus 2:14). "For God so loved the world that He gave His only begotten Son, that whosoever believes in Him should not perish but have everlasting life" (John 3:16, NKJV).

It is up to you to believe in God's Son, Jesus Christ, and choose to be with Him and enjoy eternal life, or not. "Christ on the cross, not only draws men to repentance toward God for the transgression of His law—for whom

God pardons He first makes penitent—but Christ has satisfied justice; He has proffered Himself as an atonement. His gushing blood, His broken body, satisfy the claims of the broken law, and thus He bridges the gulf which sin has made. He suffered in the flesh that with His bruised and broken body He might cover the defenseless sinner. The victory gained at His death on Calvary broke forever the accusing power of Satan over the universe, and silenced his charges that self-denial was impossible with God and therefore not essential in the human family" (Manuscript 50, 1900).

"Those who love and keep the commandments of God are most obnoxious to the synagogue of Satan, and the powers of evil will manifest their hatred toward them to the fullest extent possible. John foresaw the conflict between the remnant church and the power of evil, and said, 'The dragon was wroth with the woman, and went to make war with the remnant of her seed, which keep the commandments of God, and have the testimony of Jesus Christ.'

"The forces of darkness will unite with human agents who have given themselves into the control of Satan, and the same scenes that were exhibited at the trial, rejection, and crucifixion of Christ will be revived. Through yielding to satanic influences, men will be transformed into fiends; and those who were created in the image of God, who were formed to honor and glorify their Creator, will become the habitation of dragons, and Satan will see in an apostate race his masterpiece of evil—men who reflect his own image" (*The Review and Herald*, April 14, 1896).

"There are only two parties upon this earth—those who stand under the bloodstained banner of Jesus Christ and those who stand under the black banner of rebellion. In the twelfth chapter of Revelation is represented the great conflict between the obedient and the disobedient [Revelation 12:17, 13: 11-17 quoted] (MS 16, 1900)" (*The SDA Bible Commentary*, vol. 7, p. 974).

"The great conflict now being waged is not merely a strife of man against man. On one side stands the Prince of life, acting as man's substitute and surety; on the other, the prince of darkness, with the fallen angels under his command [Ephesians 6:12, 13, 10, 11 quoted]" (*The Review and Herald*, February 6, 1900).

Chapter 13

The Dragon and Mark of the Beast

Revelation 13:1, 2

"And I stood upon the sand of the sea, and saw a beast rise up out of the sea, having seven heads and ten horns, and upon his horns ten crowns, and upon his heads the name of blasphemy. And the beast which I saw was like unto a leopard, and his feet were as the feet of a bear, and his mouth as the mouth of a lion: and the dragon gave him his power, and his seat, and great authority."

John saw a beast rising out of the sea. Let's decode the symbols to understand this prophecy. A beast represents a kingdom (Dan. 7:17, 23). The sea represents multitudes, peoples, and nations (Rev. 17:15). The dragon represents Satan, the devil, that old serpent who deceived the whole world (Rev. 12:9). Mountains represent religious and political power (Jer. 51:24, 25).

So, this beast that John saw rising from the sea means that it is an established kingdom that came out from among the people and nations. Then the question is who is this kingdom, and how did he receive his power and authority from the dragon, Satan? For the answers we have to turn to the Old Testament in the book of Daniel to find out about the beast/kingdom. We've proven before how the Old and the New Testaments parallel each other; so here is more proof.

According to Daniel 2, 7, and 8, God revealed the future of this world to King Nebuchadnezzar, Daniel, and ultimately us. He showed us the four world kingdoms or powers that will rule this earth and the last eternal kingdom of Jesus Christ that will overthrow them all at the end of the world and rule for eternity. God revealed the future of this earth by letting us know which kingdom will be in command until His Second Coming when He will set up

The Dragon and Mark of the Beast

His eternal kingdom that will last forever and ever and ever. Please note that you do not have to pay psychics large sums of money to be told lies about the future. God revealed the future to us free of charge. I've learned that if you want to know the future, you need to read the Bible, especially the books of Daniel and Revelation. Following Daniel is describing the vision of the world history in Daniel 7:2-8:

"Daniel spoke, saying, 'I saw in my vision by night, and behold, the four winds of heaven were stirring up the Great Sea. And *four great beasts* came up from the sea, each different from the other. The first was like a lion, and had eagle's wings. I watched till its wings were plucked off; and it was lifted up from the earth and made to stand on two feet like a man, and a man's heart was given to it. And suddenly another beast a second, like a bear. It was raised up on one side, and had three ribs in its mouth between its teeth. And they said thus to it: "Arise, devour much flesh!"'

"'After this I looked, and there was another, like a leopard, which had on its back four wings of a bird. The beast also had four heads, and dominion was given to it. After this I saw in the night visions, and behold, a fourth beast, dreadful and terrible, exceedingly strong. It had huge iron teeth; it was devouring, breaking in pieces, and trampling the residue with its feet. *It was different from all the beasts that were before it, and it had ten horns.* I was considering the horns, and there was another horn, a little one, coming up among them before whom three of the first horns were plucked out by the roots. And there, in this horn, were eyes like the eyes of a man, and a mouth speaking pompous words'" (NKJV).

This vision was difficult for Daniel to comprehend, so he went and asked those who stood by for its meaning (Dan. 7:15-28). And it was given to him as follows:

"'Those great beasts, which are *four*, are four kings which arise out of the earth. But the saints of the Most High shall receive the kingdom, and possess the kingdom forever, even forever and ever.' Then I wished to know the truth about the fourth beast, which was different from all the others, exceedingly dreadful, with its teeth of iron and its nails of bronze, which devoured, broke in pieces, and trampled the residue with its feet; and the ten horns that were on its head, and the other horn which came up, before which three fell, namely, that horn which had eyes and a mouth which spoke pompous words, whose appearance was greater than his fellows.

"I was watching; and the same horn was making war against the saints, and prevailing against them, until the Ancient of Days came, and a judgment was made in favor of the saints of the Most High, and the time came for the saints to possess the kingdom. Thus he said: '*The fourth beast shall be a fourth kingdom on earth, which shall be different from all other kingdoms, and shall devour the whole earth.* Trample it and break it in pieces. The ten horns are ten kings who shall arise from this kingdom. And another shall rise after them; He shall be different from the first ones, and shall subdue three kings. He shall speak pompous words against the Most High, shall persecute the saints of the Most High, and shall intend to change times and law. Then the saints shall be given into his hand for a time and times and half a time" (Dan. 7:17-25, NKJV).

Revelation 13:3-10

"And I saw one of his heads as it were wounded to death; and his deadly wound was healed: and all the world wondered after the beast. And they worshipped the dragon which gave power unto the beast: and they worshipped the beast, saying, Who is like unto the beast? who is able to make war with him? And there was given unto him a mouth speaking great things and blasphemies; and power was given unto him to continue forty and two months. And he opened his mouth in blasphemy against God, to blaspheme his name, and his tabernacle, and them that dwell in heaven.

"And it was given unto him to make war with the saints, and to overcome them: and power was given him over all kindreds, and tongues, and nations. And all that dwell upon the earth shall worship him, whose names are not written in the book of life of the Lamb slain from the foundation of the world. If any man have an ear, let him hear. He that leadeth into captivity shall go into captivity: he that killeth with the sword must be killed with the sword. Here is the patience and the faith of the saints."

So, here God revealed to Daniel the vision about the four earthly world powers that will rule. But, you know, God is a consistent God who speaks the truth. He also revealed the same four kingdoms that will rule this earth to the curious King Nebuchadnezzar (Dan. 2). Please read Daniel 2 before you continue reading the analysis in the next few pages of the book.

Now that you've read it, let's review the prophecies and the history of the world powers to see who they are and how it came to pass.

"But there is a God in heaven who reveals secrets, and He has made known to King Nebuchadnezzar *what will be in the latter days*. Your dream, and the visions of your head upon your bed, were these: As for you, O king, thoughts came to your mind while on your bed, about what would come to pass after

The Dragon and Mark of the Beast

this; and He who reveals secrets has made known to you what will be. But as for me, this secret has not been revealed to me because I have more wisdom than anyone living, but for our sakes who make known the interpretation to the king, and that you may know the thoughts of your heart

"You, O king, were watching; and behold, a great image! This great image, whose splendor was excellent, stood before you; and its form was awesome. This image's head was of fine gold, its chest and arms of silver, its belly and thighs of bronze, its legs of iron, its feet partly of iron and partly of clay. You watched while a stone was cut out without hands, which struck the image on its feet of iron and clay, and broke them in pieces. Then the iron, the clay, the bronze, the silver, and the gold were crushed together, and became like chaff from the summer threshing floors; the wind carried them away so that no trace of them was found. And the stone that struck the image became a great mountain and filled the whole earth" (Dan. 2:28-35, NKJV).

Starting in verse 37, Daniel gives the interpretation of the dream to the king as God had revealed it to him. "You, O king, are a king of kings. For the God of heaven has given you a kingdom, power, strength, and glory; and wherever the children of men dwell, or the beasts of the field and the birds of the heaven, He has given them into your hand, and has made you ruler over them all—you are this head of gold. But after you shall arise another kingdom inferior to yours; then another, a third kingdom of bronze, which shall rule over all the earth. And the fourth kingdom shall be as strong as iron, inasmuch as iron breaks in pieces and shatters everything; and like iron that crushes, that kingdom will break in pieces and crush all the others. Whereas you saw the feet and toes, partly of potter's clay and partly of iron, the kingdom shall be divided; yet the strength of the iron shall be in it, just as you saw the iron mixed with ceramic clay. And as the toes of the feet were partly of iron and partly of clay, so the kingdom shall be partly strong and partly fragile. As you saw iron mixed with ceramic clay, they will mingle with the seed of men; but they will not adhere to one another, just as iron does not mix with clay. And in the days of these kings the God of heaven will set up a kingdom which shall never be destroyed; and the kngdom shall not be left to other people; it shall break in pieces and consume all these kingdoms, and it shall stand forever" (Dan. 2:37-44, NKJV).

In summary, Daniel tells us that the king was on his bed wondering what would happen after he was gone. So God in His mercy revealed to him the other kingdoms that would follow him, including Jesus' final kingdom that will last forever and ever.

The Revelation of Jesus Christ

The four kingdoms according to Bible prophecies and our world history are as follows:

Babylon – The head of gold signified King Nebuchadnezzar's rule. Babylon was famous for worshiping the sun and idols (Jer. 50:2, 38).

Medo-Persia – The Medes and Persians overtook Babylon, Egypt, and Lydia and were depicted as a bear with three ribs in its mouth. The Medes and Persians were famous in making laws that couldn't be changed (Dan. 6:8).

Greece – Greece overtook Medo-Persia and ruled the world. The Greeks were famous for seeking wisdom (1 Cor. 1:20).

Rome – Rome was the last earthly kingdom, and it ruled the longest. It was later divided into the ten western European countries. Hence the ten toes of clay and iron from which the beast/little horn will come (Dan. 8:9). Rome was famous for its power, strength, and persecution of others (Dan. 2:40).

The last eternal kingdom will be that of Jesus Christ the King of kings. The stone cut out without hands, which struck the image on its feet of iron and clay and broke them in pieces and then became a great mountain and filled the whole earth, will be that of Jesus's eternal kingdom that He will rule forever and ever and ever. Please note that no other country will overtake Rome's kingdom. It was divided into ten European kingdoms. The only kingdom that will overtake Rome and its divided kingdoms is Jesus's eternal kingdom.

You see, there are no losers on the side of Jesus. If you choose Jesus, you can be sure that you are on the winning team because no one can defeat Jesus. He's God and the King of kings. Now let's compare the visions in Daniel with Revelation 13 to find out some parallels with the beast, the little horn, and the antichrist.

World Powers	Daniel 2	Daniel 7	Daniel 8	Revelation 13
1 – Babylon	Head of gold	Lion		Lion's mouth
2 – Medo-Persia	Chest and arms of silver	Bear	Ram with two horns	Feet of a bear
3 – Greece / divided into four	Belly and thighs of bronze	Leopard	Goat divided into four	Like leopard beast
4 – Rome / divided Rome into ten European kingdoms	Legs of iron, feet and ten toes of clay and iron	Terrible and fearful beast with ten horns and a little horn coming up which plucked out three horns by the roots	King of fierce countenance and understanding of dark senences (Dan. 8:23-24). Little horn (Dan. 8:9).	Composite beast with ten horns

The Revelation of Jesus Christ

According to history, Rome was divided into ten kingdoms: Anglo-Saxon (England), Alemanni (Germany), Burgundians (Switzerland), Franks (France), Lombards (Italy), Suevi (Portugal), Visigoths (Spain), Vandals, Ostrogoths, Heruli. And according to the prophecy, the *little horn* that arose from the Roman empire came out after these ten divided kingdoms and became great, plucking three of the kingdoms on its way to power, which were the Vandals, Ostrogoths, and Heruli, by the roots. Therefore, they were never again mentioned in history or their place found in Western Europe.

Now the question that we want to know is who is this little horn that rose from the Roman empire and came after the ten horns and the beast? Let's review Daniel 7 and Revelation 13 again to learn about the characteristics of this little horn:

- It will arise from the old Roman empire after the ten horns
- It will be different from all the other ten kingdoms
- It will uproot three kingdoms as it rises to power
- It will speak great words against the Most High
- It will make war with the saints and prevail
- It will think to change times and laws
- It will rule for three and a half prophetic times (1,260 years).

Based on these specifications the protestant reformers—Martin Luther, John Calvin, John Wycliffe, John Wesley, and many others—concluded that the pope was the antichrist and thus this little horn.

According to *Revelation Speaks Messages of Hope for a World in Turmoil*, "Near the beginning of the fourth century, the emperor Constantine moved the capital of the Roman Empire from Rome to Byzanitium/Constantinople. Who was left in Rome to fill the vacuum that was created? Who took over when the emperor left?

"'*The Roman Church in this way privily pushed itself into the place of the Roman World-Empire, of which it is the actual continuation*; the empire has not perished, but has only undergone a transformation.... That is no mere "clever remark," but the recognition of the true state of the matter historically, and the more appropriate and fruitful way of describing the character of this Church. It still governs the nations.... It is a political creation, and as imposing as a World-Empire, because of the continuation of the Roman Empire. The Pope, who calls himself "King" and "Pontifex Maximus," is Caesar's successor.'—Harnack, Adolf. *What Is Christianity?* trans. by Thomas Baily Saunders. 2nd ed. rev.; (New York: Putnam, 1901), pp. 269, 270. [9BC 841 #1359].

"'*The mighty Catholic Church was little more than the Roman Empire baptized.* Rome was transformed as well as converted. *The very capitol of the old Empire became the capitol of the Christian Empire* [p. 149]. *The office of Pontifex Maximus was continued in that of Pope....* Even the Roman language of the Roman Catholic Church went down through the ages.'—Flick, Alexander Clarence, *The Rise of the Medieval Church*, reprint (New York: Burt Franklin, 1959), pp. 148, 149. [9BC 841 #1358].

"'By the eighth century the Bishop of Rome had become a temporal prince, so that the philosopher *Hobbes could truthfully say of the Papacy that it was "the ghost of the Roman Empire, crowned and seated on the grave thereof."*—Hyde, Walter Woodburn, *Paganism to Christianity in the Roman Empire* (Philadelphia: University of Pennsylvania Press, 1946), pp. 6, 7. [9BC 842 #1360].

"'...[Pope] Boniface VIII at the jubilee of 1300 ... seated on the throne of Constantine, girded with the imperial sword, wearing a crown, and waving a sceptre, ... shouted to the throng of loyal pilgrims: "I am Caesar—I am Emperor."'—Flick, Alexander Clarence, *The Rise of the Medieval Church*, reprint (New York: Burt Franklin, 1959), pp. 148, 149. [9BC 841 #1358]" (p. 109).

Now, going back to our question, who is the beast or which kingdom is the one that John saw having seven heads with blasphemous names on his heads and ten horns? And how did the dragon give this beast its power, throne, and authority? The papal system of religion, which derived from pagan Rome, is the beast that is mentioned in Revelation 13. Please note that we are talking about a system and not individuals in particular.

Characteristics of the Little Horn, the Beast, and the Papal System

Daniel 7 Little Horn	Revelation 13 The Beast	World History Papal System
• Arise from the old Roman empire	• Rises from the sea; an established kingdom from people, tongues, and nations—from the Roman empire	• The papal system came from the old Roman empire.
• Different from the other kingdoms. • Has great appearance, has eyes of a man and a mouth speaking great things. • A religious power. • Will make rules (Dan. 8).	• Composite of the four beasts of Daniel 7:2. • Composite beast will make rules of idol and sun worship and make laws that won't change, forcing people to worship idols and on Sunday. • Quest for wisdom and will persecute those who go against their belief or church tradition.	• Religious head of the church • Religious power • Pagan traditions
• Very strong and powerful but not of its own power (Dan. 8:23, 24)	• Satan gave the beast its power, seat, and great authority. Power was given it over all kindreds, tongues, and nations.	• The whole earth marvels at the papal system. The Vatican is rich, powerful, and majestic. • Many nations respect and worship the pope. By some it is considered a universal church.
• It will uproot three kingdoms		• Papal Rome took over the Vandals, Ostrogoths, and Heruli as they came to power.

The Dragon and Mark of the Beast

Daniel 7 Little Horn	Revelation 13 The Beast	World History Papal System
• Speak great words *against* the Most High.	• Mouth speaking blasphemy.	• Pope claimed to be the "Vicar of the son of God" (see John 10:33). • Priest forgives sins (Luke 5:21). • "The Pope is not only the representative of Jesus Christ, but he is Jesus Christ himself, hidden under the veil of flesh" (*Catholic National*, July 1895).
• Made war with the saints. • Persecute and wear out the saints of the Most High.	• Make war with the saints	• Christians experienced persecution during the Middle and Dark Ages.
• Will think to change times and laws	• "All that dwell upon the earth shall worship him, whose names *are not* written in the book of life of the Lamb slain from the foundation of the world" (verse 8). • Mysterious number 666	• Tampered with God's Ten Commandments by omitting the second commandment and changing the fourth commandment in the Catechism. • God's law will never be changed. Therefore, he "thinks" to change times and laws. • Mark of the beast • Sunday Law • Vicar of god – 666

Daniel 7 Little Horn	Revelation 13 The Beast	World History Papal System
• He shall rule for time and times and the dividing of time, which equals 1,260 years (Dan. 7:25; 11:36)	• Power was given him to continue forty and two months (1,260 years)	

According to the specifications of the little horn and the beast, the papal system is the only one who fits all the specifications.

Through a careful study of Revelation 13, I've learned that only four different kingdoms or world powers will rule this earth before Jesus sets His own eternal kingdom. And according to history Babylon has come and gone, the Medes and Persians have come and gone, and Greece has come and gone. We are living in the days of the last kingdom, which is of Rome's divided kingdoms of the ten European kingdoms, just as predicted in the Bible. Prophecy tells us that we are in the last days of this earth's history before Jesus sets up His eternal kingdom for His saints. But in the meantime, Satan, the adversary, liar, and old serpent, is working hard to deceive as many people as possible to prevent them from choosing Jesus' side and His eternal kingdom.

As we know Satan, the dragon, that old serpent, the devil, deceived Eve to sin against God, and he worked through pagan Rome to try to kill Baby Jesus when He was born. It is this same Satan who worked through the name of religious-church leaders to kill God's saints and faithful servants. Therefore, it is of no surprise that this same Satan will give the beast, the papal system, his seat, throne, and power to do its final act before Jesus sets up His eternal kingdom.

According to *Revelation Speaks Messages of Hope to a World in Turmoil*, "To whom did pagan Rome give its seat of government? How did it take place? History is clear about what happened. Professor Labanca of the University of Rome declares: 'To the succession of the Caesars came the succession of the Pontiffs in Rome. When Constantine left Rome he gave his seat to the Pontiff'

"'The popes filled the place of the vacant emperors at Rome, inheriting their power, prestige, and titles from paganism.... Constantine left all to the Bishop of Rome.... The papacy is but the ghost of the deceased Roman Empire, sitting crowned upon its grave. Pagan Rome gave its authority to papal Rome.' —*Stanley's History*, p. 40" (p. 105).

The Dragon and Mark of the Beast

I want to apologize to my Catholic, Jewish, and Protestant brothers and sisters. It is not my intention to offend anyone, but it is my desire for you to know the truth and receive Jesus Christ's free gift of eternal life. My mother served the Catholic church, and my father served a Protestant church until they learned the biblical truth that I am sharing with you in this book. Per my mother's account and history, the Catholic church has done a lot of good deeds for widows, orphans, the poor, and the sick. The church has also built schools and hospitals to serve the people. But in love I must share with you all that God has revealed to me and what I've learned about in the book of Daniel and Revelation.

I pray that you too might see the light and ask Jesus and His Holy Spirit to illuminate your mind and open your heart to the truth and accept Jesus Christ as your personal Savior. The Bible tells us to, "Cry aloud, spare not, lift up thy voice like a trumpet, and shew my people their transgression" (Isa. 58:1). "If thou turn away thy foot from the sabbath, from doing thy pleasure on my holy day; and call the sabbath a delight, the holy day of the LORD, honourable; and shalt honour him, not doing thine own ways, nor finding thine own pleasure, nor speaking thine own words: then shalt thou delight thyself in the LORD" (verses 13, 14).

Let's turn our attention back to the beast. I've learned that based on the descriptions of the beast, which is also the little horn, it tells us that the papacy power is the only power in history that can possible fit these specifications. Let's review them one by one:

"The beast rising up out of the sea" (Rev. 13:1, NKJV). We've learned that the sea represents people, nations, and tribes. So this kingdom is already an established kingdom that rises from among many people and from the Roman empire. It's a universal religio-political power, which fits the papal system (the "mother church").

The beast was "**like a leopard**, his feet were like the **feet of a bear**, and his **mouth like the mouth of a lion**," and he has seven heads and ten horns (verse 2, NKJV). From Daniel 2 we learned about the four different kingdoms: the lion, the bear, and the leopard. So this fourth Roman empire beast is a continuation of the previous kingdoms before him. He uses the same pagan system from the time of Babylon to the Roman empire in worshiping of idols and sun worship. If you notice, every Catholic church has carved images everywhere in their churches. Everyone is taught to worship Mary, the mother of Jesus. My mother worshiped her faithfully until she learned about the true worship of God and God alone.

"The dragon gave him his power, his throne, and great authority" (verse 2, NKJV). The dragon, working through the Roman empire, gave the papal system his power and great authority. Further down we will cover some of the authority and power that the papal system used to blaspheme God's name and to persecute, kill, burn, and destory God's saints.

"One of his heads ... had been mortally wounded, and his deadly wound was healed" (verse 3, NKJV). In February 1798 Alexander Berthier, a French commander under Napoleon, took Pope Pius VI captive and abolished the papal system. (The pope died in August 1799.) Many thought that this would end the papal system, but after this setback, the papacy system came back in full force. Thus, its deadly wound was healed.

"All the world marveled and followed the beast" (verse 3, NKJV). So "they worshipped the dragon which gave power unto the beast: and they worshipped the beast, saying, Who is like unto the beast? who is able to make war with him?" (Rev. 13:4). Many people, nations, tongues, and tribes are currently worshiping the pope. They tell each other that the pope is holy and they love him and feel compelled to revere and worship him. They do not know that by worshiping the pope they are worshiping the devil himself.

According to prophecy the dragon is the devil and the beast is the papal system. And the devil gave his authority to the beast; and by worshiping the beast, people are actually worshiping the devil. Please note that Jesus in His Ten Commandments said: "I am the LORD thy God... Thou shalt have no other gods before me.... Thou shalt not make unto thee any graven image, or any likeness of any thing that is in heaven above, or that is in the earth beneath, or that is in the water under the earth. Thou shalt not bow down thyself to them, nor serve them" (Exod. 20:2-5).

In John 14: 21 Jesus said, "He who has My commandments and keeps them, it is he who loves Me. And he who loves Me will be loved by My Father, and I will love him and manifest Myself to him" (NKJV). So we do not need any other human being, carved images, Mary the mother of Jesus, the apostles, the pope, idols, or the church to reach God. We can go directly to God through prayer in the name of His Son, Jesus Christ. John 14:6 says, "I am the way, the truth, and the life. No one comes to the Father except through Me" (NKJV). Jesus is the only way to the Father, and no human being can pray for us or take us to God the Father. Only Jesus can take us to His Father.

"And he was given a mouth speaking great things and blasphemies, and he was given authority to continue for forty-two months" (verse 5, NKJV). Please note that anyone who acts in the place of God or claims to be a god who can forgive sins commits blasphemy (Luke 5:21; John 10:33). Ironically that's exactly what the popes have done. They even carry the name "Vicar of Christ" or "Vicarius Filii Dei"—Vicar of the Son of God. Please note that these are not my words. This information came directly from various publications of or affiliated with the Roman Catholic Church. Let's review them.

"Q. Who is the Holy Father or Pope?

"A. The Holy Father or Pope is the Visible Head of the Church, the Successor of St. Peter and the Vicar of Christ on earth" (Peter Geiermann C. SS. R, *The Convert's Catechism of Catholic Doctrine,* p. 28).

"The Saviour Himself is the door of the sheepfold: 'I am the door of the sheep.' Into this fold of Jesus Christ, no man may enter unless he be led by the Sovereign Pontiff; and only if they be united to him can men be saved, for the Roman Pontiff is the Vicar of Christ and His personal representative on earth." Pope John XXIII made this statement in his homily to the bishops and those assisting at his coronation on November 4, 1958.

Wow! When I read that, I was in shock. No wonder Jesus warned us that many false prophets will come in His name and that we should not believe them. This is one of them. My brothers and sisters, if the statement above about the pope being the Vicar of Christ confuses you, please read 1 Timothy 2:5, 6 to receive clarification and an understanding of what is truth. It says, "For there is *one God* and *one Mediator* between God and men, the Man Christ Jesus, who gave Himself a ransom for all, to be testified in due time" (NKJV).

The Bible tells us that Peter was "filled with the Holy Spirit" and spoke to the Jewish leaders and elders and said that the stone, Jesus Christ, whom they rejected has become the chief Cornerstone and not Peter. He also added that "there is no other name under heaven given among men by which we must be saved" (Acts 4:12, NKJV). Only Jesus can save us. No one else. No pope, no pastor, no pontiff, no leader, no religious leader, no government, no parents, no one. *Only Jesus Christ.*

Let's review a few more blasphemies that Jesus warned us about:

"To pardon a single sin requires all the omnipotence of God... The Jews justly said: 'Who can forgive sins but God alone?' But what only God can do by His omnipotence, the Priest can also do by saying 'Ego te absolve a peccatis tuis" [I absolve you from your sin]" (Alphonsus de Liguori, *Dignity and Duties of the Priest,* pp. 34, 35).

"Seek where you will, through heaven and earth, and you will find but one created being who can forgive the sinner ... that extraordinary being is the priest, the (Roman) Catholic priest" (Michael Muller, *The Catholic Priest*, p. 78).

"Q. What day was the Sabbath?

"A. The seventh day, our Saturday.

"Q. Do you keep the Sabbath?

"A. No. We keep the Lord's Day.

"Q. Which is that?

"A. The first day: Sunday.

"Q. Who changed it?

"A. The Catholic Church" (James Bellord, *A New Cathecism of Christian Doictrine and Practice for School and Home Use*, pp. 86, 87).

"Q. How prove you that the church hath power to command feast and holy days?

"A. By the very act of changing the Sabbath into Sunday, which Protestants allow of; and therefore they fondly contradict themselves by keeping Sunday strictly, and breaking most other feasts commanded by the same church.

"Q. How prove you that?

"A. Because by keeping Sunday they acknowledge the church's power to ordain feasts, and to command them under sin" (Henry Tuberville, *An Abridgment of the Christian Doctrine*, p. 58).

"Q. Have you any other way of proving that the church has power to institute festivals of precept?

"A. Had she not such power, she could not have done that in which all modern religionists agree with her—she could not have substituted the observance of Sunday the first day of the week, for the observance of Saturday the seventh day, a change for which there is no Scriptural authority" (Stephen Keenan, *A Doctrinal Catechism*, p. 174).

I was happy to learn that other people became offended by the blasphemies from the papal system, and they not only spoke out but they also wrote about them. Let's review some of them:

Martin Luther (1483-1546): "[Luther] proved, by the revelations of Daniel and St. John, by the epistles of St. Paul, St. Peter, and St. Jude, that the reign of Antichrist, predicted and described in the Bible, was the Papacy.... And all the people did say, Amen! A holy terror seized their souls. It was Antichrist whom they beheld seated on the pontifical throne. This new idea, which derived greater strength from the prophetic descriptions launched forth by Luther into the midst of his contemporaries, inflicted the most terrible blow on Rome" (J. H. Merle D'Aubigne, *History of the Reformation of the Sixteen Century*, book 6, p. 215).

Based on prophetic studies, in August 1520 Martin Luther finally declared, "We here are of the conviction that the papacy is the seat of the true and real Antichrist" (LeRoy Froom, *The Prophetic Faith of Our Fathers*, vol. 2, p. 121).

John Wycliffe: "When the western church was divided for about 40 years between two rival popes, one in Rome and the other in Avigon, France, each pope called the other pope antichrist – and John Wycliffe is reputed to have regarded them as both being right: 'two halves of Antichrist, making up the perfect Man of Sin between them" (Ibid.).

John Wesley (1703-1791): Speaking of the Papacy, John Wesley wrote, "He is in an emphatical sense, the Man of Sin, as he increases all manner of sin above measure. And he is, too, properly styled the Son of Perdition, as he has caused the death of numberless multitudes, both of his opposers and followers ... He it is ... that exalteth himself above all that is called God, or that is worshipped ... claiming the highest power, and highest honour ... claiming the prerogatives which belong to God alone" (John Wesley, *Antichrist and His Ten Kingdoms*, p. 110).

Roger Williams (1603-1683): "the pretended Vicar of Christ on earth, who sits as God over the Temple of God, exalting himself not only above all that is called God, but over the souls and consciences of all his vassals, yea over the Spirit of Christ, over the Holy Spirit, yea, and God himself... speaking against the God of heaven, thinking to change times and laws; but he is the son of perdition (II Thess. 2)" (LeRoy Froom, *The Prophetic Faith of Our Fathers*, vol. 3, p. 52).

The Westminster Confession of Faith (1647): "There is no other head of the church but the Lord Jesus Christ. Nor can the pope of Rome in any sense be head thereof; but is that Antichrist, that man of sin and son of perdition that exalteth himself in the church against Christ and all that is called God" (The Creeds of Christendom, With a History and Critical Notes, III, p. 659).

Please note that according to Daniel and Revelation it is the dragon (Satan) who gave the beast/papal system his power and authority. Not God, nor His Son, Jesus Christ. Jesus, while on earth, never asked the Catholic Church to speak on His behalf. No where in the sacred scriptures will you find God the Father or Jesus Christ authorizing the Catholic Church to change His laws or scriptures and institute holy festivals. No wonder God calls their act "blasphemy."

"He opened his mouth in blasphemy against God, to blaspheme His name, His tabernacle, and those who dwell in heaven" (Rev. 13:6, NKJV). Blasphemy according to the Bible is anyone who takes the place of God or His tabernacle or claims to be God and claims to forgive sins (Isa. 43:25; Mark 2:6, 7). Let's review some of the blasphemies that came from the Roman Catholic Church:

"The Pope is not only the representative of Jesus Christ, but he is Jesus Christ, Himself, hidden under the veil of human flesh" (*Catholic National*, July 1895).

"The Pope and God are the same, so he has all power in Heaven and earth" (Pope Pius V, quoted in Barclay, Chapter XXVII, "Cities Petrus Beranous," p. 218).

"We hold upon this earth the place of God almighty" (Pope Leo XII, Encyclical Letter, June 20, 1894).

"Indeed, there is but one universal Church of the faithful outside of which no one at all is saved" (Pope Innocent III, Fourth Lateran Council, 1215; Denz. 151).

"He is a heretic who does not believe what the Roman Hierarchy teaches" (*The American Textbook of Popery*, "Directory for the Inquisitors," p. 164).

"A heretic merits the pains of fire. By the Gospel, the canons, civil law, and custom, heretics must be burned" (*The American Textbook of Popery*, "Directory for the Inquisitors," p. 164).

"The church may by divine right confiscate the property of heretics, imprison their person, and condemn them to flames. In our age, the right to inflict the severest penalties, even death, belongs to the church. There is no graver offense than heresy, therefore it must be rooted out" (Public Eccliastical, vol. 2, p. 142).

Now the question is, how did the pope blaspheme God's name, tabernacle, and those who dwell in heaven? By thinking to change the holy Scriptures, God's laws and time. Please note that God's laws and times are forever;

therefore, no one can change them. They might tamper with them and force people to follow their mandates, but in actuality no human being can change God's laws, ever.

So how did the pope tamper with God's Ten Commandments? Let's review the blasphemies of how the Roman Catholic Church says they did it:

"We confess that the Pope has power of changing Scripture and of adding to it, and taking from it, according to his will" (Roman Catholic Confessions for Protestants Oath, Article XI, [Confessio Romano-Catholica in Hungaria Evanelics pulice praescripta te proposita, editi a Streitwolf], as recorded in Congressional Record of the U.S.A., House Bill 1523, Contested election case of Eugene C. Bonniwell, against Thos. S. Butler, Feb 15, 1913).

My brothers and sisters, please note that God *does not* appreciate those who speak for Him, change, or add to what He has said. In Revelation 22 God said, "If anyone adds to these things, God will add to him *the plaques* that are written in this book; and if anyone takes away from the words of the book of this prophecy, God shall take away his part from the Book of Life, from the holy city, and from the things which are written in this book" (verses 18, 19).

The time will come in the end time when the papal system will enforce their laws and rules, forcing everyone to follow their teachings and to keep their false sabbath, which is Sunday worship. This is where God's servants need to stay virgin and not defile themselves with the woman (Catholic teachings). They will have to stand for God's Word and keep His commandments and His holy Sabbath, Saturday, as He commanded. (Please note that Catholics refer to their church as "she," or the mother of all churches, in their writing).

The next question is how did the pope change, add, and omit the Bible and God's holy law, the Ten Commandments? The pope accomplished this by removing the second commandment; changing the sequence of God's law; changing the timing of the beginning and closing hours of the Sabbath (instead of counting from sundown Friday to sundown Saturday they count from midnight to midnight), adding the six precepts of the church, omitting part of the fouth commandment that deals with time, day of worship, and the Creator of heaven and earth; and changing the holy Sabbath day of worship to Sunday.

Again, please note that these are not my words. We can find this in *The Convert's Catechism of Catholic Doctrine* by Rev. Peter Geiermann, C. SS. R.:

"Q. What is the Law of God?

"A. The Law of God is the will of God, binding the liberty of man in conscience.

The Revelation of Jesus Christ

"Q. Where is the Law of God summed up?

"A. The Law of God is summed up principally in the Ten Commandments of God and in the Six Precepts of the Church.

"Q. Which are the Ten Commandments?

"A. The Ten Commandments are:

> (1) I am the Lord thy God; thou shalt not have strange gods before me.
>
> (2) Thou shalt not take the name of the Lord thy God in vain.
>
> (3) Remember thou keep holy the Sabbath day.
>
> (4). Honor thy father and thy mother.
>
> (5). Thou shalt not kill.
>
> (6). Thou shalt not commit adultery.
>
> (7) Thou shalt not steal.
>
> (8) Thou shalt not bear false witness against thy neighbor.
>
> (9) Thou shalt not covet thy neighbor's wife.
>
> (10) Thou shalt not covet thy neighbor's goods" (pp. 36-38).

Ironically, according to the Catholic's revision of God's true Ten Commandments, they broke it, changed it, omitted part of it, and taught others to do the same. Thus, they committed willful sin by literally breaking God's law. I pray for the innocent ones who are accepting these lies from the Catholic Church that Jesus will have mercy on them and show them the light.

The other sin that the Roman Catholic Church committed in regards to God's law is when they changing God's Sabbath from Saturday to Sunday. Let's review the Catechism again to learn how they did it.

"Q. Which is the Sabbath day?
"A. Saturday is the Sabbath day.

"Q. Why did the Catholic Church substitute Sunday for Saturday?

"A. The Church substituted Sunday for Saturday, because Christ rose from the dead on the Sunday, and the Holy Ghost descended upon the Apostles on a Sunday.

"Q. By what authority did the Church substitute Sunday for Saturday?

"A. The Church substituted Sunday for Saturday by the plenitude of that divine power which Jesus Christ bestowed upon her.

I have read and studied the Bible from cover to cover and have never found anything that says that Jesus Christ bestowed divine power on the Roman Catholic Church and asked them to change God's Saturday, Sabbath. to Sunday. Please search the Bible for yourself and see if you can find it. I guarantee you that you will not find it becase it does not exist.

"Q: Have you any other way of proving that the Church has power to institute festivals of precept?

"A: Had she not such power, she could not have done that in which all modern religionists agree with her—she could not have substituted the observance of Sunday the first day of the week, for the observance of Saturday the seventh day, a change for which there is no Scriptural authority" (Stephen Keenan, *A Doctrinal Catechism* [FRS Bi, 7.] (3rd American ed., rev.: New York, Edward Dunigan & Bro., 1876), p. 174).

"So the papacy is here saying that they changed Sabbath to Sunday and that virtually all churches accepted the new holy day. Thus, the papacy claims that Sunday as a holy day is the mark, or symbol, of her power and authority" (Amazing Facts Study Guide, "The Mark of the Beast," p. 7).

When Jesus spoke to Peter in Matthew 16:18, 19, the Rock or the chief Conerstone was Jesus Himself and not Peter. Ephesians 2:20, 21 says, "having been built on the foundation of the apostles and prophets, Jesus Christ Himself being the chief cornerstone, in whom the whole building, being fitted together, grows into a holy temple in the Lord" (NKJV).

I've learned that Peter himself claimed that Jesus was the living stone that was rejected by men. "Coming to Him as to a living stone, rejected indeed by men, but chosen by God and precious ... 'A chief cornerstone, elect, precious, and he who believes on Him will by no means be put to shame'" (1 Pet. 2:4-6, NKJV; see also Ps. 118:22; Isa. 28:16).

Now let's review God's true Ten Commandments that were written by God's own hand (Exod. 20):

1. Thou shalt not have no other gods before me.

2. Thou shalt not make unto thee any graven image, or any likeness of

any thing that is in heaven above, or that is in the earth beneath, or that is in the water under the earth. Thou shalt not bow down thyself to them nor serve them for I the LORD thy God am a jealous God...

3. Thou shalt not take the name of the LORD thy God in vain; for the LORD will not hold him guiltless that taketh his name in vain.

4. Remember the sabbath day, to keep it holy. *Six days* shalt thou labour, and do all thy work: but the seventh day is the sabbath of the LORD thy God: in it thou shalt not do any work, thou, nor thy son, nor thy daughter, thy manservant, nor thy maidservant, nor thy cattle, nor thy stranger that is within thy gates: *for in six days the LORD made heaven and earth, the sea, and all that in them is, and rested the seventh day: wherefore the LORD blessed the sabbath day, and hallowed it.*

5. Honour thy father and thy mother: that thy days may be long upon the land which the LORD thy God giveth thee.

6. Thou shalt not kill

7. Thou shalt not commit adultery

8. Thou shalt not steal

9. Thou shalt not bear false witness against thy neighbour.

10. Thou shalt not covet thy neighbour's house, thou shalt not covet thy neighbour's wife, nor his manservant, nor his maidservant, nor his ox, nor his ass, nor any thing that is thy neighbour's.

"It was given unto him to make war with the saints, and to overcome them" (Rev. 13:7). And authority was given him over every tribe, tongue, and nation. History tells us that many Christians and others were killed by the Roman Catholic Church because of "heresy" according to their laws. But God already warned us that she would kill, persecute, and wear out His saints for time and times and half of time or 42 months prophetic time.

"All that dwell upon the earth shall worship him, whose names are not written in the book of life of the Lamb slain from the foundation of the world" (verse 8). Many people innocently are worshiping the pope thinking that they are worshiping God. I pray that if you are one of those people that you will pray to God directly through His Son, Jesus Christ, and ask for His Holy Spirit to teach you the right way and not humanity's way or the church's way. This

The Dragon and Mark of the Beast

is your chance, before it is too late, to repent and turn away from idol worship. If you have been worshiping the pope and the church's false idols, now is the time to stop and turn around. Ask God to forgive you for taking true worship away from Him. Don't continue to worship the dragon—Satan. He is a liar and is deceiving many people into thinking that they are worshiping God, but in actuality they are worshiping him. Now is your time to choose to obey and worship God or disobey and worship Satan.

Please note that in the beginning of our world God gave our first parents a test of their loyalty and obedience to Him. "God commanded the man, saying, 'Of every tree of the garden you may freely eat; but of the tree of the knowledge of good and evil you shall not eat, for in the day that you eat of it you shall surely die'" (Gen. 2:16, 17, NKJV). Our first parents were deceived by Satan disguised in the form of a serpent, and they sinned against God. God in His mercy, instead of letting them or their children (you and me) die because of their sin, came and died for us all. What an amazing love.

As we are living in the end of times, God is giving us, the children of Adam and Eve, a test of our loyalty and obedience to Him. God commands us to "'Fear God and give glory to Him, for the hour of His judgment has come; and worship Him who made heaven and earth, the sea and springs of water' … 'If anyone worships the beast and his image, and receives his *mark* on his forehead or on his hand, he himself shall also drink of the wine of the wrath of God, which is poured out full strength into the cup of His indignation. He shall be tormented with fire and brimstone in the presence of the holy angels and in the presence of the Lamb'" (Rev. 14:7-10, NKJV).

Are we going to disobey God as our first parents did, or are we going to stand for Him come what may? We have an advantage because we know how the devil deceived our first parents, plus God revealed to us how Satan is going to deceive us again through the enforced Sunday-law worship. Are you ready to go through this test? But remember, you are not alone. God sends us His Comforter, the Holy Spirit. Jesus Himself said, "I am with you always, even to the end of the age" (Matt. 28:20, NKJV).

We have nothing to fear as long as we are ready to obey Jesus and worship Him and Him alone. I pray that you will choose to obey and worship God and His Son, Jesus Christ. Why don't you bow your head right now and repeat this prayer. "Our heavenly Father, I was deceived to think that by worshiping the pope, Mary the mother of Jesus, Budha, Allah, Harikrishna, or other false gods that I was worshiping You. Please forgive me and send thy Holy Spirit to convict my heart and give me strength and courage to serve and worship you only. In Jesus' holy name, amen."

The seven-headed beast with ten horns is a system of worship and rulership with different heads or leaders that follow the same pagan system created by Satan. Please note that the final conflict between good and evil (God and Satan) will focus on two different worship systems—the true Sabbath worship of God, the Creator of this world, and His Ten Commandments, and the false Sunday worship of Satan, the father of lies. Please keep this seven-headed beast with ten horns in mind because we will discuss it further in the coming chapters.

In the beginning of this world our first parents were deceived by Satan in the form of a snake. At the end of this world, Adam and Eve's children, or desendents, the remnant of the earth, will be deceived by Satan again, but this time through religious figures and worship.

Satan uses mediums of animals, people, kings, government, and religious people to get his diabolical agenda completed. He will be so cunning that he might deceive even the very elect. Therefore, you need to study the Bible and ask God to open your understanding and give you wisdom so that you can discern the lies from the adversary. He's using the same tactics today.

When Adam and Eve ate of the forbidden fruit, their eyes were opened, and they noted that they were naked and thus felt uncomfortable. Right away they sewed some fig leaves together to cover their nakedness (Gen. 3:21). Thank God for His Son, Jesus Christ, who came to Adam and Eve and gave them the blessed hope of a Savior—the good news of salvation and eternal life. Jesus explained to them that they were made to live forever but now that they had sinned they must one day die. However, He also explained to them that He would die in their place to save them and us from eternal death. Right away He conducted the first sacrifice that pointed to His own sacrificial death to save humanity. He sacrificed a lamb and made clothes with its fur for Adam and Eve. This was to prove to them that one day He, Jesus, would be the sacrificial Lamb who would die on the cross for our sins and clothe us with the white garment of His righteousness. Just as He traded our forefathers fig leaf clothes for lamb's fur, He will change our filthy garments for His white linen of righteousness.

"And I will put enmity between you and the woman, and between your seed and her Seed; He shall bruise your head, and you shall bruise His heel" (Gen. 3:15, NKJV). This promise was fulfilled in the life and death of Jesus Christ (Heb. 2:14). Cain, out of jealousy and rage, killed his brother, Abel, because God had acknowledged Abel's sacrifice of a lamb, which pointed to

Jesus Christ, the Lamb of God, and did not accept Cain's sacrifice of fruits and vegetables. God recognized Abel's sacrifice because it pointed toward the true Lamb of God—Jesus Christ who was prophesied would come and save us from our sins. There was no blood or resemblance of Jesus Christ in the fruits and vegetables that Cain used as a sacrifice. Therefore, Cain's sacrifice was not acknowledged by God.

The lesson I learned from this tragic story is that God will bless everyone who obeys and follows His guidelines the way He wants it to be done. He does not like it when people change His ways or words and pretend that He will still bless them. They will not be blessed if they fail to follow His ways. Everyone who does God's will and chooses to follow Jesus Christ is the seed of the woman, and everyone who lies and does evil is of the devil (John 8:44). Satan's children and God's children are enemies of each other.

Looking again at Cain and Able, Cain tried to change what God said by making a sacrifice of his fruits and vegetables, and when God did not acknowledge his sacrifice, he got upset and jealous of his brother and killed him.

In the last days of the end of this world, history will repeat itself. God blessed His special seventh-day Sabbath and asked us to keep it holy. This is the only commandment that God asked us to remember. But again man changed His Sabbath day of worship to Sunday, and many expect God to bless their Sunday worship. Not only that, they, like Cain, will get upset with the ones who keep God's Sabbath day holy and will try to kill them or blame them for their misfortunes.

The lesson we all need to learn from this is that what God says He means. No one should change or do things their way or because of tradition, thinking that God will "understand." God requires *obedience,* not sacrifice.

Revelation 13:11

"And I beheld another beast coming up out of the earth; and he had two horns like a lamb, and he spake as a dragon."

Here John saw another beast, but this one was coming up out of the earth and had two horns like a lamb but spoke as a dragon. The question is who is this beast? This is a different beast that comes from an unpopulated area and not from among the people or nations. It arose and became prominent during the time that the papal system received his deadly wound. Its two horns are lamb like, denoting a passive and gentle appearance.

Please note that this beast does not have any crown, which symbolizes a different type of government. This beast will eventually make an image to the first beast and force everyone to worship it. This kingdom is the United States of America. Think about it. America did not come to power by overthrowing another empire. It grew up quietly and patiently with its republican and democrative form of government. It opened its doors to the Christians who were being persecuted. It eventually became a world superpower that polices the world. But according to prophecy it will one day lose all of its innocence and become a persecuting power for the first beast or papal system. It will make an image for the papal system to enforce its Sunday law, and it will force *everyone* to worship it or be killed.

"The United States established two separate authorities—political and religious. The principle of complete separation between church and state was represented by the 'two horns like a lamb.' The United States has a republican form of government. People sought 'a country without a king, and a church without a pope.' This is why the horns of the lamb-like beast have no crowns" (*Revelation Speaks Messages of Hope for a World in Turmoil*, p. 114).

Speaking about the United States, Ellen White says: "And the lamblike horns, emblems of innocence and gentleness, well represent the character of our government, as expressed in its two fundamental principles, republicanism and Protestantism" (*The SDA Bible Commentary*, vol. 7, p. 975).

"Prophecy represents Protestantism as having lamblike horns, but speaking like a dragon. Already we are beginning to hear the voice of the dragon. There is a satanic force propelling the Sunday movement, but it is concealed. Even the men who are engaged in the work, are themselves blinded to the results which will follow their movement. Let not the commandment-keeping people of God be silent at this time, as though we gracefully accepted the situation. There is the prospect before us of waging a continuous war, at the risk of imprisonment, of losing property and even life itself, to defend the law of God, which is being made void by the laws of men" (*The Review and Herald*, January 1, 1889).

"Religious powers, allied to heaven by profession and claiming to have the characteristics of a lamb, will show by their acts that they have the heart of a dragon, and that they are instigated and controlled by Satan. The time is coming when God's people will feel the hand of persecution because they keep holy the seventh day. Satan has caused the change of the Sabbath in the hope of carrying out his purpose for the defeat of God's plans. He seeks to make the commands of God of less force in the world than human laws. The man of sin, who thought to change times and laws, and who has always oppressed the

The Dragon and Mark of the Beast

people of God, will cause laws to be made enforcing the observance of the first day of the week. But God's people are to stand firm for Him. And the Lord will work in their behalf, showing plainly that He is the God of gods" (*The SDA Bible Commentary*, vol. 7, p. 975).

Ellen White goes on to say, "The Word of God plainly declares that His law is to be scorned, trampled upon, by the world; there will be an extraordinary prevalence of iniquity. The professed Protestant world will form a confederacy with the man of sin, and the church and the world will be in corrupt harmony" (*The General Conference Bulletin*, April 13, 1891).

So God revealed to us ahead of time the things that will come to pass. According to Revelation prophecies, America will one day repudiate it's heritage of being the land of religious freedom and will unite with the beast/pope and become a persecuting power of the true Christians who keep the commandments of God and have the testimony of Jesus Christ. The United States of America will be instrumental in creating an image for the pope and forcing everyone—world leaders, governments, nations, kings, queens, tribes, tongues, people, free, slave, rich, or poor—to worship the pope on the day he demands to be worshiped on.

As we learned above, the day that the pope will demand to be worshipped on is Sunday, the first day of the week, instead of Saturday, which is God's holy seventh-day Sabbath. Remember reading in the Catechism about who changed the day of worship and why? They even added that there was no "scriptural authority" to do so. Both the pope and the United States of America will create laws to enforce Sunday worship and will even kill those who refuse to obey or boycott them economically by restricting them from buying or selling. I've learned that some of the Protestant churches will reunite with their mother church, the Catholic Church, to enforce Sunday worship.

Please keep your eyes and ears open to this movement and other movements of the Christian Coalition because these churches are already meeting and planning how they are going to bring this Sunday law observance into existence. But we should not keep quiet; we must sound the trumpet and protect God's true Sabbath day of worship and let everyone know the truth so that they can make an informed consent who they want to worship and on which day. I pray that everyone will follow God's mandate to worship on His seventh-day Sabbath and receive His blessing.

"When the legislature frames laws which exalt the first day of the week, and put it in the place of the seventh day, the device of Satan will be perfected" (*The Review and Herald*, April 15, 1890). Congress and the legislators will create laws regarding the day of worship and will force all those who worship on God's true holy Sabbath day to be killed for not worshipping on Sunday.

"History will be repeated. False religion will be exalted. The first day of the week, a common working day, possessing no sanctity whatever, will be set up as was the image at Babylon. All nations and tongues and peoples will be commanded to worship this spurious sabbath. This is Satan's plan to make of no account the day instituted by God, and given to the world as a memorial of creation.

"The decree enforcing the worship of this day is to go forth to all the world. In a limited degree, it has already gone forth. In several places the civil power is speaking with the voice of a dragon, just as the heathen king spoke to the Hebrew captives.

"Trial and persecution will come to all who, in obedience to the Word of God, refuse to worship this false Sabbath. Force is the last resort of every false religion. At first it tries attraction, as the king of Babylon tried the power of music and outward show. If these attractions, invented by men inspired by Satan, failed to make men worship the image, the hungry flames of the furnace were ready to consume them. So it will be now. The Papacy has exercised her power to compel men to obey her, and she will continue to do so. We need the same spirit that was manifested by God's servants in the conflict with paganism" (*The Signs of the Times,* May 6, 1897).

"A time is coming when the law of God is, in a special sense, to be made void in our land. The rulers of our nation will, by legislative enactments, enforce the Sunday law, and thus God's people be brought into great peril. When our nation, in its legislative councils, shall enact laws to bind the consciences of men in regard to their religious privileges, enforcing Sunday observance, and bringing oppressive power to bear against those who keep the seventh-day Sabbath, the law of God will ... be made void in our land; and national apostasy will be followed by national ruin" (*The Review and Herald,* December 18, 1888).

Jesus told us that at the end of this world these things will happen before His Second Coming so that we won't be surprised when it happens. He also promises us that "lo I will be with you till the end of the world" (Matt. 28:20). And just as he fed the children of Israel in the wilderness, he'll feed you and I as long as we hold fast to His Ten Commandments, His Sabbath, and His testimonies.

Now that we've identified the beast as the papacy system and the second beast as the United States of America, our next question is what is the mark of the beast or the number 666 (which is the number of his name)?

For the answer let's go back to the Bible in Daniel 7 and *The Convert's Catechism of Catholic Doctrine*.

In Daniel 7:25 God revealed to us that the beast/papacy will intend to *change time and law*, which is God's Ten Commandments. In *The Convert's Catechism* tells us how the Catholic Church changed God's Ten Commandments and Sabbath worship and why they did it (Peter Geiermann, *The Convert's Catechism of Catholic Doctrine*, p. 50). Please note that they did not say that God or Jesus asked them to modify or change His holy day. They did it because "the Church substituted Sunday for Saturday, because Christ rose from the dead on a Sunday, and the Holy Ghost descended upon the Apostles on a Sunday" (*The Convert's Catechism of Catholic Doctrine*, p. 50). Please note it says *the church* substituted Sunday for Saturday. This is a fulfillment of God's prophecy that this beast, which represents the papacy, will think to change God's time and law.

Please read and judge for yourself. These are not my words; they came from the Catholic Church:

James Cardinal Gibbons said, "You may read the Bible from Genesis to Revelation, and you will not find a single line authorizing the sanctification of Sunday. The Scriptures enforce the religious observance of Saturday, a day which we [Catholics] never sanctified" (*The Faith of Our Fathers*, 63rd ed., pp. 111, 112).

Dwight Moody said, "The Sabbath was binding in Eden, and it has been in force ever since. This fourth commandment begins with the word 'remember.' Showing that the Sabbath already existed when God wrote the law on the tables of stone at Sinai. How can men claim that this one commandment has been done away with when they will admit that the other nine are still binding?" (*Weighed and Wanting*, p. 47).

By reading what the Catechism said above, I asked myself, if God or His Son, Jesus, wanted to change the sacred Sabbath day, the one that He *blessed* and *sancified*, then why didn't Jesus change it when He was on earth with His disciples and while He was teaching the multitude? Or even after Jesus rose on Sunday and met with His disciples, why didn't He tell them that from now on they weren't supposed to worship on Sabbath anymore because He had just risen on Sunday and wanted them to worship on Sunday and teach the rest of His disciples to do the same. No where in the Bible does it say that Jesus wanted to change His holy Sabbath day to Sunday. Instead, Jesus said, "I did not come to destroy but to fulfill" the law (Matt. 5:17, NKJV).

The Revelation of Jesus Christ

Right away this tells me that God or His Son, Jesus Christ, or even Peter, the apostle of Christ, did not ask the Catholic Church to change or substitute the Sabbath day for Sunday. My brothers and sisters, if you are worshiping on Sunday, the day that God did not bless or sanctify, this is your chance to pray to God and ask him to convict your heart and show you what to do. You still have time because the Sunday law is not in effect yet.

Once the Sunday law is enforced by the government and the religious leaders from the Catholic Church and the United States of America, you will be forced to worship on Sunday or suffer the consequences of pain or death. And if you choose to worship on Sunday as it is being enforced through the legislation and laws, then you will receive the mark of the beast, which means that you are automatically worshiping the dragon, which is Satan himself. This is what God is trying to tell you and me so that we will not be deceived. He is telling us these things ahead of time so that when it happens we won't be caught by surprise. We will know with conviction what is going on and who we should choose to worship.

We are living in the end time of this world. Jesus is getting ready to set up His eternal kingdom, and He wants all those who stand for Him to live with Him forever and ever. He wants you to be part of His kingdom. He has beautiful things in store for us. But you must choose. He's not going to force you. The choice is yours to love Him and keep His commandments, or worship the beast and receive its mark. Soon the time will come when Sunday worship will be the law of the land and everyone will be forced to obey it. And many will obey it for fear of death or because of lack of knowledge about the truth behind the Sunday law. But Jesus promises us that He will be with us till the end of the world. So, if you love Jesus, keep His commandments and not people's false commandments. Worship God and Him only. Search the Scriptures for yourself, and ask the Holy Spirit to open your mind and understanding to follow what God has commanded.

My mother was a devoted Catholic who planned to die as a Catholic. But God's Holy Spirit opened her understanding, and she accepted Jesus Christ as her personal Savior. She died a seventh-day Sabbathkeeper with the blessed hope of being resurrected in the first resurrection by Jesus Christ when He comes. She also taught her children, (she had 15 children) to choose Jesus. Before she died she gave all her living children Jesus. She did not leave millions of dollars behind for us, but she left us with Jesus, the source of all treasures and true happiness. In my opinion she left the best gift a parent could give to her children. I chesish this gift even today and thank God that she taught us the right way.

The Dragon and Mark of the Beast

As we discussed before, some people say that the fourth commandment about the Sabbath is only for the Jews. But what about the rest of the commandments? Are they only for the Jews? Let's process this realistically. Do you believe that the other nine commandments are for the Gentiles and the fourth commandment is only for the Jews? Does that make sense? No wonder Jesus had to make it clear for us to understand it. Jesus said, "The Sabbath was made for man, and not man for the Sabbath" (Mark 2:27, NKJV). Please note that Jesus did not say that the Sabbath was made for the Jews only—it says "Sabbath was made for *man*." That means everyone. Therefore, everyone must keep all of God's Ten Commandments and not only nine.

So God's mark, seal, or sign is His holy seventh-day Sabbath. "How could anyone dare attempt to change God's holy day? Answer: We ask the papacy, 'Did you really change Sabbath to Sunday?' She replies, 'Yes, we did. It is our symbol, or mark, of authority and power.' We ask, 'How could you even think of doing that?' It's a pertinent question. But the question the papacy officially asks Protestants is even more pertinent. Please read it carefully:

"'You will tell me that Saturday was the Jewish Sabbath, but that the Christian Sabbath has been changed to Sunday. Changed! But by whom? Who has authority to change an express commandment of Almighty God? When God has spoken and said, Thou shalt keep holy the seventh day, who shall dare to say, Nay, thou mayest work and do all manner of wordly business on the seventh day; but thou shalt keep holy the first day in its stead? This is a most important question, which I know not how you can answer. You are a Protestant, and you profess to go by the Bible and the Bible only; and yet in so important a matter as the observance of one day in seven as a holy day, you go against the plain letter of the Bible, and put another day in the place of that day which the Bible has commanded. The command to keep holy the seventh day is one of the ten commandments; you believe that the other nine are still binding; who gave you authority to tamper with the fourth? If you are consistent with your own principles, if you really follow the Bible and the Bible only, you ought to be able to produce some portion of the New Testament in which this fourth commandment is expressly altered.' Library of Christian Doctrine: *Why Don't You Keep Holy the Sabbath-Day?*" (Amazing Facts Study Guide, "The Mark of the Beast," pp. 8, 9).

Let's review some of the Catholic Church's quotes about their mark:

"Sunday is our mark or authority…the church is above the Bible, and this transference of Sabbath observance is proof of that fact" (*Catholic Record of London*, Ontario, September 1, 1923).

"Of course the Catholic church claims that the change [i.e. Sabbath to Sunday] was her act, and the act as a mark of her ecclesiastical authority in religious things," said H.F. Thomas, the chancellor to Cardinal Gibbons.

"The Catholic Church for over a thousand years before the existence of a Protestant, by virtue of her divine mission changed the day from Saturday to Sunday" (*Catholic Mirror*, September 23, 1983).

"She [the Catholic Church] took pagan Sunday, dedicated to Balder [an Icelandic god identified with Sun worship], became the Christian Sunday, sacred to Jesus" (*Catholic World*, 1894, p. 809).

"You may read the Bible from Genesis to Revelation, and you will not find a single line authorizing the sanctification of Sunday. The scriptures enforce the religious observance of Saturday, a day which we never sanctify" (Cardinal Gibbons, *The Faith of Our Fathers*, p. 111).

"…of course the Catholic Church claims that the change was her act. And the act is a mark of her ecclesiastical power and authority in religious matters," wrote H.F. Thomas, the chancellor of Cardinal Gibbons, in answer to a letter regarding the change of the Sabbath.

"No! Keep the first day of the week, and lo, the entire civilized world bows in reverent obedience to the command of the holy Catholic church." "It's the mark of our authority to over-rule God's law" (Father Enright C.S.S.R. of the Redemptoral College, Kansas City, Mo., *History of the Sabbath*, p. 802).

So we've learned that the mark of the Catholic Church (the beast) is her act of changing God's Sabbath worship to Sunday worship—"the Lord's day" as they call it. They were bold and honest to say that God did not give them the authority to change it. That tells you right there that you should not follow their mandates if it did not come from God. Don't waste your time. You need to follow God's mandates and His mandates only. Do not follow tradition. Jesus said, "Follow Me." He did not ask anyone to follow tradition. As a matter of fact, He was opposed to Jewish tradition. The Jewish leaders also changed His words and taught others to follow their traditions, which God is against. "Well did Isaiah prophesy of you hypocrites, as it is written: 'This people honors Me with their lips, but their heart is far from Me. And in vain they worship Me, Teaching as doctrines the commandments of men.' For laying aside the commandment of God, you hold the tradition of men … 'All too well you reject the commandment of God, that you may keep your tradition" (Mark 7:6-9, NKJV; see also Isa. 29:13).

So my brothers and sisters, don't follow man's traditions; follow God's commandments, and you will be on the side of God and His Son, Jesus Christ.

Revelation 13:12-18

"And he exerciseth all the power of the first beast before him, and causeth the earth and them which dwell therein to worship the first beast, whose deadly wound was healed. And he doeth great wonders, so that he maketh fire come down from heaven on the earth in the sight of men, And deceiveth them that dwell on the earth by the means of those miracles which he had power to do in the sight of the beast; saying to them that dwell on the earth, that they should make an image to the beast, which had the wound by a sword, and did live.

"And he had power to give life unto the image of the beast, that the image of the beast should both speak, and cause that as many as would not worship the image of the beast should be killed. And he causeth all, both small and great, rich and poor, free and bond, to receive a mark in their right hand, or in their foreheads: And that no man might buy or sell, save he that had the mark, or the name of the beast, or the number of his name. Here is wisdom. Let him that hath understanding count the number of the beast: for it is the number of a man; and his number is Six hundred threescore and six."

The United States of America, being the superpower and police of the world, will force all people—great, small, rich, poor, free, or slave—to worship the beast on the false Sabbath, which is Sunday, and receive the mark of the beast on their foreheads and right hand. This is the mark Jesus is warning us against. Each one of Eve's children has the opportunity to decide for themselves if they want to disobey God and listen to the serpent and receive its mark or obey God and receive the seal of God in their foreheads. The choice is yours.

We've discovered that the beast is the papacy and its mark is the change of God's Sabbath to Sunday, so what does the mysterious number 666 mean? Revelation 13:18 says, "Here is wisdom. Let him who hath understanding count the number of the beast: for it is the number of a man; and his number is Six hundred threescore and six." And in Revelation 15:2 God gave us more clues about this: "And I saw something like a sea of glass mingled with fire, and those who have the *victory over the beast, over his image and over his mark and over the number of his name*, standing on the sea of glass, having harps of God" (NKJV).

So let's put all the clues together to find out who the mysterious number 666 is referencing.

Clue #1 – it is the number of a man.

Clue #2 - it is the number of the beast.

Clue #3 – it is the number of his name.

We've already learned that the beast represents the papacy, so the next question is what's the papacy's name and number? The Latin name that all the popes use is "Vicarius Filii Dei" or "Vicar of the Son of God." So let's calculate the number of this name.

V = 5; I = 1; C = 100; A = 0; R = 0; I = 1; U = 5; S = 0
F = 0; I = 1; L = 50; I = 1; I = 1
D = 500; E = 0; 1 = 1

The total of all these numbers equals 666. So putting it all together, the papacy is the beast, its mark is the change of God's holy Sabbath day of worship to Sunday worship as claimed by the Roman Catholic Church itself, and its number is 666, which is the sum total of its name.

Some people might argue that there are many other names that will total the number 666 if you add their numbers together. That is correct; however, God gave us specific clues to find out which name He was talking about. The specific clues are as follows:

- This man must fit all the specifications of the beast (we've covered how the papacy fits all the specifications of the beast above)
- This man must be the one to tamper and think to change God's law (the papacy changed God's holy Sabbath day for Sunday)
- This man must persecute, kill, and wear out God's saints
- This man must have the name with the number 666.

So according to history the only man that fits *all these specifications* is the papacy. So this is the "mark" of the beast that God warns His people about. This is the mark that God says if you receive it on your forehead or right hand and if you worship him or his image then you will receive the wine of God's wrath in full strength. My brothers and sisters, you don't want to receive God's wrath. So try your best to stay on God's side, and don't worry about being persecuted and forced to worship this beast and his image and even be killed if you refuse. If you stand for God and refuse the mark of the beast, then God and His Son, Jesus Christ, the Holy Spirit, and all God's angels will protect you.

History has a way of repeating itself. In Germany the devil used the same tactic above to separate people. The Jews had to wear a swastika, which meant that they were restricted and isolated from the rest of the population. Their businesses were taken from them; they couldn't sell or buy without identifying themselves. This satanic system is nothing new. In the end time he will use the same system with the mark of the beast to separate his people from Jesus' people. He'll place his mark on their foreheads, meaning they will consent to choose and worship the beast, or on their right hand, meaning they will work with their hands to support this beast and capture others to choose this mark as well.

"The United States is a land that has been under the special shield of the Omnipotent One. God has done great things for this country, but in the transgression of His law, men have been doing a work originated by the man of sin. Satan is working out his designs to involve the human family in disloyalty" (*The SDA Bible Commentary,* vol. 7, p. 975).

Ellen White also said, "The Lord has shown me clearly that the image of the beast will be formed before probation closes; for it is to be the great test for the people of God, by which their eternal destiny will be decided ... [Revelation 13:11-17 quotes.] ... This is the test that the people of God must have before they are sealed. All who proved their loyalty to God by observing His law, and refusing to accept a spurious sabbath, will rank under the banner of the Lord God Jehovah, and will receive the seal of the living God. Those who yield the truth of heavenly origin and accept the Sunday sabbath, will receive the mark of the beast" (Letter 11, 1890).

"When the Protestant churches shall unite with the secular power to sustain a false religion, for opposing which their ancestors endured the fiercest persecution; when the state shall use its power to enforce the decrees and sustain the institutions of the church—then will Protestant America have formed an image to the papacy, and there will be a national apostasy which will end only in national ruin" (*The Signs of the Times,* March 22, 1910).

"The sins of the world will have reached unto heaven when the law of God is made void; when the Sabbath of the Lord is trampled in the dust, and men are compelled to accept in its stead an institution of the papacy through the strong hand of the law of the land. In exalting an institution of man above the institution ordained of God, they show contempt for the great Lawgiver, and refuse his sign or seal" (*The Review and Herald,* November 5, 1889).

"As Christ was hated without cause, so will His people be hated because they are obedient to the commandments of God. If he who was pure, holy, and undefiled, who did good, and only good, in our world, was treated as a base criminal, and condemned to death, his disciples must expect but similar treatment, however faultless may be their life and blameless their character. Human enactments, laws manufactured by satanic agencies under a plea of goodness and restriction of evil, will be exalted, while God's holy commandments are despised and trampled underfoot. And all who prove their loyalty by obedience to the law of Jehovah must be prepared to be arrested, to be brought before councils that have not for their standard the high and holy law of God" (*The Review and Herald,* December 26, 1899).

"We are living in a momentous period of this earth's history. The great conflict is just before us. We see the world corrupted under the inhabitants thereof. The man of sin has worked with a marvelous perseverance to exalt the spurious sabbath, and the disloyal Protestant world has wondered after the beast, and has called obedience to the Sabbath instituted by Jehovah disloyalty to the laws of the nations. Kingdoms have confederated to sustain a false sabbath institution, which has not a word of authority in the oracles of God (*The Review and Herald,* February 6, 1900).

Ellen White also wrote, "The Sabbath question is to be the issue in the great final conflict, in which all the world will act a part. Men have honored Satan's principles above the principles that rule in the heavens. They have accepted the spurious sabbath, which Satan has exalted as the sign of his authority. But God has set His seal upon His royal requirement. Each Sabbath institution, both true and false, bears the name of its author, an ineffaceable mark that shows the authority of each. The great decision now to be made by every one is, whether he will receive the mark of the beast and his image, or the seal of the living and true God" (*The Signs of the Times,* March 22, 1910).

Are you ready to follow God's laws or humanity's laws? Please pray and ask God and His Son, Jesus Christ, and the Holy Spirit to help you make the right decision to follow and obey God's Ten Commandments and not the traditions of this world.

Chapter 14

Jesus's Last Three Messages of Warning

Revelation 14:1-5

"And I looked, and, lo, a Lamb stood on the mount Sion, and with him an hundred forty and four thousand, having his Father's name written in their foreheads. And I heard a voice from heaven, as the voice of many waters, and as the voice of a great thunder: and I heard the voice of harpers harping with their harps: And they sung as it were a new song before the throne, and before the four beasts, and the elders: and no man could learn that song but the hundred and forty and four thousand, which were redeemed from the earth. These are they which were not defiled with women; for they are virgins. These are they which follow the Lamb whithersoever he goeth. These were redeemed from among men, being the firstfruits unto God and to the Lamb. And in their mouth was found no guile: for they are without fault before the throne of God."

Here God is giving John a sneak preview of the end of world history and the reward for those who have made it through the last time of trouble in this world. John saw the 144,000 standing on Mount Zion with the Lamb, which is Jesus Christ, having the name of God written on their foreheads. Who are they? They are the ones ransomed from the world who did not defile themselves with the woman. Now remember, we learned that a woman represents a church, and we also learned that there will only be two churches or two choices at the end of the world. Jesus' true church, which will be made up of those who love Him and keep His commandments, including His holy seventh-day Sabbath, and the testimonies of Jesus Christ, is the first choice. The other church is Satan's church, which is the ones who are against Christ and disobey His

The Revelation of Jesus Christ

Ten Commandments and His holy seventh-day Sabbath and do not have the testimonies of Jesus Christ.

At the end of this world it does not matter what denomination you belong to—Baptist, Methodist, Church of God, Jehovah Witness, Orthodox Jew, Catholic, Reformed Jew, Buddist, Muslim, Hindu, Islam, Rashashana, Protestant, Pentecostal, Episcopal, Congregationalist, Reformed Chuch, Seventh-day Adventist, Church of Christ, Methodist, Lutheran, Presbyterian, Church of Satan, a cult, or an atheist—you will belong to either God's seventh-day Sabbathkeepers or Satan's first-day Sundaykeepers. Those are the only two choices who will exist. The ransomed who have not defiled themselves with women means that they have not aligned themselves or obeyed the enforced Sunday worship that the Roman Catholic Church, with assistance from the United States of America, will enforce. In this chapter God is giving us His final warning. He's telling us not to receive the mark of the beast because if we do we'll receive God's wrath and fury. And we've already learned that this mark is the enforced Sunday worship.

For further study please read Daniel 7:13 about Jesus' Second Coming and Isaiah 21:9 regarding Babylon with all its idols.

Now my brothers and sisters, if you are a Christian or a member of any other church denomination who is currently worshiping on Sunday, this important message is for you. You have not chosen the mark of the beast yet because the Sunday law has not been enforced. It is only after the enforcement of the Sunday law that Sunday worship will become the mark of the beast. Once this Sunday law is passed and enforced, you will be forced to make your choice. God is telling you this way in advance so that you will not be caught by surprise when it happens.

You have time to study the Bible from cover to cover to learn about God's holy Sabbath, the day that He blessed and sanctified. Now is the time for you to search the Scriptures for yourself with the assistance of the Holy Spirit so that you can understand the law of God and His Sabbath. At the end of time when the legislators make Sunday worship into law, thus making it official that everyone must worship on Sunday instead of the true Sabbath, you will have to choose with your heart, mind, and soul which of the two churches you want to belong to. Therefore, it is imperative that you search the Scriptures so that you will be informed before you consent to anything.

If you are currently worshiping on Sunday, please pray and ask God to show you which day is the true day He wants you to worship on. To those who have an ear from every nation, tribe, tongue, and people, this message

Jesus's Last Three Messages of Warning

is for you. If you are from Europe, Africa, Asia, Antartica, North and South America, Australia, Greenland, or anywhere else in this world, this message is for you! Now is the time for you to read the Bible, listen, and obey God's Word and commandments. This is the reason of our existence. The Bible is the only Word of God. No other book in this world will bring you to God—the Bible, which is the Word of God, is the only book that can do that. And as we learned before, Jesus is the Word of God.

Think about these things from the pen of inspiration: "Sundaykeeping is not yet the mark of the beast, and will not be until the decree goes forth causing men to worship this idol sabbath. The time will come when this day will be the test, but that time has not come yet" (*The SDA Bible Commentary*, vol. 7, p. 977).

"Revelation 14:1-5 is closely connected with chapter 13:11-18. The 144,000 are portrayed here as being with Christ (the Lamb) on Mt. Zion (in heaven) to indicate their triumph over the beast and his image. The 144,000 were first presented in chapter 7 as those who had been sealed by God in their foreheads. This becomes especially significant in the light of the third angel's message in chapter 14. Because they have the 'seal of the living God' (chap. 7:2), they will be protected during the time when those who do not have it will be destroyed.

"Verses 4 and 5 thus identify what it means to have God's name or seal in the forehead. They are 'redeemed from among men' and have not been defiled by the religious impurities that mark the last great deception of Satan. Having been covered by Christ's robe of righteousness and sharing with Him the final victory over Satan and sin, they are pictured as standing 'faultless' at last before the throne of God.

"Later in the book of Revelation (chap. 18:1-4), another angel is introduced who echoes the proclamation of the second angel of chapter 14. This 'fourth' angel's message is added to that of the previous three in a final note of warning to the world. The messengers he represents are to give this last call in 'great power' and the world will be 'lightened' with the 'glory' of their message.

"They not only proclaim the fall of Babylon, whose spiritual fall and apostasy is clearly evident at the time this proclamation is issued, but bid God's people still united with all systems of perversion and apostasy (every 'foul spirit' and 'unclean and hateful bird') to 'come out' and not be partakers of her sins or the plaques that are about to be poured out on those who persist in apostasy in spite of God's clear call (see chaps. 15 and 16)" (G.C. Ministerial Association pamphlets).

The Revelation of Jesus Christ

Revelation 14:6-8

"And I saw another angel fly in the midst of heaven, having the everlasting gospel to preach unto them that dwell on the earth, and to every nation, and kindred, and tongue, and people, Saying with a loud voice, Fear God, and give glory to him; for the hour of his judgment is come: and worship him that made heaven, and earth, and the sea, and the fountains of waters. And there followed another angel, saying, Babylon is fallen, is fallen, that great city, because she made all nations drink of the wine of the wrath of her fornication."

Revelation 14 in a nutshell is God's final warning to the world. God and His Son, Jesus Christ, with the assistance of the Holy Spirit is telling us that there is still a little time left for us to know the truth and make our choice to be part of God's kingdom. God also wants us to share this gospel, the good news, with others. We should not keep it to ourselves. Just as we were blessed and received a blessed hope, we need to share it with others. God in His mercy sends us warnings so that when the fires of destruction come we cannot blame anyone but ourselves. I've learned that Jesus' pure church is made up of people who keep His Ten Commandments, His holy seventh-day Sabbath, and the testimonies of Jesus Christ.

Jesus is appealing to you to choose Him and be part of His pure church. He is the Creator of everything and worship belongs to Him only. It is His seventh-day Sabbath that He wrote with His own finger on the tables of stone that will stand forever. Sunday worship was never approved or sanctioned by God. If you pray and search the scriptures, God will reveal it to you. Why don't you bow your head right now and ask Jesus to come into your heart and show you His will. He is ready to impress your heart and lead you in the right direction. He said in John 14:6, "I am the way, the truth, and the life" (NKJV). John 14:15 says, "If you love Me, keep My commandments" (NKJV; see also 1 John 2:3; 5:2-6).

We've learned that angels are God's messengers, but we can be God's messengers to others, too. God is willing to use us if we are connected to Him. Thus, this angel that John saw flying in the midst of heaven with the everlasting gospel to the world saying "Fear God ... and worship him that made heaven, and earth, and the sea, and the fountains of water" is very important (Rev. 14:7). God is telling you today to worship Him and Him alone.

Next John saw another angel proclaiming that Babylon is fallen, that great city. Why? "Because she [has] made all nations drink of the wine of the wrath of her fornication" (verse 8). Please note that it says "she has made." That means God is talking about the church that has changed His laws and made all nations worship on a false day of worship. Thus, everyone who follows the false church will drink of the wrath of God. Again, the only church that, by their own account, confessed of changing God's law and will force all naions to worship on Sunday is the Roman Catholic Church.

I've also learned that God told Isaiah of Babylon's fall way before it was revealed to John. Please see Isaiah 21:9: "'And look, here comes a chariot of men with a pair of horsemen!' Then he answered and said, 'Babylon is fallen, is fallen! And all the carved images of her gods He has broken to the ground.'"

Look around any church and ask yourself which church has carved images in their sanctuaries? Now is the time for you to follow what God purposes in your heart to do. Salvation is individual. It is not what your parents tell you, nor what your pastor, friends, children, government, priest, pope, or family tell you to do but what *God* tells you to do.

Revelation 14:9-13

"And the third angel followed them, saying with a loud voice, If any man worship the beast and his image, and receive his mark in his forehead, or in his hand, The same shall drink of the wine of the wrath of God, which is poured out without mixture into the cup of his indignation; and he shall be tormented with fire and brimstone in the presence of the holy angels, and in the presence of the Lamb: And the smoke of their torment ascendeth up for ever and ever: and they have no rest day nor night, who worship the beast and his image, and whosoever receiveth the mark of his name. Here is the patience of the saints: here are they that keep the commandments of God, and the faith of Jesus. And I heard a voice from heaven saying unto me, Write, Blessed are the dead which die in the Lord from henceforth: Yea, saith the Spirit, that they may rest from their labours; and their works do follow them."

We already learned from the previous chapter that the mark of the beast, by the Roman Catholic Church's own account, is the change that they made from God's seventh-day Sabbath worship to Sunday worship. That is the mark of the pope's authority. Here again in plain language God is making His final warning against the ones receiving this mark. You have no excuse now. It is right here plain and simple. If you receive the mark of the beast and worship him, then you will receive the wine of God's wrath undiluted. The choice is yours.

Again and again I've learned that this world has only two choices or two parties—Jesus or Satan. Jesus is the way, the truth, and life; whereas, Satan is

The Revelation of Jesus Christ

a liar, and his destructive ways lead to death. Jesus offers eternal life; whereas, Satan offers eternal death. The choice is yours. You have to choose. You can't serve two masters.

Revelation 14:14, 15

"And I looked, and behold a white cloud, and upon the cloud one sat like unto the Son of man, having on his head a golden crown, and in his hand a sharp sickle. And another angel came out of the temple, crying with a loud voice to him that sat on the cloud, Thrust in thy sickle, and reap: for the time is come for thee to reap; for the harvest of the earth is ripe."

When this happens it is because everyone has made their decision whom they will serve. So now God is going to separate the two groups so that they can receive their reward of eternal life or eternal death. Have you decided which group you want to be part of? Only you can make that decision.

This world can't continue to exist in sin forever. God has its appointed time to put an end to it. We don't know the day and time that it will happen, but God gave us enough clues to let us know the things that will happen before the end of this world. If we stay close to Jesus, He will reveal to us everything that we need to know to be ready.

Revelation 14:16-20

"And he that sat on the cloud thrust in his sickle on the earth; and the earth was reaped. And another angel came out of the temple which is in heaven, he also having a sharp sickle. And another angel came out from the altar, which had power over fire; and cried with a loud cry to him that had the sharp sickle, saying, Thrust in thy sharp sickle, and gather the clusters of the vine of the earth; for her grapes are fully ripe. And the angel thrust in his sickle into the earth, and gathered the vine of the earth, and cast it into the great winepress of the wrath of God. And the winepress was trodden without the city, and blood came out of the winepress, even unto the horse bridles, by the space of a thousand and six hundred furlongs."

This is the end of the world. Those who are on God's side will be ransomed from this world and receive the reward of eternal life in Jesus' kingdom that will last forever and ever. On the other hand, those who chose to worship the beast and receive its mark, the papal system and their enforced Sunday worship that they call "the Lords's day," will receive God's eternal punishment. My brothers and sisters, please choose God's side and live. If you are in doubt, just pray and ask God's Holy Spirit to illuminate your mind so that you can make the right decision and choose Jesus' side. Time is running out. Now is the time to make your decision to stand for Jesus Christ before it is too late. We are living in the end time of this world. A great crisis and catastrophe is coming and only Jesus can protect you and keep you safe. Your money, your government, nothing on this earth can save you—only Jesus Christ can save you.

Chapter 15

The Bowls of God's Wrath

Revelation 15:1-4

"And I saw another sign in heaven, great and marvellous, seven angels having the seven last plagues; for in them is filled up the wrath of God. And I saw as it were a sea of glass mingled with fire: and them that had gotten the victory over the beast, and over his image, and over his mark, and over the number of his name, stand on the sea of glass, having the harps of God. And they sing the song of Moses the servant of God, and the song of the Lamb, saying, Great and marvellous are thy works, Lord God Almighty; just and true are thy ways, thou King of saints. Who shall not fear thee, O Lord, and glorify thy name? for thou only art holy: for all nations shall come and worship before thee; for thy judgments are made manifest."

This chapter begins with a wonderful picture of the redeemed standing on the sea of glass holding harps that God gave them, and they were singing the song of Moses. They've made it. They stood firm for God's law, His Ten Commandments and the testimonies of Jesus Christ. Here again God is giving John a sneak preview of the redeemed—those who did not receive the mark of the beast and worship his image or his enforced Sunday worship. The redeemed are those who have victory over his image, his mark, and over the number of his name.

I thank God for showing us the end of the story even before it happens. This gives me courage that even though the time of trouble is going to be bad if we persevere we will make it. Why? Because God has showed us in Revelation 15 the end of the story, the end of the controversy way before it happens. So if we trust Him and keep His commandments and His holy Sabbath as He commanded us to even when facing death from our persecuters, God will protect us and give us victory and our blessed reward. Oh what a song that will be—the last victorious song, and the beginning of true happiness!

All heaven will rejoice with us for having persevered in keeping God's commandments and the faith of Jesus. My brothers and sisters, hard times are ahead of us. We will go through a terrible time of trouble. Satan is using and will use all his tricks to deceive as many people as he can because he knows that his time is short. The collapsed economy, calamities, tsunamis, fires, earthquakes, and all sorts of catastrophes will be blamed on those who keep God's seventh-day Sabbath. Those who follow the beast will hate everyone who keeps God's laws, and they will hunt God's followers down as dogs to kill them. They will take their possessions, throw them in jail, burn them at the stake, put them in concentration camps, persecute and kill them.

Jesus has promised us that just as they did these things to Him, they will do it to His followers and servants. But He's going to be with us even to the end of the world. We just have to hold fast to His promises, and we will overcome the evil one. God has shown us that we can make it; we just need to trust Him, and He'll take care of the rest. Are you ready to trust God and His Son, Jesus Christ, today?

Ellen White wrote, "What a song that will be when the ransomed of the Lord meet at the gate of the Holy City, which is thrown back on its glittering hinges and the nations that have kept His word—His commandments—enter into the city, the crown of the overcomer is placed upon their heads, and the golden harps are placed in their hands! All heaven is filled with rich music, and with songs of praise to the Lamb. Saved, everlastingly saved, in the kingdom of glory! To have a life that measures with the life of God—that is the reward" (*The SDA Bible Commentary,* vol. 7, p. 982).

Oh what a beautiful day that will be! The beauty is that saints from all nations will be there. The question is, are you one of them? Am I one of them? I've made up my mind that by God's grace and mercy I will only serve and worship God the Father, God the Son, and God the Holy Ghost. No one else. How about you? Have you made up your mind whom you want to serve? Now is the time before it's too late.

Revelation 15:5-8

"And after that I looked, and, behold, the temple of the tabernacle of the testimony in heaven was opened: And the seven angels came out of the temple, having the seven plagues, clothed in pure and white linen, and having their breasts girded with golden girdles. And one of the four beasts gave unto the seven angels seven golden vials full of the wrath of God, who liveth for ever and ever. And the temple was filled with smoke from the glory of God, and from his power; and no man was able to enter into the temple, till the seven plagues of the seven angels were fulfilled."

The first, second, third, and fourth angel's messages are proof of God's love and mercy toward us. He gives us warnings after warnings so it won't be a surprise to us. He is patiently waiting on us to decide whom we want to serve. But He can't wait forever. At His appointed time He will bring the world to an end and give everyone his or her reward.

He has warned us about the devil and his deceptions, of how he will work through religious people to force us to worship on a day that God did not sanction. Jesus has shown us what will happen if we choose to worship the beast and its mark. He has shown us what reward we will receive if we choose to obey and worship Him on His seventh-day Sabbath and keep the testimonies of Jesus Christ.

Jesus died on the cross for us. He loves us and has given us pleanty of time to repent and come to Him and follow His commandments. The choice is ours. He's ready to judge, and His judgment is fair. He has done everything He could to save us. If we choose not to follow Him, we have no right to blame Him or curse His holy name. Again, now is the time for you to decide whom you want to follow. God is not going to force you. That is true love. He wants you to choose for yourself. It's all up to you to decide.

Chapter 16

God's Seven Last Plagues

Revelation 16:1

"And I heard a great voice out of the temple saying to the seven angels, Go your ways, and pour out the vials of the wrath of God upon the earth."

By this time when the angels are pouring the bowls of God's wrath on the earth, it's too late for you to be choosing which side or which church you want to belong to. It is time for God's wrath to be poured out on all those who refused Him and chose to unite with Satan, the beast, his image, and his mark. Don't delay in choosing God's side; tomorrow is not promised to anyone. I can understand why my mother pled with her Bible students to choose God's side, God's church, and God's Sabbath so that they wouldn't have to be among the ones to partake of the seven last plagues of God's wrath or cry to the rocks to cover them from God's face. And now, like my mother, I am pleading with you to choose God's church and His Sabbath and receive His reward before it's too late. If you hear His voice today, don't harden your heart.

Revelation 16:2

"And the first went, and poured out his vial upon the earth; and there fell a noisome and grievous sore upon the men which had the mark of the beast, and upon them which worshipped his image."

The first angel poured his vial on the earth and there came a "noisome and grievous sore" on those who had the mark of the beast. If you don't believe that God can produce sores, let's go back to Egypt to see how it happened before (Exod. 9:8-12). Here you can see that God knows all about these things, and He's telling all those who have an ear to listen and obey Him and receive His protection. Even some of the Egyptians, along with the Israelites, who

The Revelation of Jesus Christ

obeyed God's warnings were saved from these plagues. Today Jesus is giving us the warnings so that we can be saved and protected from these plagues.

Don't follow other people's rules and dictates; they can't save you. Only God can protect you because He has no equal (Exod. 9:14). The time will come when the government will force everyone to stop working on Sunday and keep it as a holy day or face death. But God said, "Remember the Sabbath day, to keep it holy" (Exod. 20:8, NKJV). So whom are you going to obey? Human beings or God? God taught His disciples and us that we must obey the laws of the land, our government, rulers, and those in power—"Render therefore to Caesar the things that are Caesar's, and to God the things that are God's" (Matt. 22:21, NKJV). However no earthly power has the authority to intervene between an individual's conscience and God. This is something personal, and therefore, when it comes to our conscience, the commands of God must supersede human laws. If any government passes laws requiring its citizens to violate God's law, God's people are always subject to the higher law of God.

If you read, listen, and obey God's Word, He will bless you and protect you from all these things that are about to take place (see Exod. 12:1-14).

In Exodus 12 God showed us that He will not do anything without warning His people about it and telling them what they need to do to be protected. Today God is doing the same for us as this world is coming to an end according to the book of Revelation. He's revealing to us the things that He's going to do and what we need to do to be protected and safe from the plagues. This is why I love the book of Revelation because it has shown me how much God the Father, God the Son, and God the Holy Spirit love us and want to protect us from the last plagues and save us.

So what are the sores? Well, we've seen leprosy, boils, cancer, aids, STDs, and many other diseases, but I believe this will be worse than all of them put together.

Revelation 16:3

"And the second angel poured out his vial upon the sea; and it became as the blood of a dead man: and every living soul died in the sea."

Let's review Exodus 7:17-21: "Thus says the LORD: 'By this you shall know that I am the LORD. Behold, I will strike the waters which are in the river with the rod that is in my hand, and they shall be turned to blood" (verse 17, NKJV).

And it happened as God commanded. The waters of Egypt turned to blood. And God is warning us that this will happen again at the end of this world.

Revelation 16:4

"And the third angel poured out his vial upon the rivers and fountains of waters; and they became blood."

Once again, read Exodus 7:17-22 to see how God manifested His power in the same way with the Egyptians, but now He's going to do it to the whole world.

Revelation 16:5, 6

"And I heard the angel of the waters say, Thou art righteous, O Lord, which art, and wast, and shalt be, because thou hast judged thus. For they have shed the blood of saints and prophets, and thou hast given them blood to drink; for they are worthy."

God said, "Vengence is mine" (Deut. 32:35, NKJV). God has His appointed time to take vengeance on those who hurt us and persecute us. We just have to be patient and wait upon His perfect timing (Rom. 12:19; Heb. 10:30).

Revelation 16:7-9

"And I heard another out of the altar say, Even so, Lord God Almighty, true and righteous are thy judgments. And the fourth angel poured out his vial upon the sun; and power was given unto him to scorch men with fire. And men were scorched with great heat, and blasphemed the name of God, which hath power over these plagues: and they repented not to give him glory."

I'm not sure where Al Gore got his idea of "global warming" from, but I know that the Creator of this universe wrote about it centuries ago warning us of the coming global warming as a result of our sins. Revelation 16 describes this global warming, and there's nothing we can do to stop it. We can go as green as we want to, but it's not going to stop what God says will happen.

If you want to be protected against global warming and scourging heat, you must obey God. Those who refuse to follow God's commandments and instead receive the mark of the beast will be scorched by the heat. But unfortunately, instead of repenting, they will curse God even more. What a shame. Here God is warning everyone who has an ear to hear in advance of this global warming, and He is inviting us to come to Him for protection.

So, my brothers and sisters, there's no green world practice that will prevent this from happening. The only way you can prevent this from happening to you is to choose God's law, obey Him, keep His commandments, worship on His holy seventh-day Sabbath, and have the testimonies of Jesus Christ. If you follow God's commands, you will be protected and kept cool during this plague. Just like the children of Israel who obeyed God and were spared from the plagues that God poured on Egypt, so He will protect you if you ask Him to (Exod. 1:17-21; 8:18; 9:1-7).

Another example that was given to us in the Bible is that of the three Hebrew boys, Shadrach, Meshach and Abed-Nego. They were thrown into the fiery furnace for refusing to bow down and worship the image that King Nebuchadnezzar made. But Jesus was right there in the fiery furnace with them to protect them. They came out of the furnace without even the smell of smoke (Dan. 3:8-25). That goes to show you that if you stand for God He will protect you come what may. This is a lesson for us all to learn from and to trust God even more.

Revelation 16:10, 11

"And the fifth angel poured out his vial upon the seat of the beast; and his kingdom was full of darkness; and they gnawed their tongues for pain, And blasphemed the God of heaven because of their pains and their sores, and repented not of their deeds.'

Exodus 10:21-23 documents the ninth plague of darkness that fell on Egypt, an atheist country that did not believe in God. How about you? Do you believe in God? Do you need any further proof to believe in what He's telling you today? He's ready to save you from these plaques if you will only trust and believe in Him.

Revelation 16:12

"And the sixth angel poured out his vial upon the great river Euphrates; and the water thereof was dried up, that the way of the kings of the east might be prepared."

Water—rivers, oceans, lakes—separates us from our fellow human beings around the globe. But for the final war, the final battle between good and evil, the Euphrates River will be dried up so that Satan and his evil angels can gather his troops for their final fight against the Son of God. But as God revealed to us, they are all losers and will go into perdition in the lake of fire. We already know the outcome of the battle—God wins!

Revelation 16:13, 14

"And I saw three unclean spirits like frogs come out of the mouth of the dragon, and out of the mouth of the beast, and out of the mouth of the false prophet. For they are the spirits of devils, working miracles, which go forth unto the kings of the earth and of the whole world, to gather them to the battle of that great day of God Almighty."

John saw three unclean spirits that looked like frogs—one came from the mouth of the dragon, which is the devil; one from the mouth of the beast, which is the papacy; and one from the mouth of the false prophet, which is the mouth of America's mandates. In our modern world they may be compared to lobbyists working for their cause. Those three unclean spirits are miracle working demonic spirits that go out to the kings of the whole inhabited world to assemble them for the war of the great day of God.

Frogs catch their prey with their mouth and tongue. So these three demonic spirits will go throughout the whole inhabited world to catch these people by convincing them to join the cause to fight. They'll convince them with the lies from their mouths and their tongue, spirits, witchcraft, sorcery, spells, and miracles that they perform. With their lies they'll convince the nations, kings, presidents, great and small rulers, and armies to join their cause.

We need to be vigilant of the signs of the time. We cannot be caught sleeping in these last days. Satan will keep us busy so that we won't pay attention as the prophecies are being fulfilled. Please be vigilant at all times because we do not know what time or hour our Lord will come. So let's be ready at all times.

Revelation 16:15

"Behold, I come as a thief. Blessed is he that watcheth, and keepeth his garments, lest he walk naked, and they see his shame."

This is the time that we should be devoting in watching and keeping our garments clean. We should be studying God's Word, praying, and asking the Holy Spirit to interpret the Scriptures to us so that we can understand and see the prophecies being fulfilled and be ready to meet our loving Savior. Now is the time to turn the TV off, spend less time with recreation and entertainment and more time in the Word of God, and share with others what God reveals to us. Time is running out!

Jesus does not want us to be searching or calculating the date that He's coming back because God the Father is the only one who knows the appointed time of Christ's return, but Jesus has instructed us to be ready because He will come as a thief, meaning that He can come at any time when we least expect it. Therefore, we should be living each day as if it's the last day of our lives. Forgive others. Love each other as we love ourselves. Keep God's Ten Commandments and the testimonies of Jesus. Have a close relationship with

The Revelation of Jesus Christ

God and His Son, Jesus Christ, and allow the Holy Spirit to guide you.

Revelation 16:16

"And he gathered them together into a place called in the Hebrew tongue Armageddon."

After the three unclean spirits are successful in convincing these kings, rulers, and governments and their armies to join the cause to fight against God, they will gather them to a place called Armageddon (Ps. 2:1, 2). This is the place for the final battle between good and evil. This is the end of the world. The final struggle between God and Satan will soon come to an end after Armageddon.

Revelation 16:17

"And the seventh angel poured out his vial into the air; and there came a great voice came out of the temple of heaven, from the throne, saying, It is done."

This is it. When God says, "It is done," then that's the end of Satan, his evil angels, and those who received the mark of the beast, the number of his name, and those who worshiped the beast. Please make your choice to be on God's side now before it's too late.

Revelation 16:18-21

"And there were voices, and thunders, and lightnings; and there was a great earthquake, such as was not since men were upon the earth, so mighty an earthquake, and so great. And the great city was divided into three parts, and the cities of the nations fell: and great Babylon came in remembrance before God, to give unto her the cup of the wine of the fierceness of his wrath. And every island fled away, and the mountains were not found. And there fell upon men a great hail out of heaven, every stone about the weight of a talent: and men blasphemed God because of the plague of the hail; for the plague thereof was exceeding great."

The seventh bowl was poured out into the air. Loud voices came out of the temple from the throne saying, "It is done!" Flashes of lightning, voices, and peals of thunder can be heard, and there was a massive earthquake such as has never occurred since humanity has been on earth.

When God speaks the earth trembles and shake out of its place. Even the elements fear God. How about us? Many people have seen and experienced an earthquake before, but this one is going to top them all. I lived in California for more than six years and was sick and tired of earthquakes. Some just shook the ground, while other did more damage. I also saw on the news the massive earthquake in Mexico City in the 1980s where hospitals were hit and a lot of people lost their lives. In January 2010 Haiti experienced a massive earthquake followed by Peru and other countries. And most recently, in March 2011, Japan was devastated by a violent earthquake. But this one will have no comparison to it; it will be terrible and will send the Richter scale through the roof.

Jesus told His disciples that only His Father knows when the end will come. Well, here is the proof. His Father declares when it will be done, and the earth will tremble (earthquake) when it hears the Father's voice. The great city will split into three parts and the cities of the nations will fall. This is the time when God will remember Babylon the great and make her drink from the cup of His raging fury. Every island will flee, and no mountains will be found. The earth will become one. Huge hail stones will fall on the people, but again the people will curse God for the plague of hail because it will be such a terrible plague.

God in His mercy is telling us these things way in advance so that we won't partake of these plagues. He's warning us that if we do not choose to be on His side and live then this is what we'll experience, and we will ultimately die the eternal death. As we discussed before, there are only two choices or two parties—life or death; Jesus or Satan; Sabbathkeeper or Sundaykeeper. Sabbathkeeping as God requires it is based on His Ten Commandments. Those who keep them will be on God's side and will be protected from the plagues and eternal death. Again, the choice is yours. Now is the time to make your decision. Time is running out. If you choose Jesus, you will live. If you choose Satan, you will die. If you do not choose at all, then that means that you've chosen Satan and death.

God does not play games with us. He loves us; He send His Son to die on the cross for our sins, and He gave us the gift of eternal life. The only thing that we have to do is accept Jesus and say thank you. If we can't do that then He's not going to force Himself on us. Not accepting His free gift and choosing to be on His side means rejecting Him and choosing Satan's side. Don't let this opportunity pass you by. Choose Jesus and choose life.

In order to prepare for the final battle, we can't have water that separates the countries. Therefore, the world will probably become one with all the islands moving from their places and the Euphrates River drying up so that the world can prepare for the battle. The mountains will be moved in the sea, and the islands will be moved from their places. Perhaps this is the time that the world will become one in geography. It will fit together like a big gigantic puzzle.

Ellen White has the following insight about the final scenes of earth's history. "John also was a witness of the terrible scenes that will take place as signs of Christ's coming. He saw armies mustering for battle, and men's hearts failing them for fear. He saw the earth moved out of its place, the mountains carried into the midst of the sea, the waves thereof roaring and troubled, and the mountains shaking with the swelling thereof. He saw the vials of God's wrath opened, and pestilence, famine, and death come upon the inhabitants of the earth" (*The Review and Herald,* January 11, 1887).

"There are only two parties in our world, those who are loyal to God, and those who stand under the banner of the prince of darkness. Satan and his angels will come down with power and signs and lying wonders to deceive those who dwell on the earth, and if possible the very elect. The crisis is right upon us. Is this to paralyze the energies of those who have a knowledge of the truth? Is the influence of the powers of deception so far reaching that the influence of the truth will be overpowered? The battle of Armageddon is soon to be fought. He on whose vesture is written the name, King of kings and Lord of lords, leads forth the armies of heaven on white horses, clothed in fine linen, clean and white (MS 172, 1899).

"Every form of evil is to spring into intense activity. Evil angels unite their powers with evil men, and as they have been in constant conflict and attained an experience in the best modes of deception and battle, and have been strengthening for centuries, they will not yield the last great final contest without a desperate struggle. All the world will be on one side or the other of the question. The battle of Armageddon will be fought, and that day must find none of us sleeping. Wide awake we must be, as wise virgins having oil in our vessels with our lamps…

"The power of the Holy Ghost must be upon us, and the Captain of the Lord's host will stand at the head of the angels of heaven to direct the battle. Solemn events before us are yet to transpire. Trumpet after trumpet is to be sounded, vial after vial poured out one after another upon the inhabitants of the earth. Scenes of stupendous interest are right upon us (Letter 112, 1890)" (*The SDA Bible Commentary,* vol. 7, p. 982).

The SDA Bible Commentary continues Ellen White's description of these final events on earth. "Two great opposing powers are revealed in the last great battle. On one side stands the Creator of heaven and earth. All on His side bear

His signet. They are obedient to His commands. On the other side stands the prince of darkness, with those who have chosen apostasy and rebellion (*The Review and Herald,* May 7, 1901).

"The present is a solemn, fearful time for the church. The angels are already girded, awaiting the mandate of God to pour their vials of wrath upon the world. Destroying angels are taking up the work of vengeance; for the Spirit of God is gradually withdrawing from the world. Satan is also mustering his forces of evil, going forth 'unto the kings of the earth and of the whole world,' to gather them under his banner, to be trained for 'the battle of that great day of God Almighty.'... Skepticism is prevailing everywhere. Ungodliness abounds. The faith of individual members of the church will be tested as though there were not another person in the world (MS 1a, 1890).

"We need to study the pouring out of the seventh vial. The powers of evil will not yield up the conflict without a struggle. But Providence has a part to act in the battle of Armageddon. When the earth is lighted with the glory of the angel of Revelation eighteen, the religious elements, good and evil, will awake from slumber, and the armies of the living God will take the field (MS 175, 1899)" (*The SDA Bible Commentary,* vol. 7, p. 983).

Have you made up your mind who you are going to serve and who you are going to recommend to your family, children, friends, neighbors, coworkers, pastor, in-laws, and church members? Think about what you've learned so far, pray about it, and ask Jesus to help you make your decision today. Things are moving fast. Legislators are finalizing the Sunday law. You need to search the Scriptures for yourself and open your eyes of what's going on in the news with the meetings of the Vatican and the United States. You can't afford to be sleeping as the ten virgins. Now is the time to study and fill your lamp with oil so that when the time for the bridegroom come, you will have enough oil in your lamp to be able to meet Him. So your task now is to read the following: the Bible, especially the books of Isaiah, Daniel, and Revelation, and *The Great Controversy* by Ellen. G. White.

Chapter 17

The Harlot Woman

Revelation 17:1-5

"And there came one of the seven angels which had the seven vials, and talked with me, saying unto me, Come hither; I will shew unto thee the judgment of the great whore that sitteth upon many waters: With whom the kings of the earth have committed fornication, and the inhabitants of the earth have been made drunk with the wine of her fornication. So he carried me away in the spirit into the wilderness: and I saw a woman sit upon a scarlet coloured beast, full of names of blasphemy, having seven heads and ten horns. And the woman was arrayed in purple and scarlet colour, and decked with gold and precious stones and pearls, having a golden cup in her hand full of abominations and filthiness of her fornication: And upon her forehead was a name written, MYSTERY, BABYLON THE GREAT, THE MOTHER OF HARLOTS AND ABOMINATIONS OF THE EARTH."

A woman in prophecy signifies a church, so which church dresses in purple and scarlet? The church that comes to mind is the Roman Catholic Church. Their pope and cardinals are known to wear red and purple. It goes on saying that the woman is adorned in gold, precious stones, and pearls and has a golden cup. Which church is this? Again the only church that is adorned with gold, precious stones, and pearls is the head of the Roman Catholic Church, the Vatican.

God has His sincere people in all different denominations, including the Catholic Church. And when they hear God's voice calling them to come out of Babylon, they will listen, respond, and follow Him. Again, we are uncovering prophecies and not pointing fingers at individuals. Although this may seem harsh to some people, Bible truth is clear and we need to study the truth to make an informed consent of whom we want to worship. As I shared before,

The Harlot Woman

my mother was a devoted Catholic until God called her out of the Catholic Church, and I believe that God has other people within the Catholic Church who will hear His voice and follow Him.

There are sincere Catholics who love Jesus and the gospel. The message of Revelation is not anti-Catholic. It's an eye opener for everyone who has an ear for the truth about God's church and prophecy. If you are a Catholic as my mother was, please read these prophecies carefully—pray, read, listen, research for yourself, and follow God's mandates instead of humanity's traditions.

The great whore in Revelation 17 is clothed in purple and scarlet. Now there might be other churches that wears purple and scarlet, but here again God is very specific in describing whom He's talking about. This church not only wears purple and scarlet but she's the "mother of whores." Here are the specifications that describe the whore: on her forehead she had a name written, "MYSTERY, BABYLON THE GREAT, THE MOTHER OF HARLOTS AND ABOMINATIONS OF THE EARTH" (verse 5). Furthermore, she was also drunk from the blood of God's people.

What is a whore? How can a church be considered a whore? Well, since the church represents a woman and if a woman is affectionate toward another man other than her husband then she's a whore. A pure woman is represented as God's pure church because she is faithful to Jesus Christ alone and she keeps His Ten Commandments and has His testimonies. So an impure church or whore represents an impure or fallen church that is unfaithful to Jesus and does not keep His Ten Commandments or have His testimonies (James 4:4-10).

God's pure church is considered His bride because His church is loyal to Him alone and does not fool around with others. The church that refuses to follow God's law, fools around with the devil and his pagan practices, and worships on the wrong day instead of being loyal to Jesus Christ is considered a whore and Babylon. In other words, any church that does not follow God's laws, which are His Ten Commandments and does not have the testimonies of Jesus Christ is a whore. And guess what? These churches, by not accepting Jesus and His Ten Commandments, are refusing His Father too (John 5:23).

"God is the husband of His church. The church is the bride, the Lamb's wife. Every true believer is a part of the body of Christ. Christ regards unfaithfulness shown to Him by His people as the unfaithfulness of a wife to her husband. We are to remember that we are members of Christ's body (Letter 39, 1902).... The church is the bride, the Lamb's wife. She should keep herself pure, sanctified, holy.... The church is the bride of Christ, and her members are to yoke up with their Leader. God warns us not to defile our garments (Letter 123 1/2, 1898)" (*The SDA Bible Commentary,* vol. 7, pp. 985, 986).

Which church has a name written on its forehead signifying that it is the "MOTHER OF HARLOTS"? It is no secret that there is only one church which claims to be the "mother church," and that is the Roman Catholic Church. And if the Roman Catholic Church is considered to be the "mother church" and a whore, then it is fitting that she's the mother of whores. Why? Because every Prothestant church that follows her traditions, festivals, and mandates and worships on the first day of the week, which the Catholic Church instituted instead of worshiping on the the seventh day as God commanded, are considered her children and whores. Thus, she is the mother of whores.

Many Protestant churches according to history protested against some of the Roman Catholic Church's interpretations of the Bible and practices and, therefore, broke away from her. However, they kept some of her practices, including worshiping on the first day of the week, which the Catholic Church instituted. So what's the difference? By practicing everything that the mother does is to be considered a whore child.

God said in John 10:27, "My sheep hears My voice" (NKJV). If you are not of the flock of Jesus, you will be among the flock of Satan. If you are not among Jesus' flock, you won't be blessed or saved. But today, Jesus is giving you the opportunity to belong to His flock. He's giving you the chance to come to Him. Pray and accept His invitation. You won't regret it.

Revelation 17:6-11

"And I saw the woman drunken with the blood of the saints, and with the blood of the martyrs of Jesus: and when I saw her, I wondered with great admiration. And the angel said unto me, Wherefore didst thou marvel? I will tell thee the mystery of the woman, and of the beast that carrieth her, which hath the seven heads and ten horns. The beast that thou sawest was, and is not; and shall ascend out of the bottomless pit, and go into perdition: and they that dwell on the earth shall wonder, whose names were not written in the book of life from the foundation of the world, when they behold the beast that was, and is not, and yet is. And here is the mind which hath wisdom. The seven heads are seven mountains, on which the woman sitteth. And there are seven kings: five are fallen, and one is, and the other is not yet come; and when he cometh, he must continue a short space. And the beast that was, and is not, even he is the eighth, and is of the seven, and goeth into perdition."

The woman was drunk from the blood of God's people, that is, from

The Harlot Woman

the blood of the people who testify about Jesus Christ. History attests to the above; many attrosities have been committed in the name of religion. The Catholic Church has a dark side for killing and torturing Christians and other people. Many Christians fled for their lives because of the persecution for their religious beliefs. Many of God's people fled and hid in the wilderness.

Revelation 17:9-11 identify the satanic system or headquarters. Let's examine each piece of the prophecy to understand what God is saying. "The seven heads are seven mountains, on which the woman sitteth. And there are seven kings: five are fallen, and one is, and the other is not yet come; and when he cometh, he must continue a short space. The beast that was, and is not, even he is the eighth, and is of the seven, and goeth into perdition."

So here is the system that the devil has crafted. He will use five kings to lay out his plans and actions before he himself will take over for a short time before he's destroyed. We learned that mountains represent kingdoms or nations (Jer. 51:24, 25). We also learned in Daniel 2, 7, and 8 of the kingdoms that Satan used to persecute God's saints—Egypt and Assyria, King Herod, Babylon, Medo-Persia, and Greece—which have all fallen.

The current kingdom that is in place is the divided kingdom of Rome where the Roman Catholic Church came from and from which will be enforcing the Sunday law on everybody until Satan, the antichrist, the one who is to come to earth for a short time, will come as the seventh. Satan himself is the beast that was from the beginning, hiding under the veil of others, and he will be the eighth, but in actuality he was of the seventh and is going to perdition. In a nutshell it is Satan who's behind all these kings, and in the end he will take over and show his true colors before he goes into perdition.

The beast according to the Bible is the dragon Satan. He will ascend out of the bottomless pit, the underworld, and go into perdition because he will be destroyed by God forever.

According to Ellen White, "In the seventeenth of Revelation is foretold the destruction of all the churches who corrupt themselves by idolatrous devotion to the service of the papacy, those who have drunk of the wine of the wrath of her fornication. [Revelation 17:1-4 quoted].

"Thus is represented the papal power, which with all deceivableness of unrigthcousness, by outside attraction and gorgeous display, deceives all nations; promising them, as did Satan our first parents, all good to those who receive its mark, and all harm to those who oppose its fallacies. The power which has the deepest inward corruption will make the greatest display, and will clothe itself with the most elaborate signs of power. The Bible plainly declares that this covers a corrupt and deceiving wickedness. 'Upon her forehead was a name written, Mystery, Babylon the Great, The Mother of Harlots and Abominations of the Earth.'

"What is it that gives its kingdom to this power? Protestantism, a power which, while professing to have the temper and spirit of a lamb and to be allied to Heaven, speaks with the voice of a dragon. It is moved by a power from beneath (Letter 232, 1899)" (*The SDA Bible Commentary,* vol. 7, p. 983).

The beast with seven heads and ten horns signifies a system of Satanic ruling. It does not matter who's currently ruling; they will all follow the same practice, the same mandates, and the same pagan system that was set up by the dragon. The only purpose of this system is to drive God's people away from Him and confuse their minds so that they can worship Satan instead of worshiping God. Here is the whoring idea again. The church that is worshiping Satan is whoring against Jesus and thus will be destroyed at the appointed time.

According to history, one of the heads of this movement was King Nebuchadnezzar. He used the system when he built the golden statue and forced everyone great and small to bow down and worship it. But God's faithful few refused to worship this idol, which represented Satan; therefore, they were thrown in the fiery furnace. But as God has promised, He will protect and bless those who stand up for Him. He was there in the fire with them (Dan. 3). Jesus said, "I will be with you ... when you walk through the fire" (Isa. 43:2, NKJV). What a reassurance to God's people that they don't need to be afraid of what people will do to them because He's there to protect them. Thank you Jesus.

Revelation 17:12-18

"And the ten horns which thou sawest are ten kings, which have received no kingdom as yet; but receive power as kings one hour with the beast. These have one mind, and shall give their power and strength unto the beast. These shall make war with the Lamb, and the Lamb shall overcome them: for he is Lord of lords, and King of kings: and they that are with him are called, and chosen, and faithful. And he saith unto me, The waters which thou sawest, where the whore sitteth, are peoples, and multitudes, and nations, and tongues. And the ten horns which thou sawest upon the beast, these shall hate the whore, and shall make her desolate and naked, and shall eat her flesh, and burn her with fire. For God hath put in their hearts to fulfil his will, and to agree, and give their kingdom unto the beast, until the words of God shall be fulfilled.

The Harlot Woman

And the woman which thou sawest is that great city, which reigneth over the kings of the earth."

After Satan takes over, he will appoint ten kings to rule with him. He will give them his power and in return they will give him their power and their allegiance. They will have one mind, meaning that they will work as one unit to get the job done. Their goal is to go to war against the Lamb of God, Jesus Christ, and His followers. But thank God that Satan and all who choose to be on his side are losers. Jesus Christ, the Lamb of God, will defeat them. He's Lord of lords and King of kings, and He already won the first battle in heaven, conquered Satan on the cross, and at the end will get rid of Satan and his followers once and for all.

According to Isaiah 2:2, 3, the stone that breaks the feet of iron and clay will become a mountain. This is the time when Jesus will set up His kingdom and burn Satan and all his followers.

Now is your chance to stand for Jesus Christ before it is too late. Jesus paid the price on the cross for you and He has promised to fight Satan and bless and protect you. He just wants you to read His Word, hear what He's saying, and do what He says, which is to keep His laws, His Ten Commandments, and His testimonies. That's how we can show that we are His disciples and that we love Him and Him only. Jesus said, "He who has My commandments and keeps them, it is he who loves Me" (John 14:21, NKJV; see also John 10:10; 14:16; 1 John 2:3; 5:2-6). To review God's Ten Commandments, read Exodus 20:1-18.

Ellen White made the following comment about Revelation 17:13: "'These have one mind' There will be a universal bond of union, one great harmony, a confederacy of Satan's forces. 'And shall give their power and strength unto the beast.' Thus is manifested the same arbitrary, oppressive power against religious liberty, freedom to worship God according to the dictates of conscience, as was manifested by the papacy, when in the past it persecuted those who dared to refuse to conform with the religious rites and ceremonies of Romanism.... In this warfare the Sabbath of the fourth commandment will be the great point at issue; for in the Sabbath commandment the great Lawgiver identifies Himself as the Creator of the heavens and the earth (MS 24, 1891)" (*The SDA Bible Commentary*, vol. 7, p. 983).

The Ten Commandments are the standard that God gave us to live by. If we follow His laws, we will never run into problems with our fellow men or God. In Matthew 22:36-40 Jesus summarized the Ten Commandments into two commandments—1) love God with all your heart, and 2) love your neighbor as yourself. The Ten Commandments are basically made of two parts that fit under these two commands. The first four commandments address our allegiance and respect toward God, and the other six address our respect toward our fellow men. Therefore, God holds everyone accountable based on these Ten Commandments. The churches that are teaching innocent members that the commandments are done away with are teaching them the wrong things. So don't rely on pastors or other people to interpret the Bible for you. You should read for yourself and ask the Holy Spirit to interpret the Scriptures for you.

Revelation 17:15 talks about the waters where the whore is sitting. This represents people, crowds, nations, and languages. We know that the Roman Catholic Church is known and respected in all the countries of the world. It has religious and political power. Countries, rulers, kings, governments will listen and obey what the Roman Catholic Church mandates.

Therefore, according to verse 18, the Roman Catholic Church is the one that rules over the kings of the earth. But her destruction is also coming because the beast and its ten horns, which is Satan, and his ten kings will turn against her, kill her, and burn her up. Why? Because God set this in their hearts to fulfill His purpose. This is a lesson for everyone. Anyone who tampers with God's Holy Word and laws and teaches others false doctrines should be prepared to deal with the consequences. God is not pleased with people changing and twisting His words.

In conclusion, we already learned that a woman in prophecy represents a church. There will only be two churches in the end time, God's pure church and Satan's harlot church. Since Revelation 17 is talking about the whore church, we already know that it is Satan's church. Mountains stand for political or religious power in prophecy. Therefore, this whore church, or Satan's church, rules the political powers of the earth. This church has gained the high status from these political powers or the kings of the earth because she has acted as a whore with them. They look up to her and follow her mandates. Who are these political powers? They are the political powers of the world.

The waters where this church rules are people, multitudes, nations, and tongues. In other words, this church will run the whole earth. I believe the word to describe this is "The New World Order" or as some people say, "The New World Disorder" that is coming. Don't be fooled when it comes. This is not of God. You will be forced to believe and follow their mandates, but be strong and courageous because Jesus will be with you until the end of the world.

In Revelation 17 the angel is showing John the judgment of the great whore church. The kings of the earth are in accordance with her ruling the world as long as they get their political gain. They are in agreement of mixing state and religion. They too will follow her teachings and put them into practice. As you know by now, this church is none other than the Roman Catholic Church that dresses in purple and scarlet. Its headquarters, the Vatican, glitter with gold, precious stones, and pearls. This same church will kill, punish, and mistreat everyone who refuses to worship on Sunday.

Here God is revealing to John and to us that this church will be drunk with the blood of God's people who testify about Jesus Christ and keep His Ten Commandments. So my brothers and sisters, if you belong to this church, this is your chance to investigate, search the Scriptures for yourself, pray, and get out before it is too late. If you don't, then you will partake of the plagues that this false church will receive.

Chapter 18

The Fall of Babylon

Revelation 18:1-4

"And after these things I saw another angel come down from heaven, having great power; and the earth was lightened with his glory. And he cried mightily with a strong voice, saying, Babylon the great is fallen, is fallen, and is become the habitation of devils, and the hold of every foul spirit, and a cage of every unclean and hateful bird. For all nations have drunk of the wine of the wrath of her fornication, and the kings of the earth have committed fornication with her, and the merchants of the earth are waxed rich through the abundance of her delicacies. And I heard another voice from heaven, saying, Come out of her, my people, that ye be not partakers of her sins, and that ye receive not of her plagues."

Today, God the Father and His Son, Jesus Christ, are calling Their people to come out of Babylon. If you belong to any whoring church, Jesus is calling you out. Now is your chance to study the truth for yourself so that you will understand and hear God's voice when He calls. This is a life-and-death matter. You need to hear God's voice and follow Him and Him only. If you don't, you will share in the plagues that the whoring churches will receive.

Revelation 18:5-19

"For her sins have reached unto heaven, and God hath remembered her iniquities. Reward her even as she rewarded you, and double unto her double according to her works: in the cup which she hath filled fill to her double. How much she hath glorified herself, and lived deliciously, so much torment and sorrow give her: for she saith in her heart, I sit a queen, and am no widow, and shall see no sorrow. Therefore shall her plagues come in one day, death, and

The Fall of Babylon

mourning, and famine; and she shall be utterly burned with fire: for strong is the Lord God who judgeth her.

"And the kings of the earth, who have committed fornication and lived deliciously with her, shall bewail her, and lament for her, when they shall see the smoke of her burning, Standing afar off for the fear of her torment, saying, Alas, alas that great city Babylon, that mighty city! for in one hour is thy judgment come. And the merchants of the earth shall weep and mourn over her; for no man buyeth their merchandise any more: The merchandise of gold, and silver, and precious stones, and of pearls, and fine linen, and purple, and silk, and scarlet, and all thyine wood, and all manner vessels of ivory, and all manner vessels of most precious wood, and of brass, and iron, and marble, And cinnamon, and odours, and ointments, and frankincense, and wine, and oil, and fine flour, and wheat, and beasts, and sheep, and horses, and chariots, and slaves, and souls of men. And the fruits that thy soul lusted after are departed from thee, and all things which were dainty and goodly are departed from thee, and thou shalt find them no more at all.

"The merchants of these things, which were made rich by her, shall stand afar off for the fear of her torment, weeping and wailing, And saying, Alas, alas that great city, that was clothed in fine linen, and purple, and scarlet, and decked with gold, and precious stones, and pearls! For in one hour so great riches is come to nought. And every shipmaster, and all the company in ships, and sailors, and as many as trade by sea, stood afar off, And cried when they saw the smoke of her burning, saying, What city is like unto this great city! And they cast dust on their heads, and cried, weeping and wailing, saying, Alas, alas that great city, wherein were made rich all that had ships in the sea by reason of her costliness! for in one hour is she made desolate."

Once again the Old and New Testaments are in harmony. Read what Isaiah has to say that mirrors what is happening in Revelation 18: "'And look, here comes a chariot of men with a pair of horsemen!' Then he answered and said, 'Babylon is fallen, is fallen! And all the carved images of her gods He has broken to the ground'" (Isa. 21:9, NKJV).

God never lies; His words are true. In Revelation 18:11 the world's businessmen and businesswomen (kings and queens of the earth) weep and mourn over Babylon's destruction because no one is buying their merchandise anymore. They were made rich by doing business with her. Now she's gone forever.

According to the Bible, the ten horns who work for Satan will turn against the harlot woman and kill her. We'll discuss that later. But in the meantime,

The Revelation of Jesus Christ

all the merchants who are her business associates will stand afar and marvel at how in one hour she's destroyed.

Did you know that the selling of humans and souls is going on right now? Musicians, artists, government officials, celebrities, rich and poor are selling their souls to the devil for fame, fortune, power and control. Parents are selling their children as slaves to buy food. Pimps are selling girls for money. Merchants are selling workers for cheap labor. This practise also goes on in the prison system. New prisoners, the minute they set foot into the prison system, are being bought or sold by the veteran prisoners. In parts of some countries such as India, Thailand, Cambodia, Haiti, and in many countries in Africa where poverty is so rampant, parents sell their own children to prostitution or slavery so that they can buy food to eat. Even in America, the land of plenty, young girls are being sold into prostitution. The pimps are rich from these practices, and Satan is the one behind all this.

Revelation 18:20-24

"Rejoice over her, thou heaven, and ye holy apostles and prophets; for God hath avenged you on her. And a mighty angel took up a stone like a great millstone, and cast it into the sea, saying, Thus with violence shall that great city Babylon be thrown down, and shall be found no more at all. And the voice of harpers, and musicians, and of pipers, and trumpeters, shall be heard no more at all in thee; and no craftsman, of whatsoever craft he be, shall be found any more in thee; and the sound of a millstone shall be heard no more at all in thee; And the light of a candle shall shine no more at all in thee; and the voice of the bridegroom and of the bride shall be heard no more at all in thee: for thy merchants were the great men of the earth; for by thy sorceries were all nations deceived. And in her was found the blood of prophets, and of saints, and of all that were slain upon the earth."

God has sent His warnings to His people from old times up to now. Because He's giving us all the opportunities to come to Him and be saved, how foolish it will be if we read, hear, and refuse to do what He says and are lost forever. Isaiah also spoke of the church with its carved images. This is not a new practice; it's a practice that came from pagan idol and sun worship.

In Revelation 18:4, God makes His final final appeal to "come out of her, my people." Now is the time to follow Jesus Christ all the way so that you will not partake of the plagues. Revelation 13 and 18 follows each other. In chapter 13 God reveals the mark of the beast, and in chapter 18 He calls His people out of this church. So, now is the time for you to choose between the pure church,

The Fall of Babylon

which is God's church, and the whore church, which is Satan's church. Satan's church and his followers will receive God's wrath and eternal death. After the destruction of the whore church, all her business associates will stand afar and mourn her because there's no more business going on for them.

If you notice this is the same message that was given by the second angel back in Revelation 14:8. Babylon is fallen. Why? "Because she has made all nations drink of the wine of the wrath of her indignation" (NKJV). What is the wine? The wine is her false teachings and doctrines. She has given to the world a false Sabbath instead of the Sabbath of the fourth commandments of God and has repeated the falsehood that Satan first told to Eve in Eden, which is the natural immortality of the soul.

Once the great city is burned, God will say to the martyrs, "Rejoice because now you have been vindicated." All the souls under the altar that John saw crying for vengeance and those who will be martyred, God is saying to them, now you can rejoice because as was promised to you at the appointed time you will be vindicated. And God's word is true. "'Vengeance is Mine,' says the Lord" (Rom. 12:19, NKJV).

To my Christian friends who already know Jesus, why not obey Him and worship Him on the day that He has established, which is the seventh-day Sabbath. There is no need to worship on the day that was sanctified by man. God blessed and sanctified only one day, and that is Saturday. "Thus the heavens and the earth, and all the host of them, were finished. And on the seventh day God ended His work which He had done, and He rested on the seventh day from all His work which He had done. Then God blessed the seventh day and sanctified it, because in it He rested from all His work which God had created and made" (Gen. 2:1-3, NKJV).

So you see, God never blessed the first day of the week, so why waste your time. Just follow what God commanded because that's what He requires of us. Nothing more; nothing less. Jesus said in John 10:27 "My sheep hear My voice" (NKJV). If you hear Jesus' voice today, why don't you follow Him? He's shown us the way, the truth, and the life. Why won't you follow Him and live? The choice is yours.

Ellen White provides the following insight into the power of the gospel message. "The proclamation of the gospel is the only means in which God can employ human beings as His instrumetalities for the salvation of souls. As men, women, and children proclaim the gospel, the Lord will open the eyes of the blind to see his statutes, and will write upon the hearts of the truly penitent his law. The animating Spirit of God, working through human agencies, leads the believers to be of one mind, one soul, unitedly loving God and keeping his commandments,—preparing here below for translation" (*The Review and Herald,* October 13, 1904).

Earlier in the same article, she wrote, "The Spirit of the Lord will so graciously bless consecrated human instrumentalities that men, woman, and children will open their lips in praise and thanksgiving, filling the earth with the knowledge of God, and with his unsurpassed glory, as the waters covers the sea. Those who have held the beginning of their confidence firm unto the end will be wide-awake during the time that the third angel's message is proclaimed with great power."

Chapter 19

Jesus the Word of God

Revelation 19:1-4

"And after these things I heard a great voice of much people in heaven, saying, Alleluia; Salvation, and glory, and honour, and power, unto the Lord our God: For true and righteous are his judgments: for he hath judged the great whore, which did corrupt the earth with her fornication, and hath avenged the blood of his servants at her hand. And again they said, Alleluia And her smoke rose up for ever and ever. And the four and twenty elders and the four beasts fell down and worshipped God that sat on the throne, saying, Amen; Alleluia."

I've learned that there will be rejoicing in heaven once the whore is gone. That tells me that the angels in heaven feel our pain and will be rejoicing with us when the struggle is over. They are involved in the affairs of man and are ready to help us at Jesus' command. Our world is their special case that they are working on until the end of the world. They are watching out for us so we are never alone. How beautiful it will be when we meet our guardian angels and thank them for everything that they have done for us. But more important is when we see Jesus and fall at His feet and worship Him for everything that He has done for us. We won't be able to stop thanking Him.

Revelation 19:5-8

"And a voice came out of the throne, saying, Praise our God, all ye his servants, and ye that fear him, both small and great. And I heard as it were the voice of a great multitude, and as the voice of many waters, and as the voice of mighty thunderings, saying, Alleluia: for the Lord God omnipotent reigneth. Let us be glad and rejoice, and give honour to him: for the marriage of the

Lamb is come, and his wife hath made herself ready. And to her was granted that she should be arrayed in fine linen, clean and white: for the fine linen is the righteousness of saints."

OK, this is it. This is the culmination celebration of the victory over evil—the marriage between Jesus and His church. This is when we, His pure church, will be taken to heaven to see Jesus face to face. Oh what a joy that will be! We have kept His commandments and testimonies, and the time has finally come when we will meet Him and receive the blessings that He has in store for His servants who have chosen to be on His side. This is a wedding that you do not want to miss. There will be nothing like it. Can you picture it? Can you see Jesus smiling and opening His arms to receive His people? There will be people of all different colors, languages, and nations! Oh what a reunion that will be. I sure don't want to miss it; I would love for you to be there, too.

Revelation 19:9-13

"And he saith unto me, Write, Blessed are they which are called unto the marriage supper of the Lamb. And he saith unto me, These are the true sayings of God. And I fell at his feet to worship him. And he said unto me, See thou do it not: I am thy fellowservant, and of thy brethren that have the testimony of Jesus: worship God: for the testimony of Jesus is the spirit of prophecy. And I saw heaven opened, and behold a white horse; and he that sat upon him was called Faithful and True, and in righteousness he doth judge and make war. His eyes were as a flame of fire, and on his head were many crowns; and he had a name written, that no man knew, but he himself. And he was clothed with a vesture dipped in blood: and his name is called The Word of God."

In this passage John saw Jesus on a white horse with His clothes dipped in blood—His sacrificial blood on our behalf. He had many crowns on His head, and His name was "The Word of God." Here God is revealing to us that His Son, Jesus Christ, is His Word. He became flesh and dwelt among us, and while He was on earth, God spoke directly to us through Him (Heb. 1:1). Praise God. Jesus is the only Mediator between His Father and us. There is no substitute for Jesus. No one can take the place of Jesus.

So right away, if you hear anyone say that he or she is God or Jesus, you should know that he or she is lying and trying to deceive people. Don't believe them. God speaks to us through the Bible, which is a revelation of Jesus Christ, so that we can test what others tell us or claim in regards to God.

John clearly defines Jesus' position and role as the Savior of this world in the following verses: "In the beginning was the Word, and the Word was with

Jesus the Word of God

God, and the Word was God. He was in the beginning with God. All things were made through Him, and without Him nothing was made that was made. In Him was life, and the life was the light of men. And the light shines in the darkness, and the darkness did not comprehend it" (John 1:1-4, NKJV). "He came to His own, and His own did not receive Him. But as many as received Him, to them He gave the right to become children of God, to those who believe in His name: who were born, not of blood, nor of the will of the flesh, nor of the will of man, but of God" (verses 11-13, NKJV; see also 1 John 1:1-6).

If you are not a Jew by blood, you don't need to worry as long as you receive Jesus and believe in His name; then you will be saved. Therefore, the Bible, the seventh-day Sabbath, and the rest of the commandments are for everyone who receives and believes in Jesus Christ.

God knew that some people wouldn't believe in His Son, Jesus, and that false prophets and teachers would come with false doctrines and teachings to confuse His people. We've learned about some of the false teachings in previous chapters, especially the one about Sunday worship. In order to prepare us, God gave us a test that we can run on them to see if they are true or false prophets.

The formula for testing prophets is found in 1 John 4:1-6: "Beloved, do not believe every spirit, but test the spirits, whether they are of God; because many false prophets have gone out into the world. By this you know the Spirit of God: Every spirit that confesses that Jesus Christ has come in the flesh is of God, and every spirit that does not confess that Jesus Christ has come in the flesh is not of God. And this is the spirit of the Antichrist, which you have heard was coming, and is now already in the world. You are of God, little children, and have overcome them, because He who is in you is greater than he who is in the world. They are of the world. Therefore they speak as of the world, and the world hears them. We are of God. He who knows God hears us; he who is not of God does not hear us. By this we know the spirit of truth and the spirit of error" (NKJV).

God also said in Isaiah 8:20: "To the law and to the testimony! If they do not speak according to this word, it is because there is no light in them" (NKJV). The law and the testimonies of Jesus are our standard to go by. So, if anyone comes to you with different teachings of doctrices and if they do not speak according to the law and the testimonies of Jesus Christ, then you already know that there is no truth in them. Don't believe them.

I can remember my mother saying that as a Catholic they never taught her and her classmates about the prophecies. The church only stressed Catholic doctrines but never examined what the Bible said about the law and the prophecies. What does that tell you about those teachings? There is no truth in them.

Revelation 19:14-16

"And the armies which were in heaven followed him upon white horses, clothed in fine linen, white and clean. And out of his mouth goeth a sharp sword, that with it he should smite the nations: and he shall rule them with a rod of iron: and he treadeth the winepress of the fierceness and wrath of Almighty God. And he hath on his vesture and on his thigh a name written, KING OF KINGS, AND LORD OF LORDS."

When Jesus comes back to set up His kingdom, He will judge those who did not believe in Him or choose Him with a sword, which means the Word of God in prophetic terms. So He is going to judge them from the Bible. He gave us His Ten Commandments as a standard of how to live, and He is going to use those same Ten Commandments to measure our actions and see where we stand. So why not practice and obey the Ten Commandments now while there is time. You'll be glad you did.

Revelation 19:17-21

"And I saw an angel standing in the sun; and he cried with a loud voice, saying to all the fowls that fly in the midst of heaven, Come and gather yourselves together unto the supper of the great God; That ye may eat the flesh of kings, and the flesh of captains, and the flesh of mighty men, and the flesh of horses, and of them that sit on them, and the flesh of all men, both free and bond, both small and great. And I saw the beast, and the kings of the earth, and their armies, gathered together to make war against him that sat on the horse, and against his army. And the beast was taken, and with him the false prophet that wrought miracles before him, with which he deceived them that had received the mark of the beast, and them that worshipped his image. These both were cast alive into a lake of fire burning with brimstone. And the remnant were slain with the sword of him that sat upon the horse, which sword proceeded out of his mouth: and all the fowls were filled with their flesh."

Then the beast and the kings of the earth and their armies gathered together under the leadership of Satan to fight Jesus and His army. But the beast was taken captive along with the false prophet, and they both were thrown into the fire that burns with sulfur. The rest of the people were killed with the sword,

Jesus the Word of God

which stands for the Bible, the Word of God, that goes out of the mouth of the rider, which is Jesus, riding on the horse. And all the birds gorged themselves on their flesh.

After Babylon has been judged by God and the plagues have been poured out, a great anthem is sung in heaven (Rev. 19:1-8). This happens before Christ's Second Coming (Rev. 19:11-21). Christ's Second Coming is then followed by the events described in Revelation 20—the millennium and final destruction of Satan and sin. The following chart breaks down the final events of earth's history.

Second Coming	First Resurection - 1,000 Years	Second Resurection -Eternity
Return of Jesus (Matt. 24:30)		Christ, saints, and New Jerusalem descend (Rev. 21:2, 10; 20:9)
Righteous dead raised (1 Thess. 4:16; Rev. 20:6)	The Millennium	Wicked dead raised (John 5:28, 29; Rev. 20:5)
Satan bound (Rev. 20:1-4)	Righteous in heaven (Rev. 15:2, 3; 20:4-6)	Satan loosed (Rev. 20:7, 8)
Living saints caught up (Matt. 24:31; 1 Thess. 4:17)	Wicked remain dead (Rev. 20:5)	Last judgment (Rev. 20:11-15; 21:8)
Wicked slain (Jer. 25:33; Matt. 13:39-42)	Satan and evil angels alive and bound on earth (Rev. 20:1-4)	Satan and sinners destroyed (Rev. 20:9, 10)
Earth desolate (Jer. 4:23-27)	Earth remains desolate (Jer. 4:23-27)	Earth cleansed and renewed (2 Peter 3:10-13; Rev. 21, 22)

Did you know that God also revealed to Isaiah about the end of the world? Please read Isaiah chapter 2 and compare it with the book of Revelation.

Chapter 20

Vacation With Jesus for 1,000 Years

Revelation 20:1-4

"And I saw an angel come down from heaven, having the key of the bottomless pit and a great chain in his hand. And he laid hold on the dragon, that old serpent, which is the Devil, and Satan, and bound him a thousand years, And cast him into the bottomless pit, and shut him up, and set a seal upon him, that he should deceive the nations no more, till the thousand years should be fulfilled: and after that he must be loosed a little season. And I saw thrones, and they sat upon them, and judgment was given unto them: and I saw the souls of them that were beheaded for the witness of Jesus, and for the word of God, and which had not worshipped the beast, neither his image, neither had received his mark upon their foreheads, or in their hands; and they lived and reigned with Christ a thousand years."

This is the time when the saints and the ones who were dead are resurrected (the first resurrection) and go to heaven to live with Jesus for 1,000 years. At this time Satan is bound in chains because he can't deceive anyone anymore. There's no human being left alive on the earth to be deceived; therefore, he's bound in chains of circumstances and thrown into the bottomless pit. The saints will be in heaven with Jesus, and the wicked ones will have been killed with the sword from Jesus' mouth. Therefore, the devil has no one left on the earth to deceive; he's symbolically put into chains.

All the saints who died from the time of Adam to the end of the world will be resurrected at the first resurrection along will join the living saints who went through the time of trouble during the end of the world, and go to heaven to live with Jesus for 1,000 years. They will rule with Jesus for this time. Satan will have 1,000 years to see the work of his hands—the suffering, destruction, killing that he has caused throughout history—he has to reflect and contemplate on his evil work, and wait for his punishment.

Again the Old Testament and New Testament go hand in hand. Read Leviticus 16:8-10, 21, 22 to learn about the scapegoat, which depicts Satan, that was used to carry everyone's sins, which Satan caused them to commit, out of the camp.

Revelation 20:5, 6

"But the rest of the dead lived not again until the thousand years were finished. This is the first resurrection. Blessed and holy is he that hath part in the first resurrection: on such the second death hath no power, but they shall be priests of God and of Christ, and shall reign with him a thousand years."

While Satan is on earth all by himself with no humans to deceive, God's saints, those who have chosen to be with Him, will be in heaven with Him receiving their reward. My brothers and sisters, you can't lose on the side of Jesus. You can only win if you choose Him.

Revelation 20:7-10

"And when the thousand years are expired, Satan shall be loosed out of his prison, And shall go out to deceive the nations which are in the four quarters of the earth, Gog, and Magog, to gather them together to battle: the number of whom is as the sand of the sea. And they went up on the breadth of the earth, and compassed the camp of the saints about, and the beloved city: and fire came down from God out of heaven, and devoured them. And the devil that deceived them was cast into the lake of fire and brimstone, where the beast and the false prophet are, and shall be tormented day and night for ever and ever."

After the 1,000 years the second resurrection will take place of those who are still dead, those who chose the side of the devil. This will be a very large group. Their numbers are as the sand of the sea. The devil will gather the nations to prepare to fight in the final battle. The multitude will march toward the city to engage in a battle with the saints who are in the New Jerusalem, which came down from heaven. As they prepare to fight, fire will come down from heaven and consume them. The devil will be thrown into the lake of fire where the beast and false prophet are, and they will be tormented forever and ever. So this will be the end of Satan and his followers.

Now ask yourself, is this the side you want to be on? The losing side? God is so good; He's showing us the good the bad and the ugly and telling us what to expect. But it is up to us to decide what we want to do. He has shown us that if we choose Him we will be winners and if we choose Satan we will be losers. The choice is yours. I pray that you will choose Jesus' side and win.

Once again, God gave us a glimpse of what will happen at the end times through the prophecies of the Old Testament. Read Ezekiel 38 and 39 to see the connection between those two chapters and the events of Revelation.

Revelation 20:11, 12

"And I saw a great white throne, and him that sat on it, from whose face the earth and the heaven fled away; and there was found no place for them. And I saw the dead, small and great, stand before God; and the books were opened: and another book was opened, which is the book of life: and the dead were judged out of those things which were written in the books, according to their works."

This is the court date for all those who chose Satan's side and died. They were killed when Jesus came back to earth. They did not make it to heaven because of their evil deeds. So now they are standing before God's throne to find out why they did not make it to heaven. Jesus opens the book of life and shows them what they did that caused them to lose out on the joy of heaven. They will have a panoramic view of their whole life, starting from birth. They will see everything they did and probably forgot about it. But God never forgets.

God's angels wrote every deed they committed in the book. Every evil thought, evil action, or evil scheme that was done was recorded. Those who are lost will see how they took other gods before God. How they worship idols instead of worshiping God. They will see how they took the holy name of God in vain and blasphemed Him. They will see how they trampled on God's holy Sabbath day. They will see how they partook in whichcraft. They will see how they dishonored their parents. They will see the day and time they stole, killed, lied, and coveted. They will see the day and time they committed adultery and fornication. They will see how they hated and despised others because of their race, color, economic status, culture, or religion. They will see how they committed abominations by marrying same sex partners. They will see how they neglected to help those in need even though they had the means to do it. They will see how they neglected to visit the sick, the prisoners, and those in need. They will see how they neglected to help and protect the widow, the fatherless, and the orphans. God in His mercy will show them everything they did in their life that caused them to lose heaven. This will be an eye opener for us.

Now is the time we need to come clean with God and ask for His forgiveness for everything that we have done wrong. Now is the time to set our record straight so that the angels can write "forgiven" next to each sin that we've committed so that it won't be counted against us. If we confess our sins to Jesus, we will be forgiven. It is useless to have another sinner forgive us of our sins; nothing happens when he or she says, "Ego te absolvo a peccatis tuis" (I absolve you from your sin). It is just words that can't erase our records in heaven or forgive our sins. Only Jesus can forgive sins through His blood. Don't go to any priest or pastor to ask for forgiveness; turn to Jesus instead.

By giving us a glimpse of the judgment, Jesus is showing us that everything we do, say, or think is being recorded in the books in heaven. This is to show us that He is a fair God and that He does things right and just. If we don't make it to heaven, we have ourselves to blame.

After the devil deceived Eve and caused her to eat from the forbidden tree, God banned them from the Garden of Eden so that they couldn't eat from the tree of life and live forever in their sin. But God sent His only begotten Son, Jesus Christ, to die the eternal death in our place so that we could have a chance of eternal life again. But He gave us a choice. We can live forever with Him in paradise if we follow His mandates and keep His commandments and His testimonies and ask Him to forgive us of our sins. Only Jesus can save us; no one else. But we must make the decision to follow Him.

Revelation 20:13-15

"And the sea gave up the dead which were in it; and death and hell delivered up the dead which were in them: and they were judged every man according to their works. And death and hell were cast into the lake of fire. This is the second death. And whosoever was not found written in the book of life was cast into the lake of fire."

What a powerful God! Can you imagine? Here God commands the sea to give up the dead who drowned in it; Hades to release bodies from it; the fire to release the bodies that was burned; and the grave or death to release the dead so that they can be judged according to their works. No wonder Jesus tells us in Luke 12:4, 5, "And I say to you, My friends, do not be afraid of those who kill the body, and after that have no more that they can do. But I will show you whom you should fear: Fear Him who, after He has killed, has power to cast into hell; yes, I say to you, fear Him!" (NKJV).

My brothers and sisters, we need to fear God because He has the power over Satan and man and eternal death. Let's strive to be on God's side so that we will not partake of the second death.

In closing, read these words by Ellen White: "When the flood of waters was at its height upon the earth, it had the appearance of a boundless lake of water. When God finally purifies the earth, it will appear like a boundless lake of fire. As God preserved the ark amid the commotions of the Flood, because it contained eight righteous persons, He will preserve the New Jerusalem, containing the faithful of all ages, from righteous Abel down to the last saint which lived. Although the whole earth, with the exception of that portion where the city rests, will be wrapped in a sea of liquid fire, yet the city if preserved as was the ark, by a miracle of Almighty power. It stands unharmed amid the devouring elements (Spiritual Gifts 3:87)" (*The SDA Bible Commentary,* vol. 7, p. 986).

Chapter 21

Starting Over in the New Earth With Jesus

Revelation 21:1-3

"And I saw a new heaven and a new earth: for the first heaven and the first earth were passed away; and there was no more sea. And I John saw the holy city, new Jerusalem, coming down from God out of heaven, prepared as a bride adorned for her husband. And I heard a great voice out of heaven saying, Behold, the tabernacle of God is with men, and he will dwell with them, and they shall be his people, and God himself shall be with them, and be their God."

God gave John a sneak preview of the New Jerusalem that God prepared for His servants—His pure church, those who chose death rather than the mark of the beast, those who kept His Ten Commandments and the testimonies of Jesus Christ. They will enjoy the New Jerusalem that God prepared for them, and God will dwell among them. What a privilege. No wonder the Bible tells us in 1 Peter 2:9 that "you are a chosen generation, a royal priesthood, a holy nation, His own special people, that you may proclaim the praises of Him who called you out of darkness into His marvelous light" (NKJV).

We do not deserve the New Jerusalem, but God send His Son to die for us and save us. God gave us a choice to worship Him and be blessed or worship the beast and his image and be destroyed. This is our reward and a fulfillment of His promise that He would prepare mansions for us and give us the gift of eternal life again. I have to agree that we are a peculiar people and royal priesthood loved by God and His Son, Jesus Christ.

Revelation 21:4

"And God shall wipe away all tears from their eyes; and there shall be no more death, neither sorrow, nor crying, neither shall there be any more pain: for the former things are passed away."

Once this world is cleansed by fire and the redeemed are saved, God will wipe away every tear from their eyes. There will be no more crying for the family member or friend who did not make it to heaven. There will be no more sorrow for being taken advantage of. No more pain or suffering. We are with Jesus, and now is time for our blessings and reward. All those who have suffered at the hands of the devil and his followers will enjoy their eternal reward with Jesus, His Father, the Holy Spirit, and His angels.

Revelation 21:5-7

"And he that sat upon the throne said, Behold, I make all things new. And he said unto me, Write: for these words are true and faithful. And he said unto me, It is done. I am Alpha and Omega, the beginning and the end. I will give unto him that is athirst of the fountain of the water of life freely. He that overcometh shall inherit all things; and I will be his God, and he shall be my son."

This corrupt and sinful world will be made new again. All the spores of evil will be killed by fire. God's Word is true. It is up to us to believe and accept Him. And if we do, God will freely give us the water of life. And if we stay faithful to Him and obey His commandments, we will inherit all the things that He has promised us. We will be God's sons and daughters, and He will live among us forever and ever and ever.

Revelation 21:8

"But the fearful, and unbelieving, and the abominable, and murderers, and whoremongers, and sorcerers, and idolaters, and all liars, shall have their part in the lake which burneth with fire and brimstone: which is the second death."

My brothers and sisters, if you are a coward, one who does not believe in God, a murderer, someone who commits sexual sins or worships idols, or is a liar, you are in big trouble. But guess what? You still have time to clean up your life. Now is the time to stop doing evil and ask God to forgive you and help you to keep His Ten Commandments. By keeping God's Ten Commandments, you will not commit any of the above sins. No wonder God wants us to keep His Ten Commandments as He originally wrote them, without any changes.

Revelation 21:9-14

"And there came unto me one of the seven angels which had the seven vials full of the seven last plagues, and talked with me, saying, Come hither, I will shew thee the bride, the Lamb's wife. And he carried me away in the spirit to a great and high mountain, and shewed me that great city, the holy Jerusalem, descending out of heaven from God, Having the glory of God: and her light was like unto a stone most precious, even like a jasper stone, clear as crystal; And had a wall great and high, and had twelve gates, and at the gates twelve angels, and names written thereon, which are the names of the twelve tribes of the children of Israel: On the east three gates; on the north three gates; on the south three gates; and on the west three gates. And the wall of the city had twelve foundations, and in them the names of the twelve apostles of the Lamb."

According to John 1:11-13 all Gentiles can become children of God. So the Bible, the Ten Commandments, and salvation are not only for the Jews. Everyone can receive Jesus Christ as their Savior. "He [Jesus] came to His own, and His own did not receive Him. But as many as received Him, to them He gave the right to become children of God, to those who believe in His name: who were born, not of blood, nor of the will of the flesh, nor of the will of man, but of God" (NKJV).

If you were not born a Jew, you can still receive God's blessings if you believe in Jesus Christ and receive Him as your personal Savior. Praise God. We all have a chance to become children of God if we so choose. The choice is yours.

Revelation 21:15-27

"And he that talked with me had a golden reed to measure the city, and the gates thereof, and the wall thereof. And the city lieth foursquare, and the length is as large as the breadth: and he measured the city with the reed, twelve thousand furlongs. The length and the breadth and the height of it are equal. And he measured the wall thereof, an hundred and forty and four cubits, according to the measure of a man, that is, of the angel. And the building of the wall of it was of jasper: and the city was pure gold, like unto clear glass.

"And the foundations of the wall of the city were garnished with all manner of precious stones. The first foundation was jasper; the second, sapphire; the third, a chalcedony; the fourth, an emerald; The fifth, sardonyx; the sixth, sardius; the seventh, chrysolyte; the eighth, beryl; the ninth, a topaz; the tenth,

The Revelation of Jesus Christ

a chrysoprasus; the eleventh, a jacinth; the twelfth, an amethyst.

"And the twelve gates were twelve pearls: every several gate was of one pearl: and the street of the city was pure gold, as it were transparent glass. And I saw no temple therein: for the Lord God Almighty and the Lamb are the temple of it. And the city had no need of the sun, neither of the moon, to shine in it: for the glory of God did lighten it, and the Lamb is the light thereof.

"And the nations of them which are saved shall walk in the light of it: and the kings of the earth do bring their glory and honour into it. And the gates of it shall not be shut at all by day: for there shall be no night there. And they shall bring the glory and honour of the nations into it. And there shall in no wise enter into it any thing that defileth, neither whatsoever worketh abomination, or maketh a lie: but they which are written in the Lamb's book of life."

God is giving us a sneak preview of what He's preparing for us. As parents, when we buy something for our children that we know they are going to like, we can hardly wait to show it to them. That's how God is; He desires that we will choose Him so that we can enjoy the beautiful things that He has in store for us. You see, you can't lose if you are on the side of Jesus. You will end up a winner.

"Heaven and earth will pass, but My words will by no means pass away" (Matt. 24:35, NKJV; see also 1 Pet. 1:23-25; 2 Pet. 3:10). This is for us to know that God's word is true and all who have an ear must listen and obey. Jesus is waiting patiently on us to respond to His love. He created us, died for our sins, and went to prepare mansions for us. It is up to us to accept these free gifts. Jesus is ready to save us. He's going to clean this earth, which is filled with sin and start all over again.

After the earth was purified by fire, John saw a clean new heaven and new earth (see also Isa. 65:17-25). After cleaning this sinful world with fire and getting rid of Satan, his evil angels, and followers, God will start all over again with a new heaven and a new earth. It will be wonderful to watch Jesus recreate the world again. I can imagine hearing Him say, "Let the air and sea bring forth animals of its own kind. Let the flowers come up, etc." I think that it will be an awesome experience that I do not want to miss for anything in this world.

Ellen White writes about our duty here on earth as we prepare for heaven: "This earth is the place of preparation for heaven. The time spent here is the Christian's winter. Here the chilly winds of affliction blow upon us, and the waves of trouble roll against us. But in the near future, when Christ comes, sorrow and sighing will be forever ended. Then will be the Christian's summer.

Starting Over in the New Earth With Jesus

All trials will be over, and there will be no more sickness or death. 'God shall wipe away all tears from their eyes; and there shall be no more death, neither sorrow, nor crying … : for the former things are passed away' (MS 28, 1886)" (*The SDA Bible Commentary,* vol. 7, p. 988).

The reward for God's people is sure. All those that hear His voice, listen, read, and do all that He asks, such as keeping His Ten Commandments and the testimonies of Jesus and going through persecution will enjoy the reward that Jesus is preparing for His servants. This will be our eternal vacation with Jesus and our God. What a beautiful picture. Are you willing to go on vacation with Jesus Christ and live with Him forever and ever? Now is your chance to accept Him as your personal Savior.

For further study, please read about the harmony of the prophecies in the Old and New Testaments (Lev. 26:11, 12; 2 Chron. 6:18; Isa. 7:14; 8:8, 10; 9:6; Jer 31:33, 34; Ezek. 37:27; 38:1-23; Dan 12:4; Rev. 21:5-8; 22:12).

Chapter 22

Jesus the Water of Life

Revelation 22:1, 2

"And he shewed me a pure river of water of life, clear as crystal, proceeding out of the throne of God and of the Lamb. In the midst of the street of it, and on either side of the river, was there the tree of life, which bare twelve manner of fruits, and yielded her fruit every month: and the leaves of the tree were for the healing of the nations."

Wow, have you ever seen a pure, clean, clear river and a tree that bears twelve different types of fruit? Every month this tree of life will bear a different fruit. I know that this is a new phenomenon for every human being. It is something that we can't comprehend in our finite mind. No wonder God said that "eye has not seen, nor ear heard, nor have entered into the heart of man the things which God has prepared for those who love Him" (1 Cor. 2:9, NKJV).

"Christ, the heavenly Teacher, will lead His people to the tree of life that grows on either side of the river of life, and He will explain to them the truths they could not in this life understand. In that future life His people will gain the higher education in its completeness. Those who enter the city of God will have the golden crowns placed upon their heads. That will be a joyful scene that none of us can afford to miss....

"The tree of life is a representation of the preserving care of Christ for His children. As Adam and Eve ate of this tree, they acknowledged their dependence upon God. The tree of life possessed the power to perpetuate life, and as long as they ate of it, they could not die. The lives of the antediluvians were protracted because of the life-giving power of this tree, which was transmitted to them from Adam and Eve (The Review and Herald, January 26, 1897).

"The fruit of the tree of life in the Garden of Eden possessed supernatural virtue. To eat of it was to live forever. Its fruit was the antidote of death. Its leaves were for the sustaining of life and immorality. But through man's disobedience, death entered the world. Adam ate of the tree of the knowledge of good and evil, the fruit of which he had been forbidden to touch. His transgression opened the floodgates of woe upon our race" (*The SDA Bible Commentary*, vol. 7, p. 988).

Ellen White continues to describe the tree of life in *The SDA Bible Commentary*: "Let all bear in mind that the tree of life bears twelve manner of fruits. This represents the spiritual work of our earthly missions. The Word of God is to us the tree of life. Every portion of the Scripture has its use. In every part of the Word is some lesson to be learned. Then learn how to study your Bibles. This book is not a heap of odds and ends. It is an educator. Your own thoughts must be called into exercise before you can be really benefited by Bible study. Spiritual sinew and muscle must be brought to bear upon the Word. The Holy Spirit will bring to remembrance the words of Christ. He will enlighten the mind, and guide the research (Letter 3, 1898).

"Christ is the source of our life, the source of immortality. He is the tree of life, and to all who come to Him He gives spiritual life (The Review and Herald, January 26, 1897)" (vol. 7, p. 989).

"Many seem to have the idea that this world and the heavenly mansions constitute the universe of God. Not so. The redeemed throng will range from world to world, and much of their time will be employed in searching out the mysteries of redemption. And throughout the whole stretch of eternity, this subject will be continually opening to their minds. The privileges of those who overcome by the blood of the Lamb and the word of their testimony are beyond comprehension (The Review and Herald, March 9, 1886)" (*The SDA Bible Commentary*, vol. 7, p. 990).

Revelation 22:3-11

"And there shall be no more curse: but the throne of God and of the Lamb shall be in it; and his servants shall serve him: And they shall see his face; and his name shall be in their foreheads. And there shall be no night there; and they need no candle, neither light of the sun; for the Lord God giveth them light: and they shall reign for ever and ever. And he said unto me, These sayings are faithful and true: and the Lord God of the holy prophets sent his angel to shew unto his servants the things which must shortly be done.

"Behold, I come quickly: blessed is he that keepeth the sayings of the prophecy of this book. And I John saw these things, and heard them. And when I had heard and seen, I fell down to worship before the feet of the angel which shewed me these things. Then saith he unto me, See thou do it not: for I am thy fellowservant, and of thy brethren the prophets, and of them which keep the sayings of this book: worship God. And he saith unto me, Seal not the sayings of the prophecy of this book: for the time is at hand. He that is unjust, let him be unjust still: and he which is filthy, let him be filthy still: and he that is righteous, let him be righteous still: and he that is holy, let him be holy still."

In Daniel 12:4 Daniel was instructed to seal the book until the end time, but here John was instructed not to seal the book because the time is at hand. We can see all around us that this world is coming to an end. The economy is bad, crime is increasing, all kinds of diseases, earthquakes, devastations, fires, wars, rumors of wars, and catastrophies are happening around us. People are lying, starving, and engaging in sexual immorality. We can't continue like this otherwise there won't be anyone left in this world. We will kill each other one way or another. God in His mercy will put an end to it on His appointed day and time and redeem His faithful servants.

Revelation 22:12-15

"And, behold, I come quickly; and my reward is with me, to give every man according as his work shall be. I am Alpha and Omega, the beginning and the end, the first and the last. Blessed are they that do his commandments, that they may have right to the tree of life, and may enter in through the gates into the city. For without are dogs, and sorcerers, and whoremongers, and murderers, and idolaters, and whosoever loveth and maketh a lie."

Only those who keep the commandments of God will be blessed. God will reward everyone according to his or her works be it good or bad, to eternal life or eternal death.

"Here we have the Alpha of Genesis and the Omega of Revelation. The blessing is promised to all those who keep the commandments of God, and who co-operate with him in the proclamation of the third angel's message" (*The Review and Herald,* June 8, 1897).

Revelation 22:16-21

"I Jesus have sent mine angel to testify unto you these things in the churches. I am the root and the offspring of David, and the bright and morning star. And the Spirit and the bride say, Come. And let him that heareth say, Come. And let him that is athirst come. And whosoever will, let him take the

Jesus the Water of Life

water of life freely. For I testify unto every man that heareth the words of the prophecy of this book, If any man shall add unto these things, God shall add unto him the plagues that are written in this book: And if any man shall take away from the words of the book of this prophecy, God shall take away his part out of the book of life, and out of the holy city, and from the things which are written in this book. He which testifieth these things saith, Surely I come quickly. Amen. Even so, come, Lord Jesus. The grace of our Lord Jesus Christ be with you all. Amen."

The angel showed John the river of the water of life and the tree of life. Revelation 22:7 tells us that blessed is the person who obeys the words of the prophecy written in this book.

Now that you've read and learned from God's Word, it is time for you to set your house in order and accept the water of life that God is offering to you and me free of charge. Don't delay any longer; time is running out. Tomorrow is not promised to anyone. What's your decision today? God said, "Today, if you will hear His voice, do not harden your hearts" (Heb 4:7, NKJV).

Jesus is coming back soon. Perhaps even sooner than you think. You might not have time to put it off any longer. This might be your last chance; accept Jesus in your heart today. He's ready and willing to save you. You can't afford to miss out on all He has planned for you. God the Father, the Son, and the Holy Spirit did Their part. It is now your turn to make your choice. Why don't you bow your head now and ask God to help you to make the right dicision. He's ready to save you only if you let Him.

God's Word is true. He loves you and wants you to live with Him forever and ever. Don't miss out on this special offer. There is nothing better than eternal life with Jesus Christ our Savior. The choice is yours.

As I conclude this book, I want to share a few final thoughts with you. My brothers and sisters, I have shared everything that Jesus has shared with me. I finally understand the book of Revelation, and I praise God that He has shared all these things with us, His children, way before the events will take place so that we can be prepared. As watchmen on the walls of Zion, we must give these warnings to everyone before it is too late.

A crisis and a time of trouble is soon to be upon us. The world will be in chaos with the New World Order, aliens, spirits, famines, wars, natural disasters, tsunamis, nuclear bombs, earthquakes, terrorist attacks, your rights taken away, slavery, martial law, upheaval, collapsed economies, and killings taking place. Evil will run rampant, and the government won't be able to control it. So they will hand it over to the hand of the church to put in order.

The church, with the backing of the UN (United Nations) and all the countries in the world, especially the United States, will force everyone to worship on the first day of the week, Sunday the "Lord's day."

People who do not obey this decree will be killed. These laws are already on the books waiting for the final approval to enforce them. You must read the Scriptures and see the signs of the time. This is not the time to be sleeping. This is the time for you to turn off your TV and control your appetite instead of eating and drinking things that are harmful to your body and soul. This is the time to stop looking for entertainment at amusement parks, sports events, and in the media. This is the time to plead for Jesus Christ's righteousness in your soul and ask God to send His Holy Spirit into your heart. If not, you will be caught by surprise when the crises come.

As the time of trouble and danger is creeping upon us as a thief in the night, many think they are secure and that the things that have been prophecied in God's Word will not come to pass in their generation. Well, I have news for you. These things are happening now as we speak. We are near the very end. The enforcement of the Sunday law is about to start, and you must be prepared. If you don't hear sermons about the close of probation and the end of time, then you should study for yourself to know what time we are in now and get your life right with God. Everyone has to stand on their own. You can't blame your pastor for not telling you that Jesus is coming soon and about the time of trouble that is coming.

You must study the Bible for yourself. The hours you spend watching TV should be dedicated to studying God's Word. Although everything seems as if it is the same, day after day, except for some natural disasters here and there and wars and other disturbances, the clock is still ticking. Just as it was in the days of Noah before the Flood, nothing changed until the seventh day after Noah, his family, and the animals went into the ark. Then things began to happen with great speed. But it was too late. My brothers and sisters, don't let this happen to you. Your eternal destiny is at stake. Jesus is coming soon, and you should be ready at anytime.

Right now there are religious movements that are meeting to bring the Sunday law into effect. You must keep your eyes open. Whenever they call for the churches to unite, know that it's for a common cause of worshiping on "the Lord's day," which is contrary to God's Holy seventh-day Sabbath. Be vigilant so that you will not be caught by surprise. Keep your eyes on the Christian Coalition of America, Christian Churches Together, and the Catholic Campaign for America. You must be vigilant at all times.

Jesus the Water of Life

Ellen White wrote the following in *Testimonies for the Church*: "Men and women are in the last hours of probation, and yet are careless and stupid, and ministers have no power to arouse them; they are asleep themselves. Sleeping preachers preaching to a sleeping people!" (vol. 2, p. 337).

Now is the time to wake up from your sleep and be diligently studying the Word of God and strive to conform to His Ten Commandments. The time has come for you to get worldliness and its pleasures out of your mind. You can't wait until the last minute to do so because you might not get the chance to do it. Now is the time. Ask Jesus for His Holy Spirit to anoint your eyes with eyesalve so that you can see the times that we are living in and thank Him for warning us about the time of trouble that is coming. Remember, He has promised us that He will be with us even to the end of this world. So if we keep His commandments and have the testimonies of Jesus Christ, we will be protected during this hard time. "Trust in the LORD with all your heart, and lean not on your own understanding; in all your ways acknowledge Him, and He shall direct your paths" (Prov. 3:5, 6, NKJV).

"The Lord is my shepherd; I shall not want. He makes me to lie down in green pastures; He leads me beside the still waters. He restores my soul; He leads me in the paths of righteousness For His name's sake. Yea, though I walk through the valley of the shadow of death, I will fear no evil; for You are with me; Your rod and your staff, they comfort me. You prepare a table before me in the presence of my enemies; You anoint my head with oil; My cup runs over. Surely goodness and mercy shall follow me All the days of my life; And I will dwell in the house of the LORD forever" (Ps. 23:1-6).

"Our Father in heaven, Hallowed be Your name. Your kingdom come, Your will be done on earth as it is in heaven. Give us this day our daily bread and forgive us our debts as we forgive our debtors. And do not lead us into temptation but deliver us from the evil one for Yours is the kingdom and the power and the glory forever. Amen." (Matt 6: 9-14).

"He who testifies to these things says, 'Surely I am coming quickly.' Amen. Even so, come, Lord Jesus! The grace of our Lord Jesus Christ be with you all. Amen" (Rev. 22:20, 21, NKJV).

Bibliography

A Bible Prophecy Adventure. Revelation Seminars.

Finley, Mark, Jay Gallimore, Don Gray. *Revelation Speaks Messages of Hope to a World in Turmoil.* Keene, TX: Seminars Unlimited, 1995.

Froom, LeRoy. *The Prophetic Faith of Our Fathers.* Washington, D.C.: Review and Herald Publishing Association, 1946.

Geiermann, Peter. *Convert's Catechism of Catholic Doctrine.* Charlotte, NC: TAN Books and Publishers, 1977.

Gibbons, James Cardinal. *The Faith of Our Fathers.* Charlotte, NC: TAN Books and Publishers, 2009.

Keenan, Stephen. *A Doctrinal Catechism.* New York: P.J. Kenedy and Sons, 1876.

Maxwell, C. Mervyn. *God Cares.* Vol. 2. Boise, ID: Pacific Press Publishing Association, 1985.

Smith, Uriah. *The Prophecies of Daniel and Revelation.* Mountain View, CA: Pacific Press Publishing Association, 1944.

White, Ellen G. *The General Conference Bulletin,* April 13, 1891.

White, Ellen G. *The Review and Herald.* January 28, 1909.

White, Ellen G. *The Review and Herald.* January 11, 1887.

White, Ellen G. *The Review and Herald.* October 13, 1904.

White, Ellen G. *The SDA Bible Commentary.* Vol. 7. Hagerstown, MD: Review and Herald Publishing Association, 1957.

White, Ellen G. *The Signs of the Times,* March 22, 1910.

White, Ellen G. *The Spirit of Prophecy.* Vol. 3. Hagerstown, MD: Review and Herald Publishing Association, 1870.

White, Ellen G. *Testimonies for the Church.* Vol. 2. Nampa, ID: Pacific Press Publishing Association, 2007.

White, Ellen G. Manuscript Releases. Vol. 20. Washington, D.C.: Review and Herald Publishing Association, 1989.

We invite you to view the complete
selection of titles we publish at:

www.TEACHServices.com

or write or email us your praises,
reactions, or thoughts about this
or any other book we publish at:

TEACH Services, Inc.
P U B L I S H I N G
www.TEACHServices.com
P.O. Box 954
Ringgold, GA 30736

info@TEACHServices.com

TEACH Services, Inc., titles may be purchased in bulk for educational,
business, fund-raising, or sales promotional use.
For information, please e-mail

BulkSales@TEACHServices.com.

Finally, if you are interested in seeing
your own book in print, please contact us at

publishing@teachservices.com.

We would be happy to review your manuscript for free.

www.ingramcontent.com/pod-product-compliance
Lightning Source LLC
Chambersburg PA
CBHW070550160426
43199CB00014B/2443